Creating Excellent Relationships

The Power of Character Choices

Susanne M. Alexander
Relationship & Marriage Coach

Creating Excellent Relationships: The Power of Character Choices

Version: August 2012
Published in English by Marriage Transformation LLC
Chattanooga, Tennessee, USA
www.marriagetransformation.com;
Susanne@marriagetransformation.com

International Standard Book Number/ISBN: 978-0-9816666-7-9

Cover Design: Jeff Duckworth (www.duckofalltrades.com)

Table of Contents

NOTES ABOUT THIS BOOK

Guide for Using This Material As an Individual

Goal	To learn about and strengthen your character qualities as part of empowering you in successfully preparing for being in a relationship and then, someday, marriage. To thoroughly know the character qualities of a relationship partner.
Description	Every person begins with the capacity to develop a wide range of character qualities. The strength or weakness of these qualities will significantly affect the interactions between you and someone you will date and marry. Everyone can improve his or her ability to practice character qualities. As individuals understand and strengthen their own characters, they also develop knowledge about character that will help them identify strengths and areas for growth in a partner.
Objectives	• Understand what character is and its value to a relationship • Thoroughly and in detail carry out a character self-assessment • Develop and begin carrying out a character self-development plan • Understand the character quality strengths and weaknesses in a partner • Apply effective observational practices • Distinguish between character strengths, weaknesses, and misuses • Communicate effectively with a partner about character
Length	You may find it useful to take a few weeks to go through the material and carefully observe your own attitudes and behavior related to various character qualities. Carrying out the development goals will also occur over time. Note: Some activities are marked "helpful", because they are fun and will assist you; some are marked "essential" because they are vital in moving you through the material.
Environment	Space to privately do self-assessment; opportunities to interact with other people

Guide for Using This Material with a Group

Goal	To help individuals who are interested in being in a relationship or marriage learn about and strengthen their character qualities. To strengthen the ability to thoroughly know the character qualities of a relationship partner.
Description	Every person begins with the capacity to develop a wide range of character qualities. The strength or weakness of these qualities will significantly affect the interactions between partners. It is possible for every individual to improve his or her ability to practice character qualities. As individuals understand and strengthen their own characters, they also develop knowledge about character that will help them identify strengths and areas for growth in a partner.
Objectives	• Understand what character is and its value to a relationship • Thoroughly and in detail carry out a character self-assessment • Develop and begin carrying out a character self-development plan • Understand the character quality strengths and weaknesses in a partner • Apply effective observational practices • Distinguish between character strengths, weaknesses, and misuses • Communicate effectively with a partner about character
Format	Group reading, self-reflection time, and activities; Note: Some activities are marked "helpful", because they are fun and will assist you; some are marked "essential" because they are vital in moving participants through the material.
Audience	Unmarried individuals who are not yet in a relationship or couples who are in the early stages of a relationship
Length	7-8 sessions, 2-hours each, with 1 chapter per session, or a weekend workshop
Evaluation	Group discussion at closing
Environment	Space for the group to sit in a circle; spaces for people to privately do self-assessment
Resources	Pens or pencils; check activities for other materials that may be needed for activities

Learning in Action

Generally, you read a book simply to learn new concepts. However, relationships are not merely conceptual. Therefore, this book invites you to participate in a more active adventure to learn new insights and skills. Included throughout are **Reflection** sections and **Activities**, some of which include reference to **Worksheets**—see Part 2.

The activities and worksheets are wide ranging to involve you physically, mentally, emotionally, and spiritually. This will help you in knowing yourself and understanding how character knowledge will help you prepare for a relationship. By taking the time to know yourself rather than rushing into dating, you can have a happier, more fulfilling relationship when you meet someone and are ready to get to know them well. It's hard to be patient and wait for the right person. With this material, you will learn how to make yourself ready for when that person comes along.

Some of the communication activities and tools may feel a bit strange and uncomfortable as you first use them; however, that provides opportunities to strengthen such qualities as courage or flexibility. If you take the time to be thorough, your insights and new skills will benefit you in your relationships. Note that the word is "thorough," not "perfect"! You may also develop your own activities to supplement or replace the ones provided. A few of the activities encourage engaging your creative side through using "the arts"; such as, poetry, music, or writing. Often using the arts can bring you surprising and helpful insights and perspectives.

The majority of the activities early in the book are set up for you to do on your own, assuming that you will not necessarily have someone yet who will participate in them with you. However, many you can do with a partner, and some, particularly later in the book, will be ones you will do or return to when you do have a partner. Remember that where the activity involves someone else, that participant needs to be willing, not pressured. Ideally, your partner will also have a copy of this book and be going through the same process of relationship preparation as you are.

You may want to write your general thoughts about your character in a journal, as well as your answers to the reflection questions and results of activities contained in this book. Journal writing can help you with observing and understanding significant experiences and troubling memories. It enables you to make better sense of current struggles, which helps to make them more manageable. If you are uncomfortable writing down your thoughts, consider taping or recording them.

As you set goals for your character development and begin to act in new character-filled ways, you will engage in a process of acting, assessing, learning, and then changing your words and actions if necessary. Through this active process, you will learn how to interact well with others, which will help you be a successful partner in a relationship. This discovery process is vital.

Wording Choices

It is sometimes difficult to find words that effectively describe people's roles in relationships, especially when someone is not married. I chose to use the term "partner" instead of other possibilities, such as boyfriend or girlfriend, because it includes the concept of equality and applies across a wide span of ages and various relationship stages.

This book will distribute globally, and many people reading it would not understand some of the popular expressions used in North America. As a result, I have done my best to eliminate them. For the same reason, I have minimized the use of contractions (I'll, won't, don't...) At times, this results in the text seeming a bit formal, but I hope you will agree that understanding is more important.

Having a spiritual connection between partners can strengthen a relationship, so at times this book includes spiritual terminology and encourages you to explore and try activities such as prayer, meditation, worship, reading spiritual material, and more as possibilities. The words "God," or "Creator," appear at times, but you may use a different term for a spiritual Force in your life. Please use whatever terminology fits your beliefs, and any spiritual practices that work for you in your life.

Sources

This book includes a wide variety of sources, as there is a rich array to draw on about both character and relationships. I use quotations from:

- Philosophers
- Founders of religions, religious leaders, and religious scripture from six global religions: the Bahá'í Faith, Buddhism, Christianity, Hinduism, Islam, and Judaism
- Relationship and marriage researchers and experts
- Therapists and counselors
- Authors
- Traditional wisdom

These quotations will expand your perspectives and give you insights into new choices and actions to consider in your life. I recognize these as rich sources about character and relationships, and I hope that you find them insightful. I encourage you to pursue reading many of these original sources to continue expanding your knowledge and skills.

PART 1A:

KNOWING AND GROWING YOUR OWN CHARACTER

Chapter 1
Understanding Character

INTRODUCTION

Understanding character is a vital part of the process of finding a relationship partner and developing a strong and vibrant relationship together. It can certainly be very frustrating and painful to invest a lot of time and effort in a relationship only to find out later that the person has serious character weaknesses. The frustration and pain are especially difficult if the discoveries occur after engagement or marriage.

Many people go through multiple, short-term relationships before even getting to college, some of which end in heartbreak or sadness. Others end up in marriages with people of poor character. Rather than being tangled up in meaningless dating knots or relationships that do not work, knowing yourself and how to observe a person's whole character and compatibility with you can keep you closer to love and farther from heartache.

This book is about a new, more empowering way of approaching relationships. You are taking charge of yourself and building a good foundation. If you thoroughly know and develop your own character, you will be more prepared to be an excellent partner. Through studying about character, and developing your own character strengths, you will also gain the character knowledge and skills necessary to observe a partner's words and actions and assess his or her character more quickly and effectively. When you prepare your character, you can successfully be confident while single and build a fulfilling friendship-based relationship that may someday lead to marriage.

As you gain a clear picture of your character strengths and areas in which you need to grow, you can choose how you want to grow and change. This personal understanding and development is vital to begin before being with a partner. As you proceed, you will also begin identifying what character qualities will help you succeed in a relationship.

Developing and changing yourself helps you with growing and maturing into being a good and responsible adult with healthy relationships with others. It is not wise to change yourself just with the motive of attracting someone else, such as friends or a potential partner. You may please people by becoming who they want you to be, but that change may turn out to be temporary. Not only is it not a good choice, but it makes you someone you are not. If you are not confident in yourself and know yourself well, relationships will be difficult. Change for the good because you want to better yourself and, through that mindset, you will better yourself for future partners, whoever they may be. Shallow change may not last, but character strengths are always beneficial to you and others and in all areas of life.

UNDERSTANDING CHARACTER

You may or may not be familiar with character. Simply put, **character is**:
- The sum of all the qualities you develop throughout your life as you make choices about how to speak and act; character affects the majority of your words and actions
- The spiritual essence of who you are as a human being
- Your moral compass or ethical strength that provides the unwavering drive to choose what is right, even when that choice could cause you difficulties, and even if no one else is watching you or knows what you are doing

Your reputation is what others think about you. Your character is who you truly are. And you have significant ability to practice these qualities with others for their benefit and yours, as well as to transform the ones that are weaker. You can build a good reputation for yourself by developing strong character qualities. That change comes from the inside and will naturally reflect *outward*. Reputation, instead, often affects how we then act or react *inside*.

You develop and refine your character over time as you:
- Learn about character qualities
- Try out new actions and activities
- Experience and overcome challenges
- Listen to your conscience and feelings of shame or guilt and take corrective action
- Make amends to others you have hurt; ask for forgiveness
- Make choices to strengthen your qualities, say new words, and take new actions
- Put yourself in environments and with people that encourage you to make beneficial changes

No one is perfect. However, you can make your best effort to know and develop yourself before attempting a serious relationship, marriage, and parenthood. And, since most of your character is formed early in life, an honest assessment of it now will give you a good idea of your readiness for a relationship with marriage as the eventual goal. You are probably strong in some character qualities and unskilled or uncertain about practicing others. You develop each quality according to your own willingness, choice, and effort. **The stronger your character qualities, the better you will function in the world, and the greater will be your ability to establish a strong, happy, and lasting relationship.**

The list below includes key character qualities to consider in your own self-development, to look for in prospective partners, and to practice together with a partner. What do you want to see in yourself? What do you want to look for in a future partner? What qualities mean a lot to you and affect your daily life?

Acceptance	Flexibility	Perseverance
Assertiveness	Forgiveness	Purity
Beauty	Fortitude	Purposefulness
Caring	Friendliness	Resilience
Chastity	Generosity	Respect
Commitment	Gentleness	Responsibility
Compassion	Helpfulness	Self-Discipline
Confidence	Honesty	Service
Contentment	Humility	Sincerity
Cooperation	Idealism	Spirituality
Courage	Integrity	Tactfulness
Courtesy	Joyfulness	Thankfulness
Creativity	Justice	Thoughtfulness
Detachment	Kindness	Thriftiness
Discernment	Love	Trustworthiness
Encouragement	Loyalty	Truthfulness
Enthusiasm	Mercy	Unity
Equality	Moderation	Wisdom
Excellence	Patience	
Faithfulness	Peacefulness	

You may wish to pause at this point and read more about all of these qualities in Part 3, "Powerful Character Qualities." Although you may already be familiar with many of them, you may discover aspects of them you have not thought about before. You also may not have realized that certain qualities are parts of character, not just adjectives. They are rooted much deeper than just a description of you and your actions. Reading about some of the qualities may raise happy memories, and others may trigger unhappy thoughts about difficult times in your life. You may need to reconsider some assumptions you have made, as well. Try not to stress yourself out or overwhelm yourself. At any one time, you might only focus on strengthening one or two qualities. Focusing on all of these qualities at once will be too difficult.

As you read about these qualities, think carefully about the activities you are involved in regularly. Assess how they are contributing to or interfering with your character growth. Consider what new actions and activities may help you. Chapter 3 will help you further with this process.

HELPFUL ACTIVITY

For a week or some other reasonable period, track how often an actor portraying a character or a person in the media—such as on television shows, in movies, in an Internet blog, or in magazine articles—demonstrates or discusses any character quality on this list. What thoughts do you have, and what conclusions do you draw from your observations?

CHARACTER STRENGTHS AND GROWTH AREAS

Just as exercising strengthens the muscles you use, the qualities you practice the most become strongest and become an integral part of your personal identity. Don Coyhis of the Mohican Nation says, "We need to realize the seeds we plant in the spring will be what show up in our summer season of growth and will be the fruits that we will harvest in our fall season. We really have a lot to do with what shows up in our lives."[1]

Perhaps you have consistently practiced patience, in part because you had to wait after school for a sibling. Now, as manager at a retail store, you patiently help customers. Even though you consistently practice patience in most circumstances, however, there may be moments that test you. At these times, you may become impatient. For example, you might have difficulty waiting in lines or dealing with a family member who annoys you. These experiences remind you that you need to continue strengthening your practice of patience.

There are some of the key ways from *Character Strengths and Virtues* that help you to tell whether a quality is a strength. Consider these:

- A sense of ownership and authenticity ("this is the real me")
- A feeling of excitement while displaying it, particularly at first
- Continuous learning of new ways to use the strength
- A sense of yearning or desire to act using the strength
- A feeling that you cannot help using or being affected by the strength
- Invigoration rather than exhaustion when using the strength
- The creation and pursuit of fundamental projects that revolve around the strength
- Intrinsic motivation to use the strength
- Onlookers get positive feelings and responses from watching you doing good things and using the strength
- A degree of generality across situations and stability across time[2]

None of us is perfect at practicing any of the qualities. Character growth is a process—transformation can happen a little more each day and through continued practice. Be as excellent and consistent as you can—holding high standards for yourself. However, accept and forgive yourself when you struggle and slip backward; then choose to do better in the future.

Again, like your muscles, the qualities that you do not practice very often stay ineffective or become even weaker. For instance, if you quit part way through projects when they become difficult, you demonstrate weakness in perseverance. This quality then is clearly an area for growth. You may infrequently practice some qualities because they do not seem to have any particular application in your life. Some qualities you may not be aware of, understand, or know how to practice effectively. (Part 3 will be helpful to you.)

Perhaps sometimes you flip back and forth between practicing and using one of your qualities the best you possibly can, but later begin acting more like its opposite. One week you might show compassion towards a particular family member, and the next week act distant and pay less attention to the person. Hopefully, you will see the effect of both approaches and realize how important it is for you to show compassion consistently. The positive outcome will be visible. As long as you are alive, you can continue to grow and develop, moving from weakness and ineffectiveness to strength and effectiveness in each of the character qualities. **It is possible to strive for a high level of consistent effectiveness and harmony between your inner attitudes, words, and actions.**

For example, you are consistently purposeful when working with someone on tasks. Moreover, you not only use appropriately patient words and actions while the person learns to do something for the first time, but you also are not frustrated on the inside! You are genuine in your responses from the inside out.

A character quality that has become a strength for you will serve you well throughout your life. For instance:

- Creativity and wisdom help you to gain and use knowledge
- Courage and perseverance help you to accomplish goals in the face of opposition
- Compassion and kindness help you to look after and befriend others
- Justice and service help you to reach out to others, make a difference for them, and to work well in groups
- Humility and self-discipline help you to maintain moderation in your choices (and admit your wrongs!)
- Beauty and spirituality help you to connect to the larger universe and see the joy in all areas, providing meaning and purpose in your life[3]

THE POWER OF CHOICE

Your conscience pulls you towards actions that are best for you and towards others or that cause harm. Your words, actions, and attitudes tend to match whatever choices you make. Of course, your choices then significantly affect your life and relationships. Your higher nature or best self includes your character strengths, and the stronger and more developed your character is, the easier it is to make positive choices. For example, if you see someone who is hurt, your higher nature would prompt you to be kind and helpful. Your lower nature would say to ignore the person.

The scriptures of the world's religions, the writings of great philosophers, and the work of relationship experts all stress the importance of developing character strengths. Below is a small sample.

> "Love is patient, love is kind. It does not envy, it does not boast, it is not proud. It is not rude, it is not self-seeking, it is not easily angered, it keeps no record of wrongs. ... Love never fails...." ~ *The Bible*[4]

> "But indeed if any show patience and forgive, that would truly be an exercise of courageous will and resolution in the conduct of affairs." ~ *The Qur'án*[5]

> "The light of a good character surpasseth the light of the sun and the radiance thereof." ~ *Tablets of Bahá'u'lláh* [6]

"In man there are two natures; his spiritual or higher nature and his material or lower nature. ... Signs of both these natures are to be found in men. In his material aspect he expresses untruth, cruelty and injustice; all these are the outcome of his lower nature. The attributes of his Divine nature are shown forth in love, mercy, kindness, truth and justice, one and all being expressions of his higher nature. Every good habit, every noble quality belongs to man's spiritual nature...." ~'Abdu'l-Bahá, *Paris Talks* [7]

"Make it your guiding principle to do your best for others and to be trustworthy in what you say." ~ Confucius[8]

"Virtuous action depends not just on what we do but also on doing the right thing for the right reasons, and knowing that we are acting for the right reasons." ~ Blaine J. Fowers, PhD[9]

When you make negative choices, which is acting from your lower nature or lower self, the results are usually against your best long-term interests. Your lower nature pulls you towards self-centeredness or destructive behavior.

Carefully observe how tricky your lower nature can be at times though. Sometimes your lower nature can pull you towards something that looks like fun, and you convince yourself that getting involved is a good thing. For example, it can look like fun to participate in a card game where everyone is playing for money. If you become hooked into trying to win your money back and lose more and more, you will experience more pain and problems than fun.

If someone from your past taught you that negative behavior such as lying, cheating, or stealing was okay, you may mislead yourself in this direction. However, you cannot use your past as an excuse to justify poor behavior in the present.

If you had a rigid upbringing, with excessive rules and strict consequences, you might feel guilt even when you have only done something minor or nothing wrong at all. You might struggle with perfectionism as a result, something that demands you or others behave perfectly and reject or are very unhappy with anything less. This trap actually works against your personal growth. "Authentic spirituality means giving up perfectionism for the rigorous process of developing ourselves one thought, one act, one day at a time."[10]

If your conscience is actually misleading you, it will take concentrated effort and practice to learn to assess the validity of your internal signals. You may also need someone else to help you with discernment.

Strictly avoid negative self-talk that weighs you down with destructive criticisms, such as "I am so stupid!" or "Why don't I ever do anything right?!" Self-critical people, who always focus on what they think is negative about themselves, are likely to be even more critical of others. They are less likely to notice and accentuate their strengths and those of a partner. Those who have problems with negativity may benefit from studying the qualities of humility, mercy, and joyfulness in Part 3. Celebrate even the tiniest successes and appreciate the good things you have accomplished, and determine to keep working on the things that have dragged you down. Be fair, kind, and compassionate to yourself as well as to others. Yes, the character qualities apply to how you treat yourself, too!

HELPFUL ACTIVITY

Engage your creative side by using various art or building supplies to create something that demonstrates the struggle between your good and poor choices, your higher and lower natures.

Throughout your childhood, your parents—or those who reared you—helped to form your character through the dynamic power of example, verbal guidance, and discipline. Ideally, they guided you to understand which of your actions were helpful and beneficial (higher nature), and which ones were harmful (lower nature). Perhaps your father taught you to stay confident and courteous after losing a game, instead of becoming angry. Maybe your mother taught you to speak respectfully, instead of rudely, to your grandparents and other elders. You then learn how to take what they have taught you and apply those lessons to your own life.

You continued building your character through new experiences and the choices you made. You might have practiced commitment by keeping promises to your friends, observing how this helped strengthen your friendships. Perhaps you were compassionate to a neighbor and noticed the happiness this brought to her. You might have learned respect for school property through the guidance of a teacher. A part-time job might have taught you responsibility with time and money. **Although your character continues to develop throughout your entire life, all these experiences and more formed its foundation by your late teens. This foundation then sets the stage for you to continue making choices to develop and adjust your attitudes and actions.**

Many additional sources influence your character development. For instance, TV or movies often show people making a wide variety of choices, some with positive outcomes and some more destructive, and all with varied consequences. You also learn about how people handle character choices through reading newspapers, magazines, books, and stories. As you gain understanding of people you read about, you may compare their choices to yours and to those of people you know. Are their words and actions beneficial or harmful? What about yours?

You may see people in your school or workplace make ethical and wise choices respectful of themselves and others. You also see those who choose at times to be greedy, dishonest, disrespectful, or self-centered. Perhaps a person justifies cheating on an exam, misuses an expense account, or takes property belonging to others. Prominent people throughout the world also demonstrate their character qualities as they make difficult leadership decisions that affect many people. Some leaders demonstrate poor judgment or unskillful character choices at times, adversely affecting many people. Others show more skills and strengths, instead. In every situation you observe, you can choose to follow good examples and determine not to follow the example of those who are unwise.

Whichever character qualities you did not learn how to practice while growing up are probably weak and need your intentional focus now. **You have free will to make whatever character and behavior choices you wish. The wiser your choices, the better the outcomes will be. You have the power to choose how you respond to and treat others. Your behavior does not and should not depend upon the behavior of others. You are responsible for your own character choices, your words, and your actions.** Choices made from the foundation of a strong character respect your higher nature and that of others, with positive outcomes. Consider the quotation below from Caroline Myss, PhD, about choices.

Having faith in someone commits a part of our energy to that person; having faith in an idea commits a part of our energy to that idea; having faith in a fear commits a part of our energy to that fear. ... Our faith and our power of choice are, in fact, the power of creation itself. We are the vessels through which energy becomes matter in this life. Therefore, the spiritual test inherent in all our lives is the challenge to discover what motivates us to make the choices we do, and whether we have faith in our fears or the Divine.[11]

As you choose words and actions that reflect character strengths, your self-respect and happiness will increase. "Choosing to lead [y]our lives with self-control and self-directedness is at the heart of feeling good."[12] Your self-respect and happiness will then facilitate your positive interactions with others. For example, you will more readily show kindness to a sick friend, courage when you are fearful about meeting someone new, or generosity to a neighbor in need.

HELPFUL ACTIVITY

Consider some famous people you admire and try to identify their character strengths—perhaps courage, kindness, or perseverance. You may know that these people were not perfect in every way. In spite of their imperfections, what qualities helped them in their faith communities, workplaces, or social activism? Then, look at your parents, other family members, or close friends and identify their character strengths. Finally, consider a book or movie you like and the character qualities of the people portrayed in them. What character qualities from the lives of family members, famous people, or various types of media (magazines, books, television, movies, Internet…) do you want to develop as strengths in your own life?

~ Reflection ~

1. What choices in my life show that I am practicing some character qualities effectively?
2. What new choices do I want to make?
3. What excites me about making these choices?
4. What scares me about making these choices?

MISUSING QUALITIES

(Note: This is an introduction to character strength misuses. There is more in-depth information in Chapter 6.)

You are learning that your character qualities may be strong, may need strengthening, or may be at some stage of growth in between. You are also beginning to understand how your character qualities affect your choices. In this section, you will discover another dimension of character: the misuse of qualities. **Misuse of a character quality occurs when it is a strength but you practice it too much and/or at an inappropriate time or place. Perhaps you also practice it with the wrong person! Such misuse usually results in harm to yourself and others by causing arguments, hurt feelings, or some level of disharmony or disunity.**

For example, you could practice the character strength of flexibility to excess by being so relaxed that you never make plans or set goals. It then becomes laziness. An example of practicing flexibility inappropriately would be to tell a friend you are happy to drive them anytime to the mall or their job, but you never have gas in your car when they need you. Not only will this misuse of flexibility cause conflict with others, but they will find it increasingly difficult to trust you. Others would be reluctant to work or socialize with you, and your relationships would suffer. Part 3 provides explanations of each character quality to help you practice them effectively and avoid misusing them.

Moderation and Misuses

Moderation is the middle way—an excellent balance. Moderation can help you avoid misuses of character strengths. When you practice any quality to excess, moderation helps you to tone it down. If you are practicing a quality at the wrong time and place, moderation will help you to pause and assess whether what you are saying or doing is appropriate for the situation. **Practicing moderation can help you to correct your misuse of any quality and shift to using it in a better way.** "Moderation is the silken string running through the pearl chain of all virtues."[13]

Moderating a quality does not mean "doing it half-way" instead of whole-heartedly. That would be a misuse of moderation. Excel in practicing qualities by understanding them well and making wise choices, instead. Practicing moderation along with a character strength you are misusing actually increases your ability to make wise choices. Apply this concept to dancing and see that practicing excessively or incorrectly can cause injury and frustration. When you have difficulty controlling your movements or concentrating, it is time to stop and rest. Tripping, stumbling, or stepping on your partner's toes is a signal that you might need to apply moderation. If you look at this concept of misuse from a sports angle, you see that if you practice your strength off the sports field or out of the arena and attempt to interact physically with someone in the same way, you are likely to cause an injury.

The following story illustrates what can happen when you misuse a character quality:

Paige loves to be helpful. One day she and her friend Gavin decide to help his elderly parents plant their garden. Normally Gavin's mother plants the flowers, but she is sick in bed and cannot do it now, and his father cannot do the project alone.

Gavin explains his mother's garden plan to Paige, shows her where to dig, and indicates where each of the flowers should go. Paige, however, decides to be helpful and starts digging holes where she thinks the flowers will look better. When Gavin comes over to see how she is doing, he is very annoyed to see that she changed his mother's plans and yells at her to stop. "I was only trying to help!" Paige snaps back.

After they both calm down, they discuss what happened. Gavin explains his displeasure that she made changes in the plan without asking. Paige realizes that her attempt to be helpful was actually disrespectful and caused feelings of hurt and disappointment.

Paige knew the basic skills of helpfulness. However, she caused a problem by misusing the quality. She did more than Gavin asked her to do when it was not required or wanted. Paige needs to practice moderation along with helpfulness to ensure that she is not being excessively helpful and inappropriately acting against the wishes of those she is trying to help.

Achieving moderation in practicing a character quality brings rewards. Author Linda Kavelin Popov says, in *A Pace of Grace*, "When you relax into the virtues of moderation, peacefulness, and contentment, you will find that you no longer digress into scattered, anxious multitasking. Thus, the energy you spend working on whatever task is before you will be far more purposeful and focused."[14]

~ Reflection ~

1. When have I caused harm by practicing a character quality excessively?
2. What can I do to prevent this excessive practice from happening again?
3. Which qualities am I most likely to practice excessively or inappropriately?
4. How do I respond when I realize that I have caused a problem with a character quality misuse?

Helper Qualities and Misuses

In addition to moderation, other "helper qualities" can assist you in adjusting your misuse of a character strength. For instance, in the story above, Paige could have used the helper qualities of respect and courtesy to talk with Gavin about her ideas before doing them. Gaining knowledge about the correct practice of the qualities is vital. Another example occurs when the quality of contentment allows you to be calm and to accept your life as it is. You may misuse contentment, however, and rarely get involved in anything. Drawing on assertiveness, purposefulness, or responsibility could help you practice contentment more effectively.

Here is another illustration:

Jeremiah, a student at a local college, adamantly disagrees with how one of his new professors runs the class. Jeremiah misuses assertiveness by speaking up loudly in class and arguing with or criticizing his professor in front of the other students. He objects to daily quizzes and demands formal study groups to help students improve their grades. Because he knows his fellow students are frustrated as well, he feels justified in speaking out on their behalf as well as his own.

Jeremiah's grades in this course are going down, and he is very sure he is right. However, he just does not know how to get his message across effectively. He decides to ask his close friend Sarah to help him consider what to do. One evening over dessert at the college cafeteria, Jeremiah shares his concerns about this situation. Sarah helps him to see that he is causing harm by being excessively assertive, when what he really wants to do is encourage the professor to do things differently. Jeremiah realizes, as they talk the situation through, that he has been making the situation worse with his rude comments and behaviors. He also begins to understand that he has not been fair or respectful to his professor, who is new to the college and probably doing his best to adjust.

Together, Sarah and Jeremiah work through how he can practice moderation and compassion to adjust his practice of assertiveness. They decide his professor may listen to his suggestions if Jeremiah requests a private meeting instead of openly criticizing him in class. Jeremiah can practice respect, tactfulness, and courtesy both in this private meeting and in the classroom. He can take responsibility for his behavior and apologize for disrupting the class. He also realizes that he can further improve the situation by being friendly and encouraging.

Understanding this concept of character quality misuse will contribute to your character growth, and you will learn to spot character quality misuses in a friend or partner as well. You and a partner can help each other learn how to practice character qualities more appropriately, communicating in a common language and with common understanding of the principles involved. If, instead of getting angry about your partner's behavior, you understand it as a misuse of a character strength, you will be much more effective in addressing what is happening and directing your emotional response constructively.

HELPFUL ACTIVITY
Together with a friend or a group, create a quick skit (short impromptu drama) showing someone misusing a character quality and causing a problem. Then, create a new skit using helper qualities so that the person's words and actions are effective instead. Discuss together what you observed and learned.
~ *Reflection* ~
1. When have I caused harm by practicing a character quality at the wrong time or place? What was the outcome? How can I prevent a reoccurrence?   2. When have I practiced a quality both excessively and at the wrong time and place? What was the outcome? How can I prevent a reoccurrence?

WISDOM OF CHARACTER WORK

Working through this material will increase your ability to identify your own personal character strengths, the weak areas you need to strengthen, and your quality misuses. This increased knowledge will empower you to make effective choices and take action to address areas where you need to grow. You will also more effectively identify a partner's strengths, areas for growth, and misuses. You will know what behaviors to acknowledge and encourage in a partner as well as recognize where you have cause for concern. With these skills, you can then better choose the course of your life and of your relationships.

ESSENTIAL ACTIVITY

Pause reading at this point and take some time to complete Worksheet 1: Understanding Your Character Choices in Part 2. Be both honest and gentle with yourself. The purpose of the worksheet is not to beat yourself up with self-criticism, but to help you better understand and develop your character qualities, which will be the focus of both Chapters 2 and 3. As you complete this first worksheet, note any insights that can become the focus of your character development work in Chapter 3.

∽ *Encouragement* ∾

Reflecting on your words and actions and how they affect others may be new for you. You may be tempted to glance at the "Reflection" questions and not actually take the time to answer them, or you might pass by the "Activities" and do only a few of them. Please pause and take the time to do thoroughly as many of them as possible so you prepare yourself for the best possible relationship.

REFERENCES FOR CHAPTER 1

1. From "Meditations with Native American Elders" by Don Coyhis (Mohican Nation), September 19, 2005; available from White Bison, Inc. at www.whitebison.org
2. Christopher Peterson and Martin E. P. Seligman, *Character Strengths and Virtues: A Handbook and Classification*, p. 18 and p. 21
3. Ibid, pp. 23-30
4. *The Bible* (New International Version); 1 Corinthians, 13:4, 5, 8
5. Translated by Abdullah Yúsuf 'Alí, *The Qur'án*, XLII-43
6. Bahá'u'lláh, *Tablets of Bahá'u'lláh*, p. 36
7. 'Abdu'l-Bahá, *Paris Talks*, p. 60
8. Confucius, *Confucius: The Analects*, Book IX, p. 99
9. Blaine J. Fowers, PhD, *Beyond the Myth of Marital Happiness*, p. 116
10. Linda Kavelin Popov, *A Pace of Grace*, p. 93;
11. Caroline Myss, PhD, *Anatomy of the Spirit*, p. 224
12. Khalil A. Khavari, *Spiritual Intelligence*, p. 83
13. Joseph Hall, *Christian Moderation*, introduction
14. Linda Kavelin Popov, *A Pace of Grace*, p. 139

Chapter 2

Discovering Your Own Character

INTRODUCTION

Sometimes we go through our lives without pausing to assess whether we know ourselves, what we are doing, and why. You probably have not spent much time before now looking in depth at your character. In addition, you may not have spent the time to develop the context around you and your life that helps motivate your search to understand your character. This context is having a clear understanding of your purposes in life.

It is likely that your purposes include your family and how you want your relationships with family members to be, your education or career, your contributions to others, and what you envision for your own friendships, relationships, and marriage in the future. Your character qualities affect how well you are able to achieve your goals and purposes.

As you become more knowledgeable about your character qualities, you will share yourself more accurately and honestly in a relationship. You will also improve your ability to observe and understand a partner's character and how the two of you interact together. Insights about character qualities will help you with building a sincere, honest, and intimate relationship.

Your Purposes in Life

Part of the context for developing your character is the set of broader purposes you ongoingly choose for your life. **Discerning your purposes will help you with clarifying what you want to accomplish in your life, why, and what qualities are essential to you as strengths to fulfill the purposes. Later it will also be wise to determine whether a potential partner's purposes are harmonious with yours.**

How do you consistently spend your time? You may be involved with a variety of activities and goals. When you think about your purposes, however, think beyond your day-to-day tasks. What makes you excited? When you think about the future, what motivates you? What do you care passionately about? What is most important to you? What do you want to accomplish? As you clarify your answers to these questions, you will see that effectively practicing character qualities will empower you with achieving your goals.

Rick Warren, in his book *The Purpose Driven® Life*, says that many people are driven by guilt, resentment, anger, fear, materialism, and a need for approval. He asserts that none of these will create a successful life.[1] Instead, "…make ye a mighty effort, and choose for yourselves a noble goal."[2]

Positive purposes in life can include:

- Fulfilling the potentials of my body, mind, heart, and soul
- Developing my character qualities into strengths that benefit others
- Handling challenges well and learning from them
- Loving and worshiping God and sharing my spiritual beliefs with others
- Seeking employment and excellence in work or a profession
- Earning money to support my family
- Practicing generosity through sharing and giving what I have
- Establishing strong friendships and relationships
- Building a loving, friendship-based marriage
- Raising healthy, responsible children
- Creating a strong, unified family
- Serving others
- Making the world a better place and doing my part to unify people

Whether you agree with these purposes or choose different ones, be clear what your purposes are and why they are important to you. At the same time, think about which of your purposes will be important in friendships, helped through being in a relationship, and after that applicable in a marriage. Fully developing your character may be most likely to happen within those close personal interactions.

ESSENTIAL ACTIVITY

Write a statement of your current purposes in life. What gives you direction determines your goals. What does "success" mean to you? What roles do you play and which are most important? Share your statement with a close friend or family member and then edit it based on any valuable feedback you receive. Put the statement where you will see it regularly and it will remind you to act according to it. After a few days or weeks, reassess whether this statement truly reflects your purposes, and edit the statement as needed. Do you see these as purposes that will be with you for a brief period or for a lifetime? What character strengths are you observing as you act to fulfill your purposes? Where are you stumbling due to a weak quality?

SELF-OBSERVATION AND UNDERSTANDING

Once you clarify your purposes, you can better assess your strengths, weaknesses, and misuses of character qualities. What is working well in your life and what is not? What effect do your words and actions have on others? What are people's impressions of you? Taking an objective view of yourself is not the same as self-criticism, self-blame, or focusing only on the negative. **An objective self-assessment helps you with determining the facts. This way you know what to appreciate and respect about yourself and what adjustments you need to make in your attitudes and behaviors.**

Step back and observe your actions in different situations and the effects of what you say and do on others. Ask yourself:

- Are my intentions, words, and actions lined up with each other?
- What did I do that was effective?
- Which character qualities did I practice well?
- Where did I misstep?
- Is there another character quality that would have made a difference if I had practiced it instead?
- Did I actually behave ineffectively, or did the other person's own difficulties or problems cause a negative outcome?
- How could I have spoken or acted differently to achieve a better response from the other person?

A process like this is part of strengthening the quality of **discernment** (see Part 3).

A balanced view of yourself includes appreciating your strengths and how they benefit others. You may not realize all that is wonderful about yourself and worthy of appreciation. Perhaps you are trustworthy with others' money, loyal to your friends, or enthusiastic about new ideas. Your positive qualities provide a strong foundation for your life and are likely to bring you and others happiness. Recognizing them helps you to regard yourself as a valuable and noble human being.

By assessing whether your words or actions have caused anyone hurt feelings, injury, or insult, you can determine where you could have acted better. Perhaps a generous friend loaned you a special book, which you damaged or did not return. Maybe you forgot to be tactful when giving someone an opinion about new clothing. Negative consequences from your words or actions indicate that you may need to strengthen a quality, practice it differently, or choose an alternative one to practice.

Anger or upsets between you and someone else signal that you may have a character quality that is very weak or being misused. If you are in a situation that requires honesty, courage, and commitment, but you have not often practiced them, you will be unable to behave appropriately. You can also hurt others by misusing character strengths. Perhaps you are so purposeful that you push your own ideas or plans through without considering input from others. You think your ideas are best and will help everyone. You need to carefully consider your behavior in many circumstances. Consider this scenario:

Wendy lives on her own in an apartment building in a small city. She works for an airline, checking in passengers as they arrive at the counter with their luggage and tickets. The job is often stressful, as customers frequently become annoyed or upset with flight delays or security procedures. She does her best most days to stay calm and courteous, but sometimes she does not do as well.

After a particularly difficult day when she is rude with two customers, Wendy sits at home drinking a cup of tea and considering what happened. She does not want to blame the customers and make excuses for how she behaved with them. Upon reflection, she realizes that she had stayed up too late the night before and was distracted by a call from a former partner. She forgot to focus on practicing respect and courtesy with the customers.

When you make mistakes, try to practice such qualities as honesty, responsibility, and sincerity to help with clearing up whatever problems happened. Evaluate how well your efforts work in resolving these problems. **Thinking about your behavior and handling any problems that resulted from your words or actions is a process of inner cleansing. Just as you shower or bathe your body, or tidy your home, you need to keep your internal self in a clean and orderly condition.** Chapter 3 will discuss what to do when your actions have been harmful.

As you reflect on your thoughts and feelings, assess your actions, and learn from your mistakes, you will see opportunities to act in improved ways. Just as vehicles need regular oil changes and maintenance, so your character needs regular attention. If you fail to recognize the need for or do not follow through with vehicle maintenance, the cost of repair will be far greater than if you had taken care of maintenance regularly. In the same way, reassess yourself regularly so that you can start fresh with new goals and choices.

Over time, you will learn how to practice character strengths in ways that result in smooth interactions between you and your friends, family, coworkers, neighbors, and others, no matter how diverse or difficult. If you act lovingly towards your mother, brother, and cousin each time you relate to them, being loving will become be a strength and an effective tool for you to use in other relationships.

If character assessment makes you feel a bit like an analyst, take a deep breath and remind yourself how important it is that you thoroughly know yourself. If you do not know yourself, how can you ever expect other people to know you? Self-observation and self-knowledge will help you to:

- Continually improve yourself, increasing your self-respect and your ability to make effective choices
- Accurately observe character qualities in others, particularly in a partner
- Assess quite quickly if someone else is a good match for you
- Increase your confidence and decrease your stress by understanding what is happening in your relationships, why, and what you can do differently

By making "… your ear attentive to wisdom and your mind open to discernment…. You will then understand what is right, just, and equitable—every good course."[3]

~ Reflection ~

Think back over the past few weeks, and then answer the following:
1. What action of mine benefited someone else?
2. When did I hurt, injure, or insult someone? How did I feel and respond? What character qualities do I want to work on to prevent harming others?

HELPFUL ACTIVITY

Consider the quotation below, and then discuss with someone what character growth has to do with the concept of personal transformation. Then create an artistic, dramatic, or musical representation of the concept to share with someone or along with a friend.

"What is that mystery underlying human life which gives to events and to persons the power of…transformation? If one had never before seen a seed, nor heard of its latent life, how difficult to believe that only the cold earth, the warm sun, the descending showers, and the gardener's care were needed to cause its miraculous transformation into the growing form, the budding beauty, the intoxicating fragrance of the rose!"[4]

When and How to Assess Yourself

It is a helpful practice to take a regular time each day to review your words and actions and see how well they reflected character strengths. If daily assessment feels unnatural or difficult in the beginning, experiment to determine what timing works best for you. If you allow too much time between your actions and your review, you may forget details or tend to justify or forget any negative actions. Stay focused on your own behavior and responsibility. "Each one should test his own actions…without comparing himself to somebody else…."[5]

Often when you look back on an interaction with others, you quickly spot where you could have practiced a character quality more effectively. Sometimes, however, you might feel uncertain about how you went wrong. You may get clarity by asking yourself some direct and in-depth questions related to whatever quality seems to be appropriate. You can also ask a trusted friend or relative to assist you in reflecting on your behavior. For example, you might consider the questions below about how you practice the quality of truthfulness, as well as the helper qualities of tactfulness, kindness, courage, and confidence.

• When communicating, am I careful to stick to the facts and not make up details?
• Do I withhold important information or leave out key details because they might affect how others view me?
• Do I justify lying under some circumstances? When? Why?
• When I am truthful, do I sometimes hurt others' feelings by forgetting to be tactful?
• Do I take enough time to search for the truth when solving problems, instead of rushing to an easy solution?

Here is another example of questions to ask yourself during self-review, this time about friendliness and its helper qualities of courage and confidence:

- Have I been in situations where I was friendly to only a few people and ignored or stayed away from those that I did not know?
- Did I remember to practice courage and confidence in reaching out to someone new?
- Do I sometimes practice my friendliness in a self-centered way to impress others?
- Am I sensitive about including everyone?
- Do I pretend to be friendly in order to gain something from someone else?

You can also ask yourself these more general questions:

- How well did I meet my behavior and character goals today (or this week…)?
- What character qualities did I practice well?
- When did my actions cause hurt feelings or some other negative outcome?
- What could I have done better?
- What did I have control over? What could I not control?
- What do I want to do differently tomorrow?

With courage and detachment, step back and act as an independent observer of your life and behavior. When you are too close to a situation, you can see only a small portion of it. Close to a mountain, you might see only a handful of rocks and a few trees, but from a mile away, you can see all of it. You may find it helpful to keep a journal and record your ongoing progress. This practice will assist you to make steady character development progress. Chapter 3 will assist you with goal development.

ESSENTIAL ACTIVITY

Complete Worksheet 2: Assessing Your Character Qualities in Part 2 before continuing with the rest of this book. Completing the worksheet may be a quick activity, or it may take you some time, depending on how well you already know yourself.

If you find this worksheet difficult, then you may wish to keep coming back to work on it gradually. Reward yourself after completing portions of the assessment with a fun or relaxing activity. You can then return and add to the worksheet as you become more comfortable with self-observation skills.

As you go through the worksheet, become aware of unresolved matters from your past, and make note of them in preparation for Chapter 3 activities.

ESSENTIAL ACTIVITY

Of the four qualities for development you chose on Worksheet 2 (Part 2), make a list of self-assessment questions related to the quality, such as those in the text above.

Challenges with Assessment and Change

You may be resistant to change, feel quite satisfied with how you are, or at times feel like you are being asked to change to please another person. So, why change? Consider Dr. John

Buri's response to this question as he pondered being happy with who he had become in response to his life circumstances, even though it did not work well in his marriage: "The answer was surprisingly obvious (once I saw it). I needed to change in order to become a better person. Just because I had experienced a dysfunctional home life did not make it any less true that as human beings, we are meant to have a life of connection, interdependence, relying on others, and having them be able to rely on us. In short, we are intended to have a life of love."[6]

When you are aware that your behavior is causing negative outcomes, you need courage, perseverance, and humility to look at yourself honestly and to ask others to help you with seeing yourself more clearly.

It may seem easier to make excuses for who you are or why you do what you do than to change. Other behaviors that can interfere with seeing the issues in your life and that can disrupt making changes in your attitudes and behaviors include:

- Rationalizing or blaming others for your behavior
- Lying to yourself or others about your behavior
- Justifying and defending poor behavior
- Holding on to pride
- Refusing to let others help you with seeing your blind spots
- Denying your need for change and growth
- Holding such high standards of perfection that you give up trying to improve
- Having an overly strong desire to please or change yourself for others
- Minimizing the issue and thinking that you simply did a small or isolated offense
- Deciding the other person was too sensitive
- Thinking that no one will ever find out that there is a problem
- Refusing to forgive yourself, ask for forgiveness, or offer forgiveness

Do not worry about curbing all of these tendencies at once. You may need to give yourself some time to try out a simple change before attempting a complex one. This may be especially true if you are older, as the process of personal change also often slows down (not stops!) with time and aging. Start out with catching yourself making excuses for something you have done. Listen for blaming words in your daily speech that attempt to lay the fault for something you did onto someone else. Practice eliminating these patterns and replacing them with positive words that take responsibility for your life instead. The investment of your time in this process will provide both short-term and long-term benefits to you and others.

Being honest with yourself and others and transforming your avoidance patterns will increase your self-respect and help you to have healthy and mature relationships. The more you understand and accept yourself, the easier it will be to share yourself honestly with another person. If you resist understanding and developing yourself, a partner may feel uncomfortable or uncertain about being in a relationship with you. If you are as honest with yourself as you can be, then you will be as authentic with others as you can be.

Fear of rejection, uncertainty about who you are, or self-rejection may lead you to don a mask and pretend to be someone you are not. Such pretence interferes with self-understanding and change. It also interferes with a partner's ability to get to know you. The painful outcome to behaving this way is described by relationship educators Drs. Les and Leslie Parrott:

If we wear our masks long enough, we may guard against rejection and we may even be admired, but we'll never be whole. And that means we'll never enjoy true intimacy. … When what you do and what you say do not match the person you are inside—when your deepest identity is not revealed to others—you develop an incongruent or fragmented self.[7]

People who wear masks often focus so much on the impression they make on others that they cannot focus on the other person in a relationship. They may become stuck in a pattern of looking for someone else to make them feel good about themselves. It can help you to eliminate these patterns if you get to know your character and develop your strengths. **Remember, if you feel somewhat overwhelmed by self-assessment and character development, take small steps, one at a time.** (Chapter 3 will help.)

Remember that you are not a student in school trying to earn a grade, nor an employee going through a performance review to determine if you deserve a pay raise. Do not be overly self-critical, but neither should you ignore areas of concern. Do not overwhelm yourself by trying to address every character issue or develop every quality at the same time. It's okay to take your time and be more thorough!

By starting small and being realistic, you can remain more positive about failures and remember that you are not perfect. You also will learn to be realistic about what to expect from other people. Susan M. Campbell in *Beyond the Power Struggle*, says, "As you relax your inflexible expectations of yourself, you tend also to relax your expectations of others."[8] This relaxation into flexibility then actually helps you strive to be your best.

You are simply taking an opportunity to look at how you are doing compared to a standard of character excellence. You gain a realistic perspective of yourself that will help you work towards this goal.

~ *Reflection* ~
1. What may get in the way of my ability to understand myself and my character very well?
2. What activities can I be involved in to give me greater opportunities to practice and strengthen character qualities?

RECEIVING AND RESPONDING TO FEEDBACK

Often throughout your life, you will receive positive feedback in the form of words of appreciation from others. **Positive feedback tells you what qualities others see in you as strengths.** When you hear affirmations from others, choose carefully how to respond. Let humility guide you away from arrogance. However, ensure you also let courtesy and respect for the speaker, as well as respect for your own higher nature, stop you from discounting positive feedback. Accept it with thanks, instead.

Fully understanding your character also requires you to listen and take seriously any negative feedback you receive from other people. See how this occurs for Jacques:

> Charming and outgoing with the coworkers in his office, Jacques also regularly invites his friends over for meals at his home. When shopping for food to prepare, however, he acts superior, demanding, and unfriendly to sales clerks. He believes these people are not important enough for him to make an effort to be friendly during their brief interactions.
>
> One day, Jacques' behavior reaches such an extreme that a clerk assertively requests him to stop being so rude to her. Although he is initially annoyed and defensive, this direct feedback prompts Jacques to step back and look at his behavior. He spends a few days thinking through the way he has habitually behaved in stores, and he begins to realize that his attitude and actions have actually hurt others.
>
> Jacques decides to change his behavior. For a few weeks, he intentionally practices being friendlier to clerks in a variety of stores. Later he meets Emilie at a party. As they talk, he discovers that she works as a sales clerk in a department store. He instinctively begins to withdraw from her, but stops himself and stays friendly instead. They like each other and agree to stay in touch.
>
> One day, Jacques stops by the store where Emilie works and invites her to lunch. He stands back and watches as customers interact with her. He sees Emilie being friendly to them, as they smile and thank her for her assistance. Jacques realizes that if he had not worked on this area of his character, he might have failed to get to know Emilie. He is glad they have a chance to develop a relationship instead.

Jacques was able to make a change in this situation because he did not take offense or ignore the feedback. Instead, he chose to reflect on it and make changes in both his words and his actions. Responding openly to negative feedback is not easy. It takes practice to stop yourself from reacting, becoming defensive, or attacking the person who makes critical comments to you. Practicing detachment helps you to stop your reaction and allow the necessary time to evaluate the feedback. With time and reflection, you will be able to discern what truth the feedback contains, and whether it would be wise for you to change your behavior. In the country of Guinea they say, "Those who refuse to drink from the well of knowledge will die of thirst in the desert of ignorance."[9]

You may wish to ask someone for assertive and caring input about your attitudes and behavior. You might approach your parents, close friends, a teacher, or an employer. You can also ask for assistance from a professional counselor, therapist, relationship coach, spiritual mentor or advisor, or others skilled in giving objective input and guidance. Choose people you know to be trustworthy. Explain why you are asking them for input and why you will value their perspective. People who have an interest in character growth will participate more freely and be less judgmental.

When you approach someone to request input, you might ask, "Can you share honestly with me your perspective on how I am acting in (whatever the situation is)?" or "How do you think I am doing at developing (the name of a specific character quality)?"

Sincere requests for input to assist your character development will likely bring you useful information. However, ask only those you know will give you honest answers, not just tell you what they think you want to hear. Ask for feedback both on what they see you doing well and what you can improve. Once you receive such balanced feedback, practice discernment to assess what is useful and what is not. Use the helpful feedback to grow and change in new and positive directions.

You will sometimes receive feedback without asking for it. When this happens, as it did with Jacques in the previous story, choose how you will respond. You may need to pause and detach from any hurt feelings or reactions you have to the person's words. It may help to take a walk, hammer a few nails into a board, punch a pillow, clean your desk or home, exercise, pray, sleep on it, or do whatever assists you in taking time to process the feedback. When you are calm and ready, then you can assess the person's words and learn from them. Confucius says, "When you make a mistake, do not be afraid of mending your ways."[10]

Although it may be difficult at times to view various experiences and input from others as helpful for your learning, it is in your long-term best interest to do so when you can. With practice, you can learn to regard feedback from others as a gift to assist your growth rather than as an insult.

~ *Reflection* ~
1. What feedback have I received related to the four qualities that I am choosing to develop? (from Worksheet 2)   2. How have I responded to the feedback? Do I want to do something differently? Do I need to apologize to anyone for my actions or reactions?
HELPFUL ACTIVITIES
1. Contact someone who gave you useful feedback and express appreciation for it.   2. Contact someone else and request their input about your words, actions, and attitudes. It may be wise to identify specific character qualities that you wish them to practice in the process. Consider ones such as truthfulness, gentleness, and respect.

CHARACTER IN ONLINE PROFILES

Meeting people through on-line matching services is now the choice for millions. Services give you the opportunity to review key information about a person before making contact. It is vital to know someone's character strengths (and weaknesses!) before becoming serious in a relationship or considering marrying him or her. Knowing someone's character is a process that begins from the first encounter, whether online or in person. However, most profilers offer little information on this vital topic.

Before you enter your profile on-line, think carefully about your character strengths. You will not be perfect at any of them, of course! But, which ones are you quite good at practicing consistently? How do you apply your strengths when in a relationship with someone?

The profile form will also ask what you are looking for in a partner. What qualities are vital to see in that person as strengths?

Then, narrow the list down to about five key strengths that you will emphasize in both yourself and a potential partner (because hopefully you listed more than just one or two qualities!).

Knowing Yourself and Being Honest

Many people struggle with saying things about themselves, and after all, humility is a virtue. One profile said, "I'm not really inclined to dwell at length about myself." However, character is so vital in a couple relationship that this is not the time to hide your light. Knowing what is good about yourself and how this positively affects a partner will help you be more attractive. It is simply very, very important that you are truthful and honest in the process.

If you absolutely cannot get past this barrier of talking about yourself, then at least say, "My friends say I'm …..". Here is an example: "Friends consider me warm, insightful, compassionate, strong, and a good listener, while being gently assertive." And here is another example: "I've been told that I'm generous, kind, and a gentleman."

You can also use some humor, as in this statement: "I am honest, funny, handsome, well-dressed, faithful, and fun. Always in great mood, and always laughing! Also opinionated, passionate, loyal, outgoing, shy at times (until I tend to relax), spontaneous, romantic (this list could go on)."

What is more challenging is including content that demonstrates your strengths rather than simply listing them. Here are some possible examples:

- It took *courage* for me to (climb a mountain, begin my career over again, handle my wife dying in a car accident)
- I like to have fun, but my preference is to do all things in *moderation*.
- I strive for *excellence* in my work, especially with *helping* my co-workers with projects.
- When I face challenges, I tend to *persevere* and be *patient*. I'm usually *resilient* afterward.
- When friends tell me their difficulties, I do my best to be *compassionate* and *caring*.
- I am *gentle* and *loving* with children and pets.
- I believe in working *cooperatively* with a partner, not competing with each other.
- I tend to be *enthusiastic* about new activities and adventures.
- I speak *confidently* when I am in front of groups.
- I like to do spontaneous *thoughtful* and *kind* things for my friends and a partner.
- *Truthfulness* is vital for me, both giving and receiving. Keeping my word no matter what happens is very important.
- I am very *loyal* and deeply value my family and friendships.
- I am hard working and *responsible* with paying my bills.

What You Are Looking For

Remember that character qualities once you have formed them as strengths tend to last throughout life. Today your potential partner might be willing to ride motorcycles around the country, but it may be impossible next year. Today he or she might have beautiful brown hair, but tomorrow be bald or grey. The inner qualities are the factors that will last. So, be clear with what is very important to you.

Just as with your own profile, be specific. Here are some examples from actual profiles:

- I seek a partner who is *honest*, fun, and *trustworthy*.
- I prize *kindness*, *compassion*, and a desire to make a difference for others.
- You are *responsible*, but do not take yourself too seriously.
- You have a nice balance of *humility* and *confidence*.
- You are a *friendly*, *caring*, and *spiritual* person.
- I'm passionate about people who show *kindness* and understanding where it is needed.
- I'm looking for *honesty*, *caring*, *trust*, competence, a sense of humor, and *integrity*.
- My ideal match would be a *caring*, sensitive person.
- What does excite me is *kindness*, *compassion*, intelligence, a great sense of humor, and a smile that radiates sunshine.

You are more likely to receive what you are looking for if you are clear. If you start your profile out with, "I'm just doing this for a laugh", then no one will take you seriously or respond. Focus on what is true about your character and on what you most appreciate in a potential partner, and a match will be far more likely.

∽ *Encouragement* ∾

If you are not used to self-assessment, this chapter may have been difficult for you. Developing the practice of regular self-observation is vital to your personal growth and relationship success. Therefore, you can view your full participation in this process as a major achievement that will benefit you for your entire lifetime.

REFERENCES FOR CHAPTER 2

1. Rick Warren, *Purpose Driven® Life*, pp. 27-29.
2. 'Abdu'l-Bahá, *Selections from the Writings of 'Abdu'l-Bahá*, #17
3. *Tanakh*, Mishlei (Proverbs) 2:2, 9.
4. Howard Colby Ives, *Portals to Freedom*, p. 13.
5. *The Bible* (New International Version), Galatians 6:4.
6. John Buri, PhD, "Do You Have a Tail?", quoted in *All-in-One Marriage Prep: 75 Experts Share Tips and Wisdom to Help You Get Ready Now*, pp. 74-75.
7. Dr. Les Parrott, III, and Dr. Leslie Parrott, *Relationships*, p. 32.
8. Susan M. Campbell, PhD, *Beyond the Power Struggle*, p. 86.
9. *More African Proverbs*, p. 17.
10. Confucius, *Confucius, The Analects*, I:8.

Chapter 3

Developing Your Character

INTRODUCTION

After doing the work of the last two chapters, you now understand character and your strengths and abilities more clearly. You are gaining insights about what practice and skill development you need. You learn best through awareness and experience. Hopefully you also have the help of a good teacher, coach, or friend who gives you clear feedback and encourages you to keep skill-building.

Mastering character development requires practicing qualities over and over again and learning each step of the way. Some days you may wish that your self-development were complete—no more impatience, fearfulness, or rudeness. Realistically, however, you can expect your life to be a process of ongoing growth, no matter what age you are. With each good choice you make, you will gradually become more consistent and effective. Even small changes can significantly affect you and your interactions with others.

Sometimes change is difficult, and progress takes willingness and perseverance. Often, you realize you need to change to respond to difficulties or after you have made poor choices. Ongoing personal review, encouragement from people you trust and love, apologizing, practicing forgiveness, and making amends are all aspects of personal development. Sometimes you also benefit from remembering to lighten up and not take yourself so seriously. Often the best way to handle mistakes is with a sense of humor.

Even when you become excellent at practicing qualities and have found a partner, you still need to practice and stay familiar with the best words and actions to use. If you do not keep your skills sharp, you might begin to think you need a better partner, when you really just need to improve yourself.

SMALL, CONSISTENT STEPS

The more you are engaged in actions that increase what you know about your own character, the better you will be able to monitor and evaluate your choices. This monitoring will help you to assess whether the ways you are speaking and acting are consistent with achieving your life purposes. Growth occurs as you expand your understanding of character, practice the qualities, observe how your words and actions affect others, and make improvements.

Your character assessment from Chapter 2 provides information about what you may choose to change to improve your character. Consider how this process works for Jenita:

> Jenita rapidly writes in her journal about an incident with her manager earlier in the day. "I completely lost my patience and spoke rudely to Malcolm when he wanted me to do the weekly report in a different way." Resting her pen on the notebook, she pauses to reflect. She notes that forgetting to set her alarm clock had caused her to hurry, skip breakfast, and arrive late at work. She realizes that this one small mistake resulted in her struggling with impatience the entire day. She picks up her pen and begins writing about what she can do and say to let her manager know she regrets her behavior.
>
> Jenita then decides to step back and look more broadly at other areas of her life where impatience has been a problem. She notices a pattern of conflicts that arise when she rigidly insists that something should be done her way, and then she becomes impatient with others. Through her self-assessment and new insights, Jenita recognizes that practicing the quality of flexibility will help her with being more patient with people. She decides to use these two qualities together in her work relationships for the coming week. She also decides to put an ongoing alarm setting on her cellphone to prevent her from oversleeping again.

Jenita makes a choice to change and puts together a plan to begin the process. As she acts to carry out the plan, reassesses her progress, and perseveres, she will become more consistently flexible and patient.

Changes that require "unlearning" an old habit at the same time as learning a new one will take more time. The younger you are, the easier it will be to make changes, but with a willing heart, conscious effort, and concentration, you can continue to grow throughout your lifetime.

Although it may be easy for you to keep track in your head of how you are doing, what you are learning about yourself, and where you want to improve, you are likely to gain more insights when you systematically write down your observations and conclusions. Writing focuses your attention and helps you clarify both what is happening in your life and your feelings in reaction to those events. You can set goals for and plan how you want to respond to a situation as well. Then you can record your progress towards your goals. Make specific notes about particular actions and words that show improvement. You can then look back and track your progress. How have you changed? Some people journal daily, some weekly, and others only when there is something that they are struggling to understand. Others find that writing poetry or engaging in some other creative outlet such as writing a song is more beneficial. Experiment with what works best for you.

HELPFUL ACTIVITIES

1. Create a journal to record your ongoing character self-assessment and observations, focusing especially on your practice of the four qualities you chose in Worksheet 2 (Part 2). Decorating your journal can be a creative break from all the thinking and writing. You may also find it helpful to have a sketchbook, drawing tools, and coloring materials handy to express your thoughts and feelings visually instead of in words.

2. Set a goal to write in your character journal every day for a week. At the end of the week, assess whether this frequency benefited you. If not, set a new goal to try a different frequency. After some time has passed, assess its usefulness. Keep experimenting until you discover what works best for you.

~ Reflection ~

1. What do I think and how do I feel about making changes in myself?
2. What might I gain by changing?
3. What are my concerns about responses from others?

ESSENTIAL AND HELPFUL ACTIVITIES

Essential:
1. Complete Worksheet 3: Creating Your Character Development Plan in Part 2, setting goals for improving the four character strengths you chose to work on when you completed Worksheet 2.

Helpful:
2. Write each of the four strengths you selected on Worksheet 2 and used for Worksheet 3 (Part 2) on a small piece of thick paper or cardboard. Place these four papers in a small bowl or bag and pick one each morning to focus on that day. At the end of the day, assess your behavior related to that trait. (Consider referring to the details in Part 3.) If you are in a relationship, you may wish to encourage your partner to do the same activity. At the end of the day, you can then discuss how your practices of the chosen character strengths went. You can later add other qualities you want to focus on to your container.

THE POWER OF PERSEVERANCE

Learning new ways of behavior requires perseverance and extensive practice, particularly when a behavior or character weakness is long-standing. "Spiritual growth is not automatic. It takes an intentional commitment. You must want to grow, decide to grow, make an effort to grow, and persist in growing."[1]

Dan Popov, PhD, one of the founders of The Virtues Project (www.virtuesproject.com), discusses the importance of commitment and perseverance:

Your choices matter, so make a commitment and choose a new path, even if you are uncertain about where it will lead you. Be aware—if the path feels familiar, it is not a new one. Only if you give a full 100 percent commitment, will you be able to effectively assess the value of your choice later on. Tell others about your commitment and ask for their assistance, pointing out how their involvement can benefit both of you. Call on the spiritual power of prayer and allow yourself to be guided forward.

Your commitment and choice to take a new path in your life may result in a period of turmoil calling for conscious awareness and consistent effort. At the first difficulty along the path, you may be tempted to retreat to a more familiar way, but persevere, show determination, and hold on to your commitment with integrity. Guidance, confirmation, and support often come while you are in action. Observe what happens and be honest with yourself. Be patient, flexible, and graceful. Positive change and growth will come—little by little, day by day.[2]

Some days you will feel that you are making more progress than on others. Sometimes you may even feel as if you are sliding backwards, but it is normal in the process of change to take two steps forward and one back. You will also have times when you feel as if you are standing still or stuck in one spot.

When you make changes in your behavior, people who are used to your acting in a certain way may not easily accept the changes as real. It may take some time for them to trust your commitment to the new actions. If someone gives you negative feedback while you are growing, assess its validity and helpfulness. Discern whether the person is giving you an appropriate message or just does not feel comfortable with your changing. Others may wish that you would change back to the way you were before, since that is what they are used to.

If the thought of changing or developing your character overwhelms you, try making other smaller changes instead to build your confidence. See how perseverance works and learn about your adaptability and flexibility. For example, consider making an adjustment in part of your daily routine or schedule, perhaps changing the time you eat breakfast, the order in which you do two activities, or the routines of your exercise program. Observe how long it takes before the new pattern feels "normal."

As you go through the process of personal assessment and change, make sure that you have people who assist and encourage you in your efforts. In addition, the more you anticipate, with humility, that those around you will support you in changing, the more assistance, affirmation, and confirmation you will likely receive.

HELPFUL ACTIVITIES

1. Make one small change in your environment and see how long it takes you to get used to it. You might move a piece of furniture, change a picture on the wall, or put your socks in a different drawer. Does this experiment help you with adjusting your expectations of how much time may be required for character changes in yourself or in a partner to be consistent?
2. Identify a habit you want to change. Write specific goals for your behaviors, ask someone to hold you accountable and encourage you, plan weekly rewards, and set up whatever else you can think of that will help you to succeed. Do creativity and perseverance help you?

SUCCESS IN CHANGING

The following sections provide some supportive steps for strengthening your character.

Focus on Your Strengths

Think of your character strengths as gems. You are, in fact, "...a mine rich in gems of inestimable value."[3] Throughout your life, in the mine of your character, you discover beautiful stones or dig out rough-looking rocks that you can clean, cut, and polish into beautiful gems—character strengths. These gems are gifts you can share with others and contribute to a relationship. As you share these gifts with others, you will find that you are more likely to notice and acknowledge the character gifts that others give back to you.

Do practice moderation when acknowledging your strengths. You want to increase your self-respect, not build up your ego so you can brag about how good you are. Practicing humility helps you with maintaining balance. Recognizing that your actions are not always the best helps you to see that you and your character are works in progress.

HELPFUL ACTIVITIES

1. Identify four specific gems; such as, diamonds, emeralds, sapphires, or rubies. You might locate photos of them in a book, magazine, or on the Internet. From Worksheet 2 (Part 2), choose four character qualities you consider your strengths and match each to one of the gems you chose. As you practice each quality, visualize the beautiful gem that you have associated with it. For example, you could associate a ruby with justice. Every time you act fairly or fight for justice on behalf of someone else, visualize a sparkling red ruby inside of yourself.
2. For each of the character strengths you chose to develop (Worksheet 3), identify someone you know who practices that quality effectively. You may choose from people who are deceased or still alive, real or fictional, or famous or someone you know personally. Consider what words or actions you think demonstrate the quality you associate with each person.

Try New Activities and Experiences

The choices you make each day about what to do with your time and energy reflect your priorities—what you believe is most important. Your priorities may include friends, work, spiritual activities, family, education, community service, hobbies, home maintenance, entertainment, money, sports, or pets. Finding a partner may be on your list, or transforming a current friendship into a partner relationship may also be a possibility. If you already have a partner, spending time together will be high on your list too.

Look back at the purpose statement you wrote in Chapter 2 and consider whether your use of time and energy reflects your purposes and your priorities. If not, you can make adjustments to align your purposes, priorities, and behaviors. To facilitate personal growth, you may need to choose some new activities, different experiences, and maybe even some new friends.

Find opportunities to practice new interactions to strengthen qualities in which you are weak, such as acceptance, courtesy, generosity, friendliness, and service to others. "Sensitivity to the feelings and needs of others and a willing disposition to help and serve are hallmarks of a person committed to the path of spiritual development."[4] You can look to your civic community, neighbors, religious leaders, family, education system, and other organizations for opportunities to serve. **Contributing to others will help you with developing an excellent character.**

Fulfilling promises to participate in activities allows you to practice commitment, demonstrating to others that you are trustworthy. The ability to make and keep commitments is essential to strong relationships, reduces misunderstandings, and prevents serious disagreements.

You can also strengthen weak qualities by noticing the behavior of those people with whom you associate regularly. If they encourage you to behave poorly, if you act differently around them, or you change yourself inappropriately to be with them, you would be wise to spend less time with them. If someone is openly unsupportive and critical of your choices to change, then you may want to reconsider being around that person at all. You need strong defenses against negative influences to be successful at moving forward in your life. You can choose to spend more time with people who set a positive example and encourage your character growth. With these people, you can use courage and self-discipline to practice the character strengths you want to develop and receive positive reinforcement from them.

You can also benefit from looking for opportunities to encourage others and acknowledge how well they are practicing certain qualities. The more you look for strengths in others, the more you appreciate the qualities and want to practice them yourself.

~ *Reflection* ~

1. How am I using my time? Am I happy with my choices?
2. What specific qualities can I strengthen through service to others?
3. How are other people helping me with positive choices?

ESSENTIAL ACTIVITIES

1. Look at one of the four qualities you chose to develop (Worksheet 3) and choose a new activity that would support its growth. For example, if you want to work on patience, learn to do needlework or restore an old car. If you want to work on friendliness, plan a social occasion at your home. If a chosen activity gives you good opportunities to strengthen the quality, repeat it or do something else. If it did not work well, then try a new activity.

2. Find or design a project that requires you to work cooperatively with others. You might build something, volunteer for community service, make a quilt, cook a complex meal, beautify a piece of property, or organize an event. Before you begin, choose the qualities that you want to focus on improving throughout the project. You may choose to share the qualities with your team members and ask them to assist you. Invite others involved in the activity to choose qualities to practice as well, perhaps through using the list in Chapter 1. At the end of the project, assess what you learned and what personal growth took place. How did your improved behaviors benefit others?

Get Help

Your wisdom and your understanding of character strength development will grow with time and experience. You can speed up the process, however, by looking for input and guidance from someone with valuable experience to share. A person skilled in the quality you want to develop and willing to help you, may give you advice, share insights, and encourage you.

By associating with people who are committed to excellence, you will more easily keep your character qualities strong and effective. They will set a good example for you and encourage you. Remember this thought from Buddha: "A man that stands alone…may be weak and slip back into his old ways. Therefore, stand ye together, assist one another, and strengthen one another's efforts."[5] You do not generally learn about and develop your character in isolation from others. Often your best "teachers" are the other people in your life, including a relationship partner. You learn from interacting with others.

You can find many potential sources of assistance for working through personal development and dealing with troublesome issues through research and the recommendations of others. You can talk with relatives, friends, spiritual advisors, teachers, a relationship or life coach, a therapist, or a counselor. You can join a support group or participate in educational opportunities, such as workshops or informal study groups where you can interact with others facing similar challenges.

If you have a strong streak of independence (or stubbornness!), you may resist seeking or asking for assistance. In this case, asking for help would be a great opportunity to practice acceptance and humility. Do not view asking for help as a sign of weakness, but as an indicator of courage and wisdom. Your reaching out to others also gives them the opportunity to practice important qualities; such as, helpfulness and compassion.

If you have an active addiction that is interfering with your character efforts, identify what steps might minimize harm to yourself and others. For addiction to substances such as alcohol, drugs, or food (eating disorders), you may need to join a 12-Step support group. Anyone struggling with addiction to Internet pornography should see a therapist specializing in sex-related matters and put in place electronic controls to restrict access to certain websites. Compulsive shoppers may need to limit the amount of money they carry or what credit cards they use. Support groups may also be helpful for all of these situations. As you gain help and improve your life, it will become easier to align your words and actions with the character qualities.

HELPFUL ACTIVITY
Identify someone willing to commit to serving as a listening partner for you and request his or her assistance with your character growth efforts. Promise that person what actions you will take related to the four specific qualities you chose to develop (Worksheet 3). Agree on how often you will check in with each other.

Handle Difficulties

Facing, accepting, and working through difficulties and crises develop your character. In fact, a crisis often transforms someone's life in dramatic ways. **If you take advantage of problems and treat them as valuable learning experiences, not only will you deal effectively with them, but you will also strengthen whatever character qualities you practice to solve a problem.** If you or someone close to you has an accident, illness, or injury, you have an opportunity to practice patience, compassion, and courage. Such situations draw on your character strengths and invite you to engage in personal growth.

If you have a problem with another person:
- Identify character qualities that will be particularly useful in resolving the situation
- Spend time visualizing what you would say and do while practicing that quality effectively
- Affirm internally that you can respond positively
- Choose words and actions that demonstrate the quality, even if you do not feel like practicing it
- Observe the results
- Respond to any challenges that arise in ways that strengthen your maturity and your spirituality; difficulties may remind you to practice thankfulness for the blessings you have and to turn to spiritual sources for assistance; rely on prayer to focus you outwardly on a source of comfort, instead of internally on problems.

Consider problems as learning experiences, not just negative occurrences to avoid. "Men who suffer not, attain no perfection. The plant most pruned by the gardeners is that one which, when the summer comes, will have the most beautiful blossoms and the most abundant fruit."[6] Challenges provide opportunities to grow and develop. In every crisis, you can achieve a personal victory.

HELPFUL ACTIVITY
Create a computer screensaver, poster, or other visual object to remind you of a character strength. When you are going through a difficult time, let what you created inspire you to persevere and learn from the experience. Alternatively or in addition, you might choose or create a song, poem, or quotation to encourage you.

Lighten Up

As you work on character growth and make mistakes, as we all do, humor and laughter will help with keeping you from taking yourself too seriously. If you can find the humor in your efforts or in what happened, you might gain more clarity about what to do next. Encourage others to laugh along with you as well. **Happiness and joy lighten your heart and free you to participate more fully in all of life. Practicing positive character traits effectively, and genuinely loving others, add to your happiness.**

Detachment from anxiety and thankfulness for blessings can increase your happiness, even when you have challenges in your life. Thankfulness is not just a feeling, but an attitude you can generate by specifically identifying what is positive in your life. Author Linda Kavelin Popov explains:

> Without thankfulness people would stay focused on negativity. They would do nothing but whine and complain. They would miss the beauty of life and the power of learning, especially during difficult times. … No matter how difficult or dark things become, there is always light. There is something to learn in every painful situation. In fact, sometimes when you look back at a really hard test in your life and realize what you learned, that is when you feel the most grateful of all.[7]

You can also increase your happiness by exploring ways to make others happy. Can you practice your creativity to surprise and delight someone? Can you think of a way to make someone genuinely laugh? A thankful and happy approach to life enhances your ability to develop other character strengths.

HELPFUL ACTIVITIES

1. Plan a fun activity and invite friends to join you. If you know that you tend to be too serious or overly concerned with details, ask someone else to plan something fun in which you can participate. You might try getting involved in part of the planning to learn how to be more light-hearted.
2. List 10 people or aspects of your life for which you are thankful and share the list with someone else. Review this list daily, or whenever you start thinking about the negative aspects of your life. Consider decorating the list by adding graphics or artwork and posting it in a visible place in your home.
3. For a week, at the end of each day, identify something funny that happened during the day. If possible, share the stories with someone else.

RECOVERING FROM POOR CHOICES

Sometimes the need to change becomes obvious after you have made a mistake or caused hurt, insult, or injury to someone. Sometimes when you harm someone you may lapse into denial, try to escape from problems, or blame others. Consider this approach instead:

...[T]he spiritually mature person faces whatever problems arise with relative calm and decision. He recognizes and acknowledges whatever faults he may have committed which have contributed to the problem and accepts and forgives the errors made by others. He doesn't get bogged down in talking about who caused the problem or waste energy defending himself. He concentrates on searching for a good solution, using prayer for divine guidance, meditation, and consultation with others. Then he willingly cooperates in carrying out the actions necessary to apply the solution.[8]

Whether you have made one mistake or many, you can still attempt a better choice next time. You learn as much from your mistakes, failures, and challenges, if not more, than from your successes. Choose to learn and persevere in your character transformation, determined to forgive yourself and resolve the matter, and then not make the same mistake again.

Make Apologies and Amends

When you assessed your character and choices in Worksheets 1 and 2 (Part 2), you probably identified some occasions when you caused harm by your attitude, words, or actions. Perhaps you never took action to resolve some of those incidents. You may have broken a promise to a friend, refused to cooperate with a coworker, spoken disrespectfully to a parent or teacher, cheated on an exam, lied to or otherwise mistreated someone, or any of a wide range of actions springing from your lower nature. These unresolved incidents provide opportunities to assess your character choices, take responsibility, make apologies, make amends, set development goals, and take the needed corrective actions. You need to determine what weak or misused character qualities contributed to your behavior and which qualities you need to strengthen or adjust.

It takes humility, honesty, and courage to listen to your conscience, admit when you are wrong, and take the necessary actions to address situations where you have caused harm. Whatever actions you choose for making amends must be sincere. If you can express an honest feeling of regret about what happened, and convey a true desire to do things differently in the future, you can heal a situation or relationship.

You may be clear about what responsible and constructive actions you need to take to resolve the situation you caused. If not, talk with the person most affected and together choose a path that restores integrity, justice, trust, and love to the situation. Obviously, if you owe someone money, you will likely have to pay it back. Sometimes, of course, you owe a person much more than something material. You may need to ask them to give you another chance to prove your loyalty and friendship. In essence, the person you hurt gives you the opportunity to start over. By changing your words and actions, both with the one you harmed and with others, you can prevent recurrences of such poor behavior in the future. Consider this scenario:

Pierce runs three miles over roads and hills most mornings by himself. One day, his younger sister, Annette, who usually runs in the evenings, asks Pierce if she can exercise with him. Blurting out "No way," he tells her she is too much of a grouch in the mornings to be good company.

As Pierce runs alone the next morning, he thinks about how hurt and unhappy she looked and regrets being so rude and unfriendly. They are not as close as they used to be, and he thinks perhaps running together would give them an opportunity to rebuild their relationship. Pierce calls Annette, apologizes, and invites her to run with him the next day. She forgives him, and they spend time together peacefully.

Sometimes a wrongdoing is so severe that it will be best for you to make amends by practicing detachment and staying away from the person you harmed. Avoiding contact may be necessary if you have threatened someone's life or well-being or if the person is adamant about not associating with you further. At times, however, the intervention of a legal mediator, counselor, or religious leader may be able to help you heal such a situation. 12-Step recovery and support groups (usually related to addictions) face this issue straight on by advising their participants to make direct amends with those they have harmed wherever possible, "except when to do so would injure them or others."[9]

ESSENTIAL ACTIVITY

Make a list of everyone you have harmed and not made amends with, or where a situation is unresolved, and what specifically you did that you regret. [Note: You may have begun to make this list while doing Worksheets 1 and 2 in Part 2]. This activity may take some time, so simply start a list and keep coming back to it as you remember names and situations. Be as honest as you can and resist making excuses or blaming others for your actions.

When you are certain your list is complete, plan how and when to address each unresolved matter. You may want to ask advice to determine an appropriate plan before taking action. Afterwards, assess each situation and determine whether it feels completed for you and the other person. Do your best to avoid doing anything that is likely to cause further harm. If the person you have harmed is unreachable or has died, you may be able to complete the matter through prayer or by writing the person a letter that you keep or destroy.

Note: Be encouraging and kind to yourself and seek assistance as needed. Keep in mind that you want to develop your character, clean up past mistakes, and move forward, not spend a high amount of time dwelling on your faults, errors, or inadequacies.

Request Forgiveness

For a situation to feel fully resolved, the person you harmed needs to detach from the hurt and forgive you, but the response to your request for forgiveness depends on the other person. All you can do is request forgiveness and then practice detachment yourself.

Even knowing that what you did was wrong, you may find it hard to ask for forgiveness. However, forgiveness will assist you and the other person to put the incident in the past. Depending on your beliefs, you can begin by asking God to forgive you, then focus on forgiving yourself, and finally ask the one you offended to forgive you. **Self-forgiveness is a key part of the process. Holding self-directed anger or criticism inside freezes part of your life in the past, both mentally and emotionally, and this can make you anxious and even physically ill.** Take responsibility for yourself and your choices, but do not condemn yourself or punish yourself endlessly.

Once you are ready to request forgiveness, try to do so in person. Otherwise, a phone call is probably the next best thing. On the other hand, a written request might help you organize your thoughts before speaking to the person. Be cautious about putting in writing deeply personal information, especially if the person you are giving it to has a history of breaking trust and might use your written words against you or cause problems for you. In some situations, trustworthy family members, teachers, advisors, or spiritual leaders might be able to assist you and the other person to resolve the matter. Whatever method you use, thoughtfully choose your words and do not make excuses or offer self-justifications to minimize your behavior. Be brief, clear, and sincere.

Choose the best time, place, and circumstances to talk to the person, rather than simply acting in a hurry to make yourself feel better. Your inner discomfort is a definite signal that you need to act, but the other person may be more open to forgiving you and accepting your amends if you handle the situation wisely. You and the other person may be in a more open and constructive frame of mind if you both tend to your well-being, perhaps by eating and getting well rested first. You may find it helpful to pray separately or together as well. Find a place and time when interruptions from other people or ringing telephones will not distract you. Consider what works best for the situation and the personalities of the people involved—it may be a quiet corner or a one-on-one sports activity.

Remember that it is important to *request* forgiveness, not *demand* it. Gary Chapman and Jennifer Thomas in *The Five Languages of Apology* say:

> Don't demand forgiveness. You cannot expect it. When we demand forgiveness, we fail to understand the nature of forgiveness. Forgiveness is essentially a *choice* to lift the penalty and to let the person back into our lives. It is to pardon the offense so that we might redevelop trust. Forgiveness says, "I care about our relationship. Therefore, I choose to accept your apology and no longer demand justice." It is essentially a gift. A gift that is demanded is no longer a gift.[10]

The merciful gift and act of forgiveness allows healing between you and the other person and restores at least some unity between you. However, you cannot predict the outcome of your request for forgiveness. The person you approach may not feel you deserve forgiveness, may see your request as a burden, might forgive you even before you ask, might do it instantly when you ask, might refuse to consider it, or may simply need time to think and pray about it. Forgiveness often takes time, and the person you harmed has the right to decide how long, no matter how painful the unresolved situation is for you. Do not burden others by trying to make them feel guilty if they do not offer you forgiveness right away.

If you are truly sincere in your request for forgiveness and obviously willing to make amends, hopefully the other person will forgive you. Whether the person does, or does not, be at peace with yourself if you have made your best effort and forgiven yourself.

ESSENTIAL ACTIVITY
Create or find a meditative space where you can reflect on your behavior, your self-forgiveness, and who you want to ask to forgive you. You might try playing some music to help you feel peaceful and experience inner healing. If instead you find it easier to reflect while being active, consider a cleaning or building project or exercising.

Give Forgiveness

The previous section spoke of requesting forgiveness from those you have harmed. At times, however, you will be the injured party. In either case, forgiving helps to bring closure to an issue and assists both people to move forward. However, in this case, the responsibility shifts back to you again. What character qualities will help you with forgiving another person?

Natalie Jenkins is quoted in *The Power of Commitment* as saying that when someone hurts you, forgiveness is "…giving up your perceived right to get even. It is a strategy for making things right again that does not involve revenge."[11] **When someone harms you, you can choose to hold onto your hurt or to let it go by forgiving. Forgiveness does not mean you ignore the situation or say that what happened was okay. Just as you are responsible for your actions, so others are for theirs.**

Forgiveness frees you from holding something against another person. Drs. Les and Leslie Parrott say that forgiving is choosing to reject "…vengeance, renounce bitterness, break the silence of estrangement, and actually wish the best" for the other person. As the Parrott's point out, "Forgiveness is not for the faint-hearted. Our sense of justice usually recoils at the thought of this unnatural act. Only the brave forgive."[12] In other words, forgiving takes courage.

In a relationship, refusing to forgive your partner keeps you stuck in the past and in the pain. The details of the offense stay clear in your mind and replay over and over. Resentment makes it difficult to focus on your partner's best qualities. You then struggle with moving your relationship forward. When you forgive, the details become vague, and you may even forget the incident entirely. If the topic does come up, you can talk about it without a strong emotional reaction.

Consider this perspective:

> When you forgive, you need to do more than say the words and mean them. You also have to extend a forgiving, helping hand. To truly forgive, you need to be gracious to your partner. Being kind and generous as well as granting pardon will put you back on the same footing and keep your love strong.[13]

The ability to forgive relates to the value one places on unity. The more committed you are to maintaining harmony, the more intolerance you will have for disunity, and the more quickly you will grant forgiveness. Not everyone has this ability to forgive quickly or even instantly, however, so take the time that you need, but work towards increasing your ability to forgive promptly. Be aware, however, that your forgiveness needs to be sincere. It is not wise to forgive someone automatically just because the situation is difficult or because the other person's regret moves you emotionally. If you say you forgive someone, but still hold onto significant levels of anger, sadness, or pain from the incident, the situation is not resolved. You may need to find inner healing first.

Once a situation is resolved, leave it in the past and do not bring it up again. Reminding someone about a hurtful situation may indicate that you have not completely forgiven. Keeping track of each other's mistakes and bringing up issues from the past harms relationships and interferes with love and unity. Remember, "Love is patient, love is kind. It does not envy, it does not boast, it is not proud. It is not rude, it is not self-seeking, it is not easily angered, it keeps no record of wrongs. …Love never fails…."[14]

There are also times when the primary person you may be harming by withholding forgiveness is yourself. Perhaps someone close to you has died, and you have difficulty forgiving the person for leaving you. You may be holding onto resentment for something someone did years previously, and the person is unreachable and may not even remember the incident. Holding onto anger, grief, or whatever emotions you are experiencing, keeps you stuck in the past and prevents you from moving forward powerfully with your present and future. Forgiving the other person, and forgiving yourself for holding onto the negative emotions, are both part of the healing process.

◆ Encouragement ◆

These three chapters have presented information about developing your character, which is an essential step in preparing for a relationship. By completing the activities and reflecting on the material, you have gained insights into new concepts and into yourself. You are doing great work! Reward yourself for your concentrated effort by doing something special for yourself.

Note: There is a Bonus Worksheet in Part 2 entitled "Choosing Character Qualities to Look for in a Partner". It is excerpted from the eBook *Becoming Relationship Ready*. While the character qualities are fresh in your mind, you may wish to complete it. **Choose a partner who is as interested in personal growth as you are, so that you both have the desire and determination to practice positive behaviors and character strengths consistently.** Both of you will grow by listening to your wisdom and by self-correcting or adjusting after feedback or facing difficult challenges. A partner who is not interested in personal development will challenge and frustrate you if you are trying to grow. Such a relationship may not last. Choose what is best for you for the long-term.

REFERENCES FOR CHAPTER 3

1. Rick Warren, *Purpose Driven® Life*, p. 179
2. Dan Popov, PhD, one of the founders of The Virtues Project (www.virtuesproject.com)
3. Bahá'u'lláh, *Gleanings from the Writings of Bahá'u'lláh*, p. 260
4. Joan Barstow Hernández, *Love, Courtship, and Marriage*, pp. 41-42
5. Compiled by Paul Carus, *The Gospel of Buddha*, XVII:2
6. 'Abdu'l-Bahá, *Paris Talks*, p. 51
7. Linda Kavelin Popov, *The Family Virtues Guide*, p. 250
8. Joan Barstow Hernández, *Love, Courtship, and Marriage*, p. 28
9. Alcoholics Anonymous, www.aa.org; Copyright © Alcoholics Anonymous World Services, Inc.
10. Gary Chapman and Jennifer Thomas, *The Five Languages of Apology*, p. 99
11. Natalie Jenkins quoted in Scott M. Stanley, *The Power of Commitment*, p. 205
12. Dr. Les Parrott III; Dr. Leslie Parrott, *When Bad Things Happen to Good Marriages*, p. 142
13. Howard J. Markman, Scott M. Stanley, Susan L. Blumberg, Natalie H. Jenkins, and Carol Whiteley, *12 Hours to a Great Marriage*, p. 207
14. *The Bible*; 1 Corinthians 13:4, 5, 8

PART 1B:

KNOWING A PARTNER'S CHARACTER

INTRODUCTION TO PART 1B: WHEN YOU ARE IN A RELATIONSHIP

From the first encounter you have with a potential partner, and then through all stages of your relationship, you have the vital task of ensuring you thoroughly know the person's character. At times this can be straightforward and easy. Some qualities are obvious and consistent. However, many will take significant time, experiences together, and reflection to discover.

You will have choices throughout your relationship that will affect your success. How you spend your time together can aid the process or interfere with it. Your skillfulness with observation and communication, as well as your partner's, will assist you in learning what you need to know.

Character affects virtually all of your words and actions, and the same for your partner. One of the primary goals of being in a relationship is to work towards marriage. As you assess whether your partner is someone you may wish to marry, it will be wise for you to ensure he or she has the qualities that provide a good foundation for a long-term commitment.

Marriage, like all of life, has times of peace and times of difficulty. Living together in harmony with someone and being parents or stepparents together takes knowledge and skill. If you ensure you have a foundation of compatibility and good character, you have a greater opportunity for a happy, successful marriage.

Chapter 4

Understanding Character and Partner Observation

INTRODUCTION

Every time you are with your partner, whether alone or with family or friends, you have the opportunity to engage in observing words, actions, and interactions. This is a learning-in-action process so that you thoroughly know your partner's character and are clear whether your relationship has potential to move towards marriage.

As you observe your partner, you will likely discover details you appreciate and others you find difficult to accept. For instance, someone who gets along well with your friends may annoy your mother. You will assess what you appreciate, what requires you to accept and adjust, what you can influence to change with your partner's full agreement and cooperation, and what will not work at all. It is vital that you *celebrate your harmonies* and also *pay careful attention to any warning signs*, obtaining assistance from others as needed to understand whether an issue is truly serious.

Examine whether you are staying confident that you are a well-matched couple and there is good evidence to demonstrate this. At the same time, be cautious of misleading yourself into thinking that your partner is the only possible person for you or that there is some mystical reason that fate is at work and you are "meant to be" together. Sometimes being in this state of mind can blind you to what is not working well in the relationship or to where there are true incompatibilities.

Successful observation, which includes understanding and processing what you see and hear, helps you keep "both eyes open" to clearly see your partner and to be sure you are choosing someone who is a good long-term match for you.

UNDERSTANDING THE OBSERVATION PROCESS

Observing is the process of gathering information through careful and directed attention. The more attentive and systematic your observations, the more knowledge and insights you will gain. You observe what the other person says and does—or does not say or do. Good observation skills allow you to perceive details about your partner's appearance, choices, character qualities, words, actions, and attitudes. Of course, hopefully your partner will be aware of your observation and will take care to learn about you at the same time. Your mutual honesty with each other will help this process.

Time and Infatuation

Part of the intent of observing and assessing your partner's character strengths is to avoid being blinded by infatuation. Infatuation, or being "in love," is usually an intense and short-lived passion. It's often the way a relationship begins, and it can be a special time of connection when you only see the best in each other. **However, practicing detachment and getting to know someone thoroughly will help you establish a lasting relationship built on committed love.**

Relationship expert John Van Epp, PhD, addresses the importance of taking time to know someone intimately, no matter what age you are or your level of relationship experience. He says:

> "Not until around three months into a relationship do deep-seated patterns start to become evident. ... [T]he newness of a relationship is a natural inebriating effect accompanying attraction that typically begins to wear off around the third month. We put our best foot forward until we feel a bit more secure in a new relationship. Then we slack off a bit and let our imperfections surface. This is why it is so difficult to be sure what someone is really like in the first three months. This is also why it is so essential that you keep a grip on your trust, reliance, commitment, and sexual involvement with this person during this period of time." [1]

Judgment and Respect

Your intent with observation is not to judge your partner's behavior as right or wrong, but rather to determine whether the person has the character strengths that are important to you and has the qualities that will work well in a relationship, courtship, and then marriage with you. You also need to know whether the two of you are a compatible match for each other in purposes, values, lifestyle, and more.

A delicate part of the process is learning to observe with respect and without offending your partner. Effective observation helps you with seeing a partner with "both eyes open", rather than acquiring just a superficial understanding. You need more than an online profile or a brief resume of people's life experiences to thoroughly know them, especially their character. You will miss key information about your partner if you close one eye or both eyes in denial of potential problems.

Do not take someone else's opinion about your partner as fact without checking it out. While getting to know someone, you will need to **carefully assess the accuracy of any information you get from a third party, positive or negative, that you do not directly observe or confirm yourself**. You are "...not intended to see through the eyes of another, hear through another's ears nor comprehend with another's brain. ... Therefore, depend upon your own reason and judgment...." [2]

If you want a partner with the strengths of honesty, courage, or kindness, you will need a good picture in your mind of what it looks like for a person to be honest, courageous, or kind. Knowing your own character will make you more effective at observing the character of a partner [See the work you did in Part 1A of this book]. In Part 3 of this book are the Powerful Character Qualities for your reference as you observe a partner's words and actions.

You will make some observations quickly and easily. Other aspects of your partner, however, will become clear to you only as you participate in a variety of activities and converse together at length. **Observation will help you learn how your partner handles friendships, family interactions and obligations, education, work, community service, religious or spiritual activities, commitments, and responsibilities.** These observations are especially important when you and your partner come from different family, cultural, or religious backgrounds. You will have to work harder to ensure you share similar values. Observations are especially challenging to accomplish if you are in a long-distance relationship.

You may choose to identify systematically what you want to learn about someone and record the results of your information-gathering process, perhaps in a journal. Do keep your notes in a private location and at some point destroy them, rather than risk embarrassing or angering your partner. As your relationship progresses, however, and stability and commitment increase, you will want to share your observations with your partner and find out what your partner has observed about you. Consider this couple's approach:

> Andy and Liz work side-by-side in the community center, filling boxes with cans of food. Their team will later deliver the food to low-income families in the area. Newly in a serious relationship, they decide that a service activity like this will help them with getting to know each other better. They commit to making positive comments about each other's character qualities throughout the day. They struggle at times with impatience and frustration as they experience dropped cans, fatigue, hard work, and a fellow worker's rudeness. However, they also notice and acknowledge in each other the qualities of courtesy, generosity, excellence, perseverance, and caring.

Practice tactfulness, respect, courtesy, and moderation as you gather information, remembering that **you are engaged in loving observation, not in a covert spy mission or investigating a crime.** Being sneaky, suspicious, or intrusive creates a poor foundation for a relationship and can alienate your partner. Use wisdom and discernment to evaluate the information that you gain. The goal is to engage in a systematic, thorough, and impartial search for truth, getting clarity about your partner's character strengths and life to minimize the possibility of encountering unpleasant surprises later on.

As you observe your partner, considering both the immediate and long-term future of your relationship and whether or not you should stay in it, you may feel both appreciation and some concerns. As concerns arise, discuss them with your partner, tactfully and kindly, committing yourself to **work through concerns together. Do not abandon the relationship over small and petty issues, which can actually provide opportunities for growth and learning.** If you think that you might be with someone long-term (or marry), learning to resolve differences together is especially important.

Do not expect to be perfect in this observation process, just do your best. If you believe in prayer, ask for spiritual guidance and for protection from making any major mistakes.

Avoid being so serious about observing that you forget to enjoy the relationship-building process. You may find it easy and fun to make observations and check them out with each other. You can gently tease and make lighthearted jokes (kindly, of course) that become a private language for the two of you. You may be fascinated by what you learn about yourself as well. Relax and enjoy your discoveries.

HELPFUL ACTIVITY

Begin strengthening your observation skills by pretending that you are a reporter for a news organization. Choose a location, and write down what and whom you are observing. Choose a length of time that works for you, 30 minutes, a day, or a week. Record what the people look like, what they are wearing, what they do and say, and their tones of voice. Try to be completely objective, recording only what you actually see and hear.

Once you have completed your observations, write a story in which you include the scene and conversations, using your imagination to interpret what might be happening. What do you notice about the judgments you make?

Challenges in Observing Others

Just as you sometimes resist observing and assessing yourself, you may sometimes feel it is too difficult to stay focused on observing your partner. Certain factors may act as barriers to clear observation and assessment of a partner. Awareness of barriers like these listed below will help you avoid or overcome them.

- Excessive focus on romance or projecting fantasy onto the relationship
- Lack of awareness of your partner's actions
- Snap judgments without clear facts
- Denial about what you observe and its significance
- Becoming overly attached emotionally
- Intense sexual passion
- Fear of being alone
- Excessive concern about how your partner will react if you raise an issue
- Setting your partner up on a pedestal and considering him or her nearly perfect
- Attachment to your partner's physical appearance, social position, or wealth as more important than character demonstrated by words and actions

Effective observation requires objectivity and enough detachment from your feelings that you can clearly assess the person's character. Detachment does not mean that you avoid or stay away from your partner or end your relationship. You still care about and are attracted to your partner, but you let go of some of the intensity of your emotions so you can think more clearly and make a more objective and fair-minded choice.

Keeping an open mind increases the accuracy of your observation. Prejudices, biased opinions, quick interpretations, or snap judgments can keep you from discerning the

truth about your partner. Discernment empowers you to "…make distinctions between what is real and what is an illusion."[3] Pause and consider whether you are adding your own interpretation to someone's actions or words. Accept that you may not have the full picture. Courtesy, patience, and perseverance can help you gain more information and a clearer understanding. You may also find it helpful to pray and/or meditate to strengthen respect and detachment to help you slow down and avoid jumping to false conclusions.

Pushing ahead into actions that are best left for marriage, such as sexual behavior, can interfere with the natural flow of getting to know each other. Sexual touch or fantasizing can stir up physical and hormonal reactions that interfere with your ability to make accurate observations, leading to unrealistic perceptions of your partner. You may overlook or justify serious shortcomings, failures, and character weaknesses in your partner. If you base your assessment of your partner on sexual responses, you may assume that the relationship is far more positive than it actually is.

Dave Carder, a Marriage and Family Therapist with expertise in the sexual dynamics of couples, says:

"Sexual activity while infatuated creates an artificial sense of closeness. Infatuation, combined with great sex (and it is almost always 'great' during this period of time), sets a couple up for disillusionment later in courtship or after marriage when real life and real schedules set in. Genuine closeness comes from using this sexual energy, this time of infatuation, to explore all of your differences, your values, your history, and your goals. It is always more fun to make love than conversation when you are together, but even that will end when you begin to think, after marriage, that due to your differences, you married the wrong person.

"Here's an interesting truth: Your relationship is only as 'old' as it is non-sexual. Sexual activity while infatuated keeps the relationship from developing. If your relationship is a year old but you have been sexual with each other since shortly after the first three months of dating, you have a three-month-old relationship. Why? Because, though it is always more fun to make love, it is the resolution of differences that will provide long-term potential for genuine intimacy. Lovemaking may seem more exciting than time spent talking and getting to know one another. When a couple sees each other less frequently (such as only on weekends, during college breaks, trips between military deployments, and so on), the thinking often goes like this: 'Why rock the boat by discussing what I know could create a disagreement? We have so little time together anyway.'" [4]

See Chapter 7 for more on the topic of sex and character.

When getting to know someone, you can seek observations and insights from parents, other relatives, and friends. When asking others for their opinions, word your questions carefully to avoid getting a list of your partner's negative qualities. You can ask people who know your partner, "What do you think are the strengths we have as a couple, and what problems do you foresee in our relationship?" If everyone you ask struggles to say something positive, that by itself can indicate a problem. Do your best to avoid participating in **backbiting**, which is negative, spiteful, derogatory, or defamatory words about someone who is not present. Also be cautious about **gossiping**, which is spreading personal or sensational information that is sometimes true, but often inaccurate or incomplete, and the intent or outcome are harmful.

~ *Reflection* ~
1. What helps me observe someone effectively?
2. What interferes with my ability to observe a partner objectively? How can I avoid this?
3. How does also observing myself improve my skills and increase the accuracy of my perceptions of my partner?

Observing Character

While growing up, you may have been taught to say only good things about other people and to focus on their positive qualities. Although this is an excellent practice, it may trip you up a bit when you are exploring a relationship possibility. When choosing someone with whom to be in a serious relationship or to potentially marry, you need to thoroughly identify the person's character qualities and habitual behaviors to obtain a complete picture and to assess the potential for a successful and lasting relationship. How successful would a marriage be if your partner has a large number of weak qualities and a small number of strengths? Would your marriage be harmonious or more likely full of conflict?

On the other hand, you may have learned to criticize others habitually, instead of speaking positively about them. You can achieve balance now by observing and acknowledging when your partner demonstrates character strengths. Notice the behaviors your partner repeats consistently and consider whether they indicate strengths or may cause conflict in your relationship.

It is easy to be infatuated and distracted by an attractive face or a charming personality without taking a closer look at a person's character. Objective observation can help you avoid this pitfall. To get to know someone's character and behavior takes time, patience, experience, trust in your inner voice, reflection, prayer, common sense, and perseverance. Consider this perspective from author and relationship educator Charlie Michaels:

> Although you may not consciously be aware of it, most people have created a mental picture of an ideal partner—and you probably have as well. While this is good from a character quality standpoint, it can be a hindrance if your vision includes specific physical traits as most images do. Whether you favor a dark-eyed brunette with a strong profile and a dimple, or a green-eyed, redhead with freckles and an impish grin, there will be a tendency to assign all the positive qualities of your ideal partner to anyone who matches the physical traits that appeal to you. It is crucial to separate physical attributes from character, personality, and behaviors. It is vital to hold all prospective partners to the same standards in your heart and mind. Just because someone looks the part does not mean they are the real thing.

You may have heard the saying, "appearances can be deceiving." It's true. Just because someone looks like a younger version of your beloved grandmother does not mean they have anything more than an outer shell in common. Resist the temptation to assume a new acquaintance has the interests, abilities, character qualities, or love for you that your grandmother had. Show your fairness, kindness, and maturity by eliminating the unfair expectations you have placed on this person just because he or she looks like someone with whom you had a real or imagined relationship. Save yourself from the inevitable disappointment that will come if you fool yourself into seeing attributes that are not there. Keep your eyes open and see the person before you, not the memory in your mind or the hope in your heart.[5]

As any good researcher will tell you, you must start by defining what you are looking for. In terms of character, this means paying close attention to behaviors that reveal particular qualities. For instance, you can tell whether people are friendly by the way they greet you when you meet. You consider a mother responsible because she gives her child healthy food. You watch a couple getting off a bus or out of a car, and notice that one waits courteously for the other on the sidewalk before they enter a building. You may see a person in the laundry room of your apartment building folding their clothes in a neat and careful way. These are all indications of their character qualities. Below is a reminder of the qualities to look for. You can see details on practicing and observing each of them in Part 3.

Acceptance	Flexibility	Peacefulness
Assertiveness	Forgiveness	Perseverance
Beauty	Fortitude	Purity
Caring	Friendliness	Purposefulness
Chastity	Generosity	Resilience
Commitment	Gentleness	Respect
Compassion	Helpfulness	Responsibility
Confidence	Honesty	Self-Discipline
Contentment	Humility	Service
Cooperation	Idealism	Sincerity
Courage	Integrity	Spirituality
Courtesy	Joyfulness	Tactfulness
Creativity	Justice	Thankfulness
Detachment	Kindness	Thoughtfulness
Discernment	Love	Thriftiness
Encouragement	Loyalty	Trustworthiness
Enthusiasm	Mercy	Truthfulness
Equality	Moderation	Unity
Excellence	Patience	Wisdom
Faithfulness		

Even in new friendships and relationships, you can begin to gain some knowledge of your partner's character by observing his or her behavior. Consider the couple in the story below:

> Charlene and Patrick are good friends and new partners. He invites her to meet his parents and sister, who are visiting from Ireland. During his family's visit, she enjoys watching him talk and laugh with them. She observes that he thoughtfully meets his family at the airport, flexibly adjusts to changes in plans, and suggests activities moderately, without trying to fill every minute. The love and caring Patrick feels for his family are evident to her.
>
> Charlene notices, however, that Patrick assumes his mother and sister will prepare each meal for them. He stays in the living room with his father while the women cook and then do the dishes after the meal. He bluntly states, although with a chuckle, that kitchen chores are women's work. He has shown her many great qualities, but she has questions about his helpfulness and his openness to the idea of equality.

Excellent tools that you have in your relationship toolbox are acknowledgement of your partner's positive behavior and effective use of character qualities yourself. **The more you focus on and acknowledge your partner's positive behavior, and the less you focus on the negative, the better.** If she wants to encourage Patrick's heart and spirit, Charlene will acknowledge Patrick's positive behavior.

Charlene will also need to determine through further observation and discussion with Patrick whether he might change his assumption about women's responsibilities and, therefore, change his behavior. Together they can explore how they feel about helpfulness and equality. After she learns more about his attitudes and whether he is open to change, she can then decide whether Patrick's behavior is a minor or major problem for her. She can encourage Patrick to change, but she cannot expect him to do so just to make her happy. The choice must be his.

HELPFUL ACTIVITY
Go to public places such as shopping centers, workplaces, or schools, and watch people you do not know interact with each other. What character qualities do you observe? Which behaviors do you consider positive and which ones negative? If you were friends with the people you are observing, how would you encourage their positive behaviors and address the negative?
~ *Reflection* ~
1. How do I know that I am beginning to know someone's character? 2. How might discovering something I perceive as negative behavior affect my relationship and interactions with my partner? 3. What weak character qualities or shortcomings in others might make it difficult or impossible for me to be friends or to be in a serious relationship with them? 4. What are the consequences of ineffectively assessing the character of someone with whom I am in a relationship? What surprises could cause significant problems?

Clarity and Consistency

People often have a tendency to hold parts of themselves back initially, or to be on their best behavior, to make a good first impression. Behaving well is a good idea, but it will take time for you and your partner to relax with each other enough to see the truth about each other. Confucius says, "Look at the means a man employs, observe the path he takes and examine where he feels at home. In what way is a man's true character hidden from view?"[6] He also says, "I used to take on trust a man's deeds after having listened to his words. Now having listened to a man's words I go on to observe his deeds."[7]

To get a full and accurate picture, notice how your partner consistently practices character qualities. **Consistency indicates that the behavior is deeply ingrained in your partner's character and is likely to be present throughout your relationship.** Is your partner usually loving and courteous to everyone, or polite to you and rude to others. Is your partner joyful and enthusiastic when it is appropriate? Is he or she often late to pick you up or not ready at the agreed upon time? How does your partner usually speak to his or her parents or to any children in your families? Do your partner's words match his or her actions? Does your partner keep or break promises made to you or to others?

Consistency does not mean your partner is perfect. Everyone falters at times, and few people always behave as well as they want to. However, if your partner has a quality as a strength, you can anticipate it being practiced regularly and well.

In the story below, notice how Bakari observes Kadence and assesses her consistency in practicing purity, which includes cleanliness and orderliness. Notice also what he observes about himself:

Kadence and Bakari develop a mutual friendship as they work part-time together at the library in their town. At times they also see each other outside of work. One day at the library, Bakari searches his desktop frantically, looking for a book his manager asked him to put away in the fiction department. He knows it is there, and he is confident he will find it quickly. As he sorts through the papers, books, and containers from his lunch, he looks up and notices his friend Kadence alphabetizing her cart of books by author and then by title.

Bakari sighs and thinks about how organized Kadence is. Her clothes are neat, her car is clean, and she puts her paper clips and pens away in their containers instead of leaving them scattered on the desk as he does. Bakari knows he has many great qualities, but maintaining his work environment in an orderly way is not one of them. He knows that this difference between them can present a problem if he and Kadence become more serious about each other.

Through his observations, Bakari knows that Kadence is a clean and orderly person. If someone asks him to describe Kadence, Bakari can objectively give this positive information about her.

You can often tell if you know the character of someone by how you respond when someone asks you to describe that person. Perhaps your parents or a friend says, "Tell me about him," or asks, "What is she like?" As you try to answer, perhaps all you can come up with is, "Oh, he is so nice!" or "She is wonderful!" This is an indication that it would be wise for you to spend additional time together with your partner and improve your observation skills. You can also benefit from learning more about how to describe someone's character.

Another sign that you can benefit from strengthening your character observation skills occurs when you can describe your partner only in relation to you. For instance, when asked to tell what the person is like, you might say, "He's so good *to me*," or "She is always doing things *for me*."

You want to know whether your partner is generous, friendly, or courageous generally, not just what behavior is directed towards you. A person's true character is revealed by words and actions used with all types of people, not just those used with those he or she is trying to impress.

As you observe your partner, watch for the character qualities you think are most important. If you find them in your partner, it builds confidence that you are in a good relationship. If your partner is weak in these qualities, however, reevaluate your commitment to this relationship. This is particularly true if the person is not interested in or engaged in developing these character qualities.

If you find that you are unsure about your observations or how to interpret them, you might benefit from further study of the qualities in Part 3 or of other material about character. You may also gain assistance from someone you trust.

ESSENTIAL ACTIVITIES

Complete Worksheet 4: Assessing Character Strengths in Your Relationship Partner, to assess your partner's quality strengths.

As you choose character qualities to observe in your partner, read about them in Part 3. Then, develop a set of questions to guide your observations. For example, for the quality of perseverance, you might ask: Does my partner finish projects or instead procrastinate and leave things only partially complete?

~ *Reflection* ~

1. Am I generally an accurate observer of the character of others? If not, how can I improve my skills?
2. Do others perceive me as overly judgmental, critical, or a perfectionist? Or am I the opposite, rarely noticing obvious character weaknesses in others? How might either of these tendencies affect my assessment of a partner's character?

OBSERVING BODY LANGUAGE AND CLOTHING

Everyone communicates, even without words, through choices of clothing, eye movements, touch, facial expressions, body positions, and hand gestures. How people dress and present themselves can draw you towards them, leave you feeling neutral, or push you away. The following list includes various types of body language or ways of dressing, which may invite you to talk to or spend time with someone or discourage you, depending on your tastes, experience, culture, and judgments. Some items will give you information about character. Think about how you respond when someone:

- Gives flirtatious looks
- Raises eyebrows
- Winks
- Shuffles feet
- Stares
- Touches a shoulder or hand
- Wears baggy clothes
- Wears tight clothes
- Frowns
- Hugs
- Wears heavy makeup
- Wears no makeup
- Smiles
- Wears a low-cut top or open shirt
- Wears short skirts or shorts
- Kisses (consider different types)
- Gives a shoulder or back massage
- Looks down or away
- Keeps eye contact
- Points a finger at others
- Exposes bare feet
- Wears headphones
- Has a distracted or bored facial expression

Some of these, such as wearing very revealing clothing, may seem to invite physical touch or sexual interest. This may or may not be true, since your interpretation of what is provocative may be different from that of another person or the wearer. Culture can be a factor in interpretation as well. For instance, avoiding someone's eyes by looking down or away indicates respect in some cultures and disrespect in others. Eye contact can also be interpreted differently by each gender. At times, men can interpret direct eye contact as aggression, and indirect eye contact as calming. Women can interpret direct eye contact as an intimate connection and indirect as dishonesty. Checking out each other's intended messages and interpretations rather than making assumptions is wise.

Flirting, in its mildest form, is unlikely to be harmful, but try to discern what it means when someone is flirting with you. Some people flirt to indicate that they find you attractive. Others may flirt to communicate sexual availability or to make another person jealous. If you respond to someone's flirting, either positively or negatively, based on false assumptions, you may end up in an embarrassing or difficult situation.

You will also want to notice your partner's body language and non-verbal signals, such as a compassionate smile, a frown after someone speaks rudely, a comforting squeeze of your hand during an emotional or scary moment, or a puzzled look after you have said something. Such cues express your partner's attitudes and personality and may enhance or contradict the meaning of words that are spoken. You will want to assess, therefore, the impact of your partner's words and gestures together as a complete message. Are they appropriate and pleasing, or unpleasant and perhaps even hurtful. Do your partner's gestures and facial expressions complement his or her verbal messages, or do they make the message confusing or so intense that you feel uncomfortable or anxious?

A Word of Caution: It takes highly skilled specialists to interpret body movements accurately, especially since their significance varies among different cultures and genders. **As you observe someone else's clothing choices or gestures, be mindful that you can easily misinterpret them entirely. Although these observations may give you some clues about a person, beware of making assumptions.** Talking with your partner will help you with verifying the accuracy of your interpretations.

HELPFUL ACTIVITY

Go with a friend or your partner to a shopping mall, college, city street, or some other location where you can see people wearing a variety of different clothing styles. Share your observations and interpretations of people's clothing and behavior.

~ *Reflection* ~

1. What do I like about my partner's clothing choices? Body language?
2. What judgments do I tend to make about others based on their clothing and body language? About my partner? What does my partner tend to judge about my choices?
3. What messages about character might be conveyed by clothing and behavior?
4. When have I misinterpreted someone's body language or behavior? How did I handle the situation?

OBSERVING LIFE MANAGEMENT SKILLS

Part of your observation and assessment process will be determining over time whether you and your partner can function independently and practice the character quality of responsibility effectively. This means being able to manage the details of everyday life in a mature fashion. People who can take care of themselves are better equipped to be full partners in a relationship. Which of the following indicators of maturity are most important for you to find in a partner?

Physical and Life Maturity

- Eating balanced and nutritious meals
- Practicing personal physical self-care, including exercise, cleanliness, and dental/medical care
- Obtaining and maintaining appropriate clothing
- Handling the cleaning and maintenance of a vehicle and a home
- Going to work and/or school as appropriate and completing the associated tasks in a timely and complete way
- Earning a living or gaining the education needed to do so
- Keeping debt low, paying bills on time, and maintaining savings

Mental Maturity

- Reading books and participating in ongoing learning
- Staying informed about current events
- Engaging in problem-solving discussions as needed
- Demonstrating self-respect and respect for others; not trying to control or dominate others
- Expressing one's true self openly and honestly and demonstrating a willingness to accept another person's true self as an equal partner

Emotional Maturity

- Recognizing one's feelings
- Not being overwhelmed by feelings
- Effectively expressing feelings
- Practicing joyfulness and confidence, even when life is difficult
- Handling challenges effectively and in cooperation with others
- Taking personal responsibility and not blaming others or making excuses when something does not go smoothly
- Relating well and solving problems peacefully with parents, family members, friends, neighbors, and co-workers
- Regarding a partner as a teammate and not as a parent-substitute

Spiritual Maturity

- Having faith in God
- Turning to spiritual sources for insight and help
- Praying regularly as well as during difficulties
- Meditating or reflecting
- Reading scripture or other books with spiritual content regularly
- Participating in spiritually-centered activities
- Recognizing and joyfully acting on the need to make a contribution to others in the world

Since achieving maturity may take a lifetime, some aspects of maturity may be weak or may not be present in either you or your partner when you enter a relationship. You can then discuss how you will develop any areas in which either of you still need to grow. Do not just assume someone is aware of the need to mature and is open to doing so. You may have differing perspectives on maturity. **Be sure that you agree on any important aspects of maturity being present before you commit to a serious courtship or discuss marriage.**

In the following story, consider whether you think Rachel's actions indicate that she is mature enough for a serious relationship:

Rachel enjoys working with children of all ages. She baby-sits regularly and teaches children's classes for her faith community. She tried college, but she thought it was too much work and dropped out. Many of her friends encourage her to become a teacher, but she has some fears and doubts about going back to school. She works occasionally as a clerk in a store, gets along well with her family, and generally demonstrates an optimistic attitude. When she is not working, she often ends up at local bars or clubs—wherever her friends want to go. Sometimes she drinks with them, even though she believes drinking is a bad idea and knows it is against the teachings of her faith.

As you look at this story, what do you think about Rachel's readiness for a serious relationship? What are her strengths? Does she simply lack confidence? Is she practicing friendliness appropriately? If you were Rachel, what actions would you change to build greater maturity?

How mature you are may or may not correlate with how old you are. Although maturity tends to increase through life experience, it does not always match the number of years one has lived. Mature or immature behaviors can occur at any point in someone's life. It is wise, therefore, to focus on maturity when observing a person's character, rather than making assumptions based on someone's age.

~ *Reflection* ~
1. What do I consider mature behavior in myself? In others? 2. How do I handle my responsibilities? Which ones do I particularly struggle to fulfill? 3. How does my partner handle responsibilities?
ESSENTIAL AND HELPFUL ACTIVITIES
Essential: 1. Identify three areas in which you want to demonstrate more maturity. Set specific behavioral goals and act on them. Periodically reflect on your progress and adjust your efforts as needed to ensure results. **Helpful:** 2. Play an electronic or video game with your partner or watch your partner play with someone else. Pay attention to how they respond to the content and the competition. What type of game do they choose? How violent or vulgar is it, and how do they respond to that violence or vulgarity in it? Do they become aggressive during the play or treat it as meaningless fun? How do they handle losing? How do they act when they win? What else do you observe that might indicate their level of maturity?

OBSERVING RESPONSES TO PROBLEMS

Good character information includes how your partner handles such things as disagreements, illness, or difficulties. What do you observe in your partner when things are not going smoothly? Do challenges bring out character strengths such as compassion, courage, or flexibility? Does your partner instead retreat into destructive anger, frustration, depression, or denial? How does your partner behave when feeling sad or disappointed?

Difficulties provide great opportunities for personal development. **Both you and your partner will be stronger individuals and more successful in the relationship if you learn and**

grow by responding well to challenges together. This does not mean that you should find a difficult relationship in order to aid your personal development! **Be assured that in all relationships, including marriage, plenty of challenges arise naturally. You do not need to make life more difficult by choosing to be in a relationship weighed down by behavior and character problems. If you have to struggle to maintain harmony, you will spend all of your energy trying to keep the relationship going, with little left to focus on anything else.** This may cause you to neglect your family, friends, work, spiritual commitments, and community service.

You may not easily find opportunities to observe how your partner handles problems, but this is a vital piece of your getting-acquainted process. Such opportunities can be particularly scarce if you go out on social dates only, or if you and your partner are in a long-distance relationship. Usually this type of observation occurs only when you spend time with your partner in real-life situations.

Of course you should not devise difficulties intentionally to see how the other reacts, but if your relationship is becoming serious, you will want to know how your partner responds when in a bad mood, short-tempered, tired, or frustrated. What character qualities does he or she draw on to stay calm and respond appropriately? Are any character qualities misused at such times (see Part 3)? It is also wise to see how you respond to the other's anger or upset feelings. How do the two of you resolve any hurt feelings or misunderstandings that come up between you? Do you practice acceptance, forgiveness, peacefulness, and resilience?

If the opportunity to observe how your partner handles challenges does not arise naturally, you can ask key questions to learn how your partner reacts when tired, after a long day, or when disappointed about how something turn out. You can also find challenging activities to participate in that will give you deeper experiences together. By helping clean up after a disaster in your area, traveling to and working in another country, teaching children, or doing community service you can learn how you handle problems together and how effectively you can function as a team.

ESSENTIAL ACTIVITIES

Choose two-three different challenging activities to expand your opportunities to observe your partner's words, actions, and character and so you can develop your observation and teamwork skills. You might work with or teach children, do a creative project, attend a large social occasion as partners, or work together to repair something or resolve a problem.

~ Reflection ~

1. What problems are most difficult for me to respond to effectively? For my partner?
2. How could a partner assist me with handling these problems differently? How can you assist your partner?
3. What could strengthen my ability to respond effectively to challenging circumstances?
4. What character qualities do I find helpful during difficulties? What qualities does my partner rely on? How successful are they in practice?

BEING IN A LONG-DISTANCE RELATIONSHIP

Internet-based matching services and affordable communications are reducing geographical barriers. Long-distance relationships give you the opportunity to experience diversity in ways that would not have been possible in the past. Global communications allow you to expand your access to potential partners in other countries and cultures. Long-distance relationships can be part of connecting people together as one human family.

Long-distance methods of communication may allow you and your partner to get to know each other in ways that you might not if the two of you were together in the same place regularly. Because you may feel less pressure and find it easier to remain somewhat detached about the eventual outcome of the relationship, you may experience less nervousness and be more relaxed with each other. You can learn about each other's character qualities, choices, interests, previous experiences, current involvements, and hopes for the future. You can ask focused questions that will tell you if your partner matches what you are looking for in someone. You might study the same relationship book and discuss it to learn about each other's ideas and values.

Although getting to know a partner from a distance is not the same as being together in-person, you can certainly build a friendship and explore a potential future this way. Long-distance relationships can still have many of the elements of typical relationships, but there are important differences, too.

To sustain a long-distance relationship, and because your partner does not have the advantage of constantly seeing you in person on a regular basis, be as honest as possible about the "real" you rather than portraying a "perfect" picture of yourself. Encourage your partner to do the same. Through your exchanges, you can develop an understanding of your partner and his or her attitudes and character qualities.

Take advantage of the time when you and your partner do get to see each other in person. You can use this time to further deepen your relationship, assess the reality of your impressions of each other, and learn more about each other's character. However, also be aware that when you and your partner see each other infrequently, your times together may be very intense, romantic, and almost "magical." **You may be tempted to avoid raising difficult issues or may attempt to portray an image that will be difficult to sustainIn addition, you have no effective way of knowing about each other's real-life behavior between visits.** You might view any problems that occur during your visits as resulting from the stress of being apart, assuming that being together more will prevent them. These assumptions can lead you and your partner to believe that being together in a more serious relationship or marriage will be a wonderful experience. Then, when you end up together, you may discover that neither of you really knew the other.

To counteract the risks of a long-distance relationship, spend the time that you do have together doing things that maximize getting to know each other. These might include participating in community service, spending time with family, attending a spiritual or religious event, or meeting each other's friends. Talk to your partner about which of these events is most effective for each of you. If you come from different cultures, include experiences that expand your knowledge of whichever of you is the one being visited. During your time together, continue to observe your partner's character qualities and try to assess your actual compatibility. Consider this situation:

> Lena and Zelipe, who live and work in adjoining countries, met a few months ago while attending a conference in the city where Zelipe lives. Once Lena returns home, they are able to visit each other only every few weeks. They find it difficult to be apart and express that frustration during their telephone calls and in emails. Their communications do not go smoothly.
>
> However, on the positive side, Lena and Zelipe stay with each other's parents during their visits, giving them the opportunity to get to know each other's family. One weekend, Lena invites Zelipe to attend a workshop about relationships with her. They learn new communication skills that help them to improve their long-distance interactions.

Assessing a partner's character requires many opportunities to be together over time and a high level of trust and intimacy between the two of you. Character assessments are challenging, because people have a tendency to show only their positive behavior to others. This is particularly true early in a relationship, or when you only see each other briefly and infrequently. Assessing your partner's character is not something that you can do instantly. It may be very difficult, if not impossible, to accomplish thoroughly in a long-distance relationship. Often you will best observe character qualities when your partner interacts with others, and there are fewer opportunities when you live far apart.

If you and your partner become serious about each other, it will be wise to live in the same area or visit for extended periods so that you can get to know each other in more detailed and practical ways. It may take a few months of in-person time together before you can be certain that you are seeing a partner's true self. Without this opportunity, Lena and Zelipe can miss learning many significant aspects of each other.

However, be clear that the goal in living closer is to ensure you know each other's character thoroughly. **Until you are seriously considering engagement or marriage, neither of you should consider traveling or moving to be near each other as a firm commitment to be together in the future.** You do not want to feel compelled to go forward unwisely with a marriage simply because one of you moved to be closer to the other.

Note: This book is not intended as a guide to safe Internet dating and matching practices. Be aware that there are dangers such as lying, false online profiles, money scams, and more. Do your best to make safe, wise decisions. You can access one of the many articles online about safe Internet practices.

1. What methods of communication will I be comfortable using with a long-distance partner?
2. What will help me to be successful in a long-distance relationship?
3. How can I thoroughly get to know a long-distance partner, especially his or her character, in real-life situations?
4. What character qualities do I believe I am seeing in my partner from long-distance contact or brief visits? What aspects of my partner's character might I be missing observing and knowing about?

REFLECTING AND PROCESSING OBSERVATIONS

As you reflect on what you are observing in a partner and begin to understand the dynamics of your relationship, you may want to answer the following questions:

- What do I like about my partner?
- What seems to be working well in his or her life?
- What does not seem to be going well?
- What annoys me about my partner?
- What do I like about the way we interact?
- Is my partner supportive as a friend, even when there are minor disagreements between us?
- How does my partner respond when faced with difficulties?

Your answers to these questions may change over time. The key is to stay aware. If you are mindful as you observe your partner, you will begin to understand whether he or she:

- Fulfills responsibilities and commitments with integrity
- Behaves wisely and appropriately in most situations
- Sincerely and consistently practices character strengths

A key guideline for you will be to see, "In all matters, great or small, word must be the complement of deed, and deed the companion of word: each must supplement, support and reinforce the other."[8]

Be sure to thoroughly observe how your partner:

- Acts in a group of people
- Treats children and animals
- Handles money and financial decisions
- Raises issues for discussion
- Handles stressful events
- Communicates awareness of and acts to meet your needs
- Practices personal cleanliness and courtesy
- Demonstrates an attitude of equality and partnership
- Cares for personal belongings and maintains his or her home in an orderly and clean way
- Practices patience and detachment during stressful events
- Accepts and forgives others with whom there is disagreement or who have caused hurt

- Maintains a consistent work history
- Relates to different people
- Recharges personal energy (introvert or extrovert)

Be fair and comprehensive in observing your relationship. Understand the character qualities you both bring to the relationship. Observing constructive behavior and character strengths in your partner gives you a firm, legitimate foundation on which to build a strong friendship-based relationship.

As you process your observations and assess the viability of the relationship, you have a number of choices for further action. For instance, you might:

- Participate in relationship education or coaching, work with a happily married mentor couple, seek professional counseling, or obtain spiritual or religious guidance
- End the relationship and stop spending time together
- Spend more time with mutual friends instead of alone together
- Agree to shift back to a casual friendship
- Work on strengthening your friendship
- Commit to deepening the relationship and begin to discuss the possibility of marriage

How much time you will need before you decide whether or not to continue the relationship varies. Your mutual honesty, your availability to be together as a couple, and your choice of activities will all be factors. Do not force yourselves to move at a faster pace than is wise for the growth of your relationship. There is rarely a deadline to meet, and creating an artificial one could have very unwise results.

By keeping "both eyes open" to observe your partner fully, you will gain the necessary information to make an informed choice. You may choose to accept whatever imperfections you see in your partner as a tolerable risk to your happiness. You will then not be surprised when those imperfections surface later on in the relationship. You can even decide in advance how you will deal with them through your own character strengths, such as gentleness, compassion, or forgiveness. Alternatively, you may decide the level of risk is unacceptable and choose to end your relationship.

ACTIVITY

Select someone to observe, preferably your partner. If your partner is unavailable, then observe another person you will see regularly for a few days. Complete Worksheet 5: Practicing Observation Skills.

RESPONDING TO NEGATIVE OBSERVATIONS

Anything from a toothache to a problem at work can occasionally affect someone's mood, tone of voice, or behavior. When your partner's behavior indicates negative feelings, it is important to discern the source. You will also want to discover whether this is an isolated event or a behavior pattern that may be repeated consistently over time. For instance, hormonal fluctuations or weather changes can cause predictable mood and behavior changes in some people. While you want to avoid minimizing possible problems, you certainly want to accept occasional incidents with understanding and mercy and experience your partner's ability to do the same for you.

Understanding what is happening in your partner's life helps you to moderate your emotional reaction to a partner's misbehavior. Such knowledge also helps the two of you with discussing how to handle an incident and prevent it from happening again. It also helps you avoid taking responsibility for a problem that is not yours. Your observations and knowledge can help you with discerning whether your partner's words and actions were serious enough to address, or whether it would be better to forgive and let go.

Bringing up concerns about someone's character requires tact, sincerity, and sensitivity. With casual acquaintances, new friends, or a new partner, it is best to keep your observations to yourself and not raise concerns about words and actions until your relationship is on firmer footing. If you do not yet have a foundation of trust and unity, the other person may feel your comments are rude and an invasion of privacy.

As you get to know a partner better, you will be in a better position to raise an issue carefully without causing offense. You can discuss together how the behavior affects you and explore ways to address it. **One measure of whether a relationship is ready to become more serious is if the two of you are willing and able to discuss serious issues related to character and behavior.** These might include struggles with impatience, concerns about parenting, difficulty in managing money, or differing priorities. If you and your partner are open and honest about concerns and welcome gentle input, influence, and guidance from each other, this is a positive relationship indicator. If every discussion the two of you have about serious topics causes an explosive reaction, or if one of you attempts to dominate the other, then your relationship is in difficulty.

As you learn about your partner and share your observations, avoid trying to justify intrusive questions or critical feedback by saying that you are just trying to be helpful. Be clear about your need to understand and about what you are looking for in a relationship. Premature comments based on the stage of your relationship, or critical comments about a partner's behavior, however, may cause your partner to feel defensive and perhaps under unwise pressure to change.

If discussing serious differences about character and behavior causes conflict, it would be wise to stop. Either you or your partner may need to apologize or make amends. Do not restart the discussion until the two of you can find a way to stop escalating the discussion into conflict. Are you demanding or expecting change from your partner? Is your partner overly sensitive about you raising any concern and not open to being influenced in a positive direction? Is the problem one you can work on together? Are you both willing and able to take the necessary time to work on it? Do you need assistance from someone else to see the situation clearly? **When conflict occurs, both of you contribute to it in some way. Focus on what you can change in yourself rather than pointing a blaming finger at your partner.** Make a plan to act differently next time, regardless of how your partner acts. Once your partner is willing to resume the discussion, offer calm reassurance that you have changed your attitude and are ready to proceed. Then calmly listen to your partner to understand his or her point of view.

If you find that your partner is actively engaged in improving a behavior or willing to address a character issue, you will want to determine:

- How serious the issue is to your relationship
- Whether your partner is committed to and serious about changing, if that is what is necessary
- How much change will have to happen for you to be able to stay in the relationship, and how quickly you want it to happen
- How many opportunities or chances you are willing to give the person to change
- What your boundaries, needs, and expectations are, and whether you have clearly communicated them
- What you are willing and able to do to assist your partner
- Whether this is an opportunity for you to be flexible and accepting
- Whether you are being critical about something that is also an issue in you, and you also need to change
- Whether it would be wise to just wait, without pushing for resolution of the issue, giving your partner time and space to work it through
- Whether you are seeing enough consistent behavior change that it is reasonable to believe in long-term success

Because responding to negative behavior is one of the most difficult aspects of relationships, you may at times struggle with what to say or do. You may need to obtain assistance from someone you trust to work through the issues with you individually or as a couple.

◡ Encouragement ◡

Learning good observation skills is not easy. You probably gained some practice throughout your education experiences, but character observation can be quite different. With determination and perseverance you can accomplish this task. Your happiness in the future depends on it.

REFERENCES FOR CHAPTER 4

1. John Van Epp, PhD, *How to Avoid Marrying a Jerk*, pp. 70-71
2. 'Abdu'l-Bahá, *Promulgation of Universal Peace*, p. 293
3. Linda Kavelin Popov, *A Pace of Grace*, p. 62
4. David Carder, "Using the Power of Your Infatuation for Good" essay in *All-in-One Marriage Prep: 75 Experts Share Tips and Wisdom to Help You Get Ready Now*, pp. 183-184
5. Copyright 2005 by Charlie Michaels and Mike Brown
6. Confucius, *Confucius, The Analects*, II:10
7. Confucius, *Confucius, The Analects*, V:10
8. Shoghi Effendi, *The Compilation of Compilations, Vol. II*, "Trustworthiness", p. 346

Chapter 5

Observing Friendship and Character in Action

INTRODUCTION

You now have a foundation of understanding character. You also are beginning to understand the importance of observation skills and how they work. Now it's time to get more practice and see how all of this works in action.

Remember that a wide variety of experiences together will give you increased opportunities to observe the quality of your character-based friendship and relationship, as well as with seeing a range of character qualities in action. Some experiences will be with the two of you alone. However, many of your best insights will come from experiences that include others.

Time with family is vital. Not only will you learn from those interactions, but family members who are less involved emotionally with your partner may see aspects that are invisible to you. Time with friends will also be valuable.

FRIENDSHIP-BASED RELATIONSHIP

Relationship experts John Gottman and Nan Silver define friendship as "…a mutual respect for and enjoyment of each other's company." Their research shows that "…happy marriages are based on a deep friendship." Couples in such marriages "…tend to know each other intimately—they are well versed in each other's likes, dislikes, personality quirks, hopes, and dreams. They have an abiding regard for each other and express this fondness not just in the big ways but in little ways day in and day out." This information supports the wisdom of developing a firm friendship before a relationship becomes so serious that it may lead to marriage.[1]

If you develop a friendship that provides mutual support and understanding and then decide to marry, you will ensure your marriage has a strong foundation. You will already have practiced being companions, confiding in each other, supporting and helping each other through difficulties, sharing joys, and turning to each other for fun and relaxation. Ideally, you will be closer to your spouse than to any other human being.

Understanding Friendship

Descriptions of close friendship often include the following:
- Good communication; ability to share honestly about positive and difficult matters
- Acknowledgement and affirmation of positive qualities in each other
- Enjoyment of quiet, peaceful time together
- Play, fun, and laughter
- Acceptance; allowing both partners to be themselves
- Support and appropriate sympathy, empathy, and help during difficulties
- Enthusiasm for individual and shared goals and achievements
- Loving, spiritual connection (such as through prayer, meditation, activities)
- Encouragement
- Loyalty
- Trust that shared information will kept confidential and not used hurtfully
- Reliability; trustworthiness
- Willingness to suspend judgment and avoid jumping to conclusions
- Common experiences and bonding memories
- Ability to work together on projects
- Agreed-upon boundaries and expectations
- Shared interests
- Willingness to learn together and from one another
- Ability to disagree peacefully and constructively
- Shared values
- Ability to reconnect easily after being apart
- Motivational feedback or nudging that constructively influences the other to grow
- Attitude of forgiveness, not holding grudges, and willing to grant another chance
- Respectfulness and equality

To achieve this type of friendship, you and your partner must be willing to grow as people and to learn through your interactions:
- What is helpful to others
- What is hurtful to others
- How to communicate effectively
- How to share thoughts and feelings honestly
- How to share possessions
- How to respect your own boundaries and limits and those of others
- What triggers intense emotions
- How to disagree peacefully
- When and how to joke and tease
- When and how to be serious
- How to keep private what is shared in confidence
- How to trust and be trustworthy
- How to know when a friendship is constructive
- How to know when a friendship is harmful or damaging

- How to communicate without speaking negatively about others
- How to observe and acknowledge character strengths in another person

Beginning and maintaining a friendship is often a challenge requiring commitment, time, attention, caring, and the ability to open one's self to another. Friendships grow through shared experiences, such as talking, learning new skills, playing sports, and participating together in community service and spiritual or religious activities. Poet Kahlil Gibran says, "And let there be no purpose in friendship save the deepening of the spirit."[2] **Being a steadfast and loyal friend requires patience and the ability to communicate, understand, forgive, and resolve any unpleasantness or disagreements.**

Be wary of a partner who wants to set up an exclusive friendship with you and avoid spending time with others. **Genuine friendliness reaches out to include people in a circle of caring. Genuine loyalty does not make unreasonable demands upon others, such as acting against one's beliefs, values, or nature.**

If you transition into a deeper relationship with your partner, you will still need to maintain your friendship together. **That foundation will help you with handling the changes that come with new experiences and expectations.** Author Agnes Ghaznavi comments, "As time passes and the relationship is subjected to tension and stress from all sides—personal and social—friendship becomes essential to strengthen the relationship against the forces that are tending to undermine it. Friendship also constitutes a refuge in times of stress or unhappiness."[3] Think of maintaining a car as an analogy for this experience. If you want to take a car on a long trip or one that involves hills and bumpy roads, you make sure to change the oil, put enough air in the tires, and put fuel in the tank.

Consider the couple in this story:

Margie and Frank, both of whose spouses passed away, recently moved to the same retirement community. One evening, they notice each other at the weekly community cookout and end up having a great conversation. For hours, they sit by the pool and talk about their children and grandchildren, beliefs, a common interest in historical documentaries and biographies, where they grew up, concerns about retirement, and movies they enjoy. They laugh more than they have in a long time, and they end the evening looking forward to the next time they will be together.

Over time, Margie and Frank continue to strengthen their friendship. Their conversations expand and deepen. As they participate together in a variety of activities, they begin to develop a serious relationship.

+--+
| ~ *Reflection* ~ |
+--+

1. How well do I develop and maintain friendships? What holds me back? What about my partner?
2. What specific things do I do to maintain friendships? What does my partner do?
3. What qualities make me a good friend? My partner?
4. Who are my closest friends, and what do I value about these friendships?
5. What is my history of friendships with the opposite gender? With the same gender? What have I learned from both?
6. What challenges have I experienced with friends? What have I learned?
7. What roles do spirituality, religion, and God play in my lasting friendships?
8. Do I share my spirituality openly with friends? Do I have friends who are uncomfortable when I do share? How does that make me feel about those friendships?

CHARACTER AND FRIENDSHIP

Friendships advance through various levels. According to author Bill Gothard, two people may start out as acquaintances, progress to casual friendship, move on to close friendship and fellowship, and finally become intimate friends. He describes the most intimate type of friendship as one "...based on commitment to the development of each other's character."[4]

Because friends can usually relax and be themselves, they reveal their strengths, mistakes, and the areas in which they need to grow. **Friends tend to behave naturally, without trying to impress each other and without fearing the loss of their friendship relationship. In exclusive romantic relationships with little or no foundation of friendship, however, people usually experience a greater fear of loss.** Issues that trigger lively discussions or amiable disagreements between friends can become much more emotionally charged for romantic partners.[5]

In the following story, consider how attraction to someone's character qualities provides an excellent beginning for a friendship:

> Noam and Lesley meet when they are assigned to the same team for the spring beach cleanup in their city. They quickly begin talking and joking with each other while picking up assorted trash and accumulated debris from a number of winter storms. As they work with their teammates, Lesley notices how quick Noam is to cooperate with others in picking up the larger, heavier pieces. Meanwhile, Noam notices Lesley's confidence as she becomes a leader in the group, encouraging others to keep at the task even as they tire. Lesley smiles in appreciation as she watches Noam thoughtfully hand out water bottles to the group members during a break.

Noam and Lesley begin a good friendship based on a shared interest in community service and respect for each other's character strengths. Discernment of each other's strengths during this activity solidifies the experience into a strong, positive memory for both of them.

On the other hand, as you get to know others, their behaviors may sometimes raise concerns. If you observe consistently disrespectful, irresponsible, or discourteous behaviors, you may need to listen to your inner voice and consider detaching from that person. Unless your partner is able and willing to change, you will not likely be happy in a relationship with someone whose behavior regularly offends, upsets, or angers you.

You can gain additional understanding of someone's character by getting to know your partner's friends. Consider this quotation from Joan Barstow Hernández:

> Becoming acquainted with a person's other friends and trying to understand what he has in common with them also contributes to a deeper knowledge of his character. Friends usually share some values. Therefore, if you do not see the qualities in a person's friends, which you think you see in him, it may be an indication that you do not yet know him very well, or that you have an idealized concept of him.[6]

A friendship-based relationship provides a safe place to influence the development of each other's character qualities, if you both want that to happen. As you grow closer to each other, you can talk freely and provide kind feedback, support, and understanding about character challenges. In an established relationship between close friends, your caring feedback and discussion encourages character growth. "Genuine service demands that we speak the truth in love. We do not serve each other by avoiding one another's weaknesses."[7] **When a genuine friend offers loving and compassionate feedback, it is much easier for you to accept because of your confidence that your friend knows you well and has your best interests in mind.** In a friendship-based relationship, you both help each other.

As you and your partner encourage each other's character growth, however, avoid slipping into fault-finding or focusing too much on the other person. Keep your primary focus on your own character.

> …[R]esist the natural tendency to let our attention dwell on the faults and failings of others rather than on our own. Each of us is responsible for one life only, and that is our own. Each of us is immeasurably far from being [perfect]…and the task of perfecting our own life and character is one that requires all our attention, our will-power and energy. If we allow our attention and energy to be taken up in efforts to keep others right and remedy their faults, we are wasting precious time.[8]

The description of friendship earlier in this chapter includes many character strengths—caring, truthfulness, faithfulness, enthusiasm, and loyalty, for example. Friends appreciate each other's best qualities. Author and researcher Blaine J. Fowers, PhD, describes "character friendship" as follows:

...[I]t is based on the friends' recognition of each other's good character and on the shared pursuit of worthy goals. ... [T]hey are brought together because they recognize each other's good qualities—the character strengths that make it possible for them to seek the good together. ... [C]haracter friends work together as a team or a partnership to achieve their shared goals. ... [M]utual happiness is a by-product of shared commitment and teamwork....[9]

As you develop a friendship with your partner, practice mutual courtesy, generosity, kindness, respect, patience, and other character strengths. This will deepen your appreciation for each other and strengthen your bond.

~ Reflection ~

1. When has a friend's effective practice of character strengths made a positive difference in my life?
2. When has a friend's character weaknesses been a problem for me?
3. What are the indications that my partner and I are good friends?

CHARACTER AND PRACTICING EQUALITY

Throughout the world today, there is a growing movement towards equality between women and men, prompting one of the most significant paradigm shifts underway in couple relationships. Organizations such as the United Nations and the Council of Europe (COE) have championed human rights and gender equality, which the COE defines as "...an equal visibility, empowerment and participation of both sexes in all spheres of public and private life."[10] The United Nations is vigorously promoting the rights and freedom of women to live without being subjected to physical, sexual, and psychological abuse, and to have full access to education.

Over time, each generation has explored the best ways for men and women to interact, shifting closer to the full practicing of equality. Many people have different understandings of equality and mixed responses to it as a concept. What equality will look like in relationships in the future is unknown, but there are some principles that can guide you with enhancing it in your own relationship.

A prerequisite for achieving equality is deep respect between you and your partner. This means recognizing that neither you nor your partner is better than the other and that you each have a body, mind, heart, and soul of highest value. You acknowledge the value of each other's thoughts, feelings, and contributions to your relationship. Neither you nor your partner has the right to dominate, control, force, or dictate to the other.

When you discuss any topic, you listen carefully and share your thoughts and feelings with each other. You try to make decisions in partnership that you both can wholeheartedly support. In some matters, however, if you have more knowledge and experience, your partner may defer to you. Similarly, in other matters, you will defer to your partner. Even when one of you defers, however, you both agree with, respect, and follow through on decisions made together.

Strive for equality in discussions and decision-making as you make plans to do things together or issues arise in each other's lives that affect the other. Each of you should offer ideas and share preferences as you decide together what to do. If one of you makes all the decisions, while the other simply goes along, you create an unequal relationship.

Money can be an issue related to activity choices, and who pays for an activity can have layers of significance for both of you. Historically, the male always paid when going out with a female partner. With our new understanding of equality, you and your partner may take turns paying. Sometimes you can pool your resources and share the expense, or each of you may pay your own way.

Think about the significance you place on who pays and for what. Do you see it as your responsibility to pay all the time, or do you need to pay your "fair share"? Do you think poorly about yourself or the other person based upon who pays? Are your choices based on cultural practices? Are you looking at your finances and those of your partner and making decisions based on facts? As you think about the significance you place on who pays, do your best to avoid letting money cause disunity between you and your partner. Consider how this couple handles money:

Early in their relationship, Soo and Amadi realize their perspectives on money are significantly different. As a medical technician at a small hospital, Soo earns only enough money to pay her monthly bills and save a small amount for the future. She learned from her parents that if she socializes with friends or a partner, she should pay her fair portion. Amadi, on the other hand, owns his own business and is doing very well financially. His parents taught him that he should pay when he takes women out socially.

As Amadi and Soo start doing things together, he wants to pay for Soo, but she is uncomfortable with that, feeling that she should pay for her portion. As this continues, they realize that they need to come to an agreement or money will cause difficulty for them. Amadi understands that Soo takes pride in paying at times and enjoys feeling as if she actively contributes to the relationship. Soo also understands, however, that Amadi is in better position to be generous and pay for things they do together.

Soo and Amadi sit down together one evening and discuss how they can respect each other's values about money. Soo indicates that she has been thinking about applying for a higher paying position at another hospital. Amadi encourages her to pursue this option, but they agree that for now he will pay the majority of their expenses, while Soo will occasionally contribute what she can.

In the past, relationships have often been guided by the belief that the man is the "head" of a relationship or home, with the woman responsible for "submitting" to him. Amadi could have taken this position with Soo. Traditional expectations, roles, and responsibilities grew out of customs and from religious traditions in societies dominated by men. As societies change, so do our expectations of personal relationships. Consider this alternative view of the "headship" concept from Dr. Les Parrott in *7 Secrets of a Healthy Dating Relationship*:

Headship [of a partner/wife/home] is not being the first in line. It is not being the boss or ruler. It is being the first to honor, the first to nurture, the first to meet the other's needs. A true administrator is also a servant.

A healthy relationship, whether in dating or marriage, is built on a mutual desire to submit one's needs to the other. Emptying ourselves of our self-centered desires is the bridge to a deeper and more meaningful relationship.[11]

As our desire for equality grows, we are sometimes uncertain how to interact with or treat a partner. Some think we should abandon long-held customs, such as holding a door open for a partner. The key for determining how to act is character, not customs. If you and your partner perceive holding a door open as a courtesy, then that is the standard to strive for, regardless of your gender. As in the quotation above, both partners can serve each other.

Belief in and commitment to equality should not lead to the false assumption that men and women have equal strength and physical ability. Physical capacity must be determined on an individual basis, with care to avoid stereotyped expectations. A Kenyan saying asserts that, "It is not necessary for fingers to look alike, but it is necessary for them to co-operate."[12] Equality has more to say about minds, hearts, and souls than bodies. Consider this view:

The world of humanity has two wings—one is women and the other men. Not until both wings are equally developed can the bird fly. ... Not until the world of women becomes equal to the world of men in the acquisition of virtues and perfections, can success and prosperity be attained....[13]

You practice equality in a relationship when you and your partner interact as peers, finding common interests and participating in activities as a team. The more you experience an equal partnership, the stronger the bond between you will grow. Consider what therapist Agnes Ghaznavi, MD, in *Sexuality, Relationships and Spiritual Growth*, says about developing this bond of equality:

It is…important, in a relationship of equality, to have certain common fields of interest, concern and endeavor, be it in the community, in the family and neighborhood, in art or science or business or any other field. But in the last resort even this is not sufficient. The partners have to lay a firm spiritual foundation.[14]

You and your partner can foster a spiritual bond in a number of ways. Consider some of the following:
* Explore each other's beliefs
* Practice yoga, Tai Chi, or some other meditative discipline
* Pray
* Spend time relaxing in nature and appreciating it as an awe-inspiring creation
* Attend or plan worship or devotional services

- Read and discuss spiritual books
- Serve others together
- Encourage and develop character qualities

Essentially, equality is something you work out between the two of you, a commitment you make together based on your belief in the equal value of all people. You may need both assertiveness and flexibility to achieve it cooperatively. Don Coyhis of the Mohican Nation offers this perspective:

> We all come from one Great Spirit but we are all different and unique. Nothing in the Great Creation has a twin that is identical. Even children that are twins are different. Every single person is extremely special and unique. Each person has a purpose and reason why they are on the Earth. Just like every leaf on a tree is different, each one is needed to make the tree look like it does. No leaf is better or worse than the other—all leaves are of equal worth and belong on the tree. It is the same with human beings. We each belong here and do things that will affect the great whole.[15]

ACTIVITY

Choose a project that requires cooperation to work on with your partner. This might include arranging books on a bookshelf, bringing order to CDs or DVDs, rearranging or redecorating a room, organizing a filing system, building something, landscaping, cooking, or cleaning out cupboards or a closet. Assess how well you completed the task. How did you handle differences of opinion? Were you able to respect each other's input, complete the project successfully, and maintain unity in your relationship?

Observing Your Interactions as a Couple

As you interact with a new partner, you are naturally eager to learn about each other's lives. You both ask questions and share increasingly detailed information as trust grows between you. **Observing how you and your partner communicate with each other provides vital information.**

Here are some observations you might make about your interactions with your partner:

- What questions does your partner ask or not ask you?
- Does your partner keep turning the conversation back to himself or herself?
- Does your partner ask so few questions that you question his or her interest in you?
- Does your partner ask so many questions that you feel pushed too fast in the relationship?
- Does your partner talk about himself or herself so much that it overwhelms you?
- Does your partner offer so little information that you feel you have to push to learn anything?
- Are there important subjects your partner refuses to discuss?
- Is your partner positive and respectful or negative and hurtful?
- Do your partner's eyes regularly wander to other people or parts of the room while you are talking?

- Does your partner focus more on texting others or answering the phone than listening to you?
- Does your partner ignore or discount what you say?
- Does your partner show genuine interest in your opinions and stories?
- Are you able to minimize, moderate, or pace physical touch between you while you get to know one another?
- Are you able to observe character qualities in your partner?

Rick and Sandie met through an online matching service. They emailed initially, and then had a couple of long and excellent phone conversations. At the end of talking a second time, they agreed to a first meeting. Part of what helped Sandie decide to meet Rick were the qualities she could already see might be strengths for him. He shared a story about his mother that showed his attitude of caring and love towards her. A description of how he was handling a problem showed perseverance and a sense of justice. As he was ending their call, he was on his way to help a friend.

Rick felt respected in the conversation with Sandie, and he appreciated her honesty about her current life circumstances. He liked her enthusiasm and could tell that she practiced self-discipline with exercising.

Each of them could already begin to see strengths in each other, although it will take more time to know whether these qualities are consistent. The night they first meet, they gain more information. Rick is courteous in holding the door open for Sandie, she shows compassion about a difficulty he experienced in his work history, and they are both willing to be patient in building a friendship together.

As your relationship progresses, you will notice that some character qualities and behaviors, such as cooperation, are most effective when you and your partner practice them together. Can you work effectively on something together, or do you both become frustrated and get in each other's way? Dancing is an example of a cooperative activity that can demonstrate underlying challenges in your relationship. Couples who struggle with being cooperative may experience a power struggle on the dance floor. Each partner, thinking he or she knows the steps and direction better than the other, may take the lead and perhaps try to force the other to follow. When couples argue about which way is correct or best, or when one blames the other for not doing the dance correctly, they demonstrate a belief that the dance itself or being right is more important than maintaining the relationship.

When you are with a partner, you begin to develop a "couple personality." Who you are together becomes a "we" and "us" that is a different entity from who you are individually. The more time you spend with each other developing shared positive practices and memories, the stronger will be your identity and bond as a couple. The question to ask yourself is, "Do I like the couple that we have become?" Here are some questions to consider about your couple identity:

- Are you better together, or do you regularly bring out the worst in each other?
- Are you able to be honest and your true self around your partner, or do you pretend to be someone you are not or hide key aspects of yourself?
- Are you happy or unhappy when you are together?

- Do you feel positively energized or very drained and discouraged after spending time together?
- Do you feel safe and comfortable with your partner both in public and in private?
- How do others around you act? Do others like to be around the two of you?
- Are your friends and family positive and encouraging of your relationship, or are they expressing reservations and concerns? What are they saying?
- What concerns do you have about the relationship? Are the concerns serious?
- Are you consistently seeing character strengths and words and actions that you appreciate?

Chuck and Amelie have been together for a few months. They have had many good times with each other and see character strengths in how they treat one another. However, every time they try to spend time with friends or family members, problems arise. Amelie has serious concerns about how Chuck interacts with his mother, which is often curtly and rudely. Chuck sees that Amelie is easily influenced to behave poorly when she is with her friends. Amelie is often disrespectful to servers in restaurants. Chuck is inconsistent with paying his bills on time and refuses to answer the phone when companies call him about payments. There are enough indications of character weaknesses that it is clear they are simply behaving well with each other at this stage, something that is unlikely to last over time.

OPPORTUNITIES FOR OBSERVATIONS

At times couples have difficulty thinking of activities to do together, and a variety of activities with many different people will give you the most information about your partner. Your partner will then also have more opportunities to observe your behavior.

The list below will give you a wide range of possibilities.

Sharing Time

- Take nature walks or stroll along a beach
- Visit art galleries or museums
- Visit amusement parks
- Share photographs
- Throw a party
- Watch television or movies
- Go shopping
- Study and discuss religious or spiritual materials
- Exercise at a fitness center
- Play board, card, or video games
- Listen to music
- Take a class in and/or practice meditation or yoga
- Take an educational class
- Walk with or care for a pet

- Visit the library
- Pray together
- Spend time with friends
- Go dancing
- Spend time with family
- Attend a concert
- Listen to a musical group at a restaurant, coffeehouse, or night club
- Attend religious gatherings, worship services, conferences, workshops, or summer schools
- Do home/yard work and repair
- Attend a sporting event
- Read a book aloud to each other
- Participate in a book club
- Do homework or study together
- Go out for tea, coffee, a meal, or dessert
- Have a picnic
- Go to a movie
- Participate in a hobby-related event
- Go to a comedy club
- Participate in a Toastmasters International club (learn to give public talks)
- Attend an exhibition or show (boating, jewelry, health, home & garden….)

Serving/Working

- Help with a home repair project
- Visit elders
- Plan a meeting or a conference
- Teach a children's class
- Care for children
- Handle taxes/finances
- Volunteer with a local civic organization
- Join or start a committee
- Plan and host a devotional/prayer meeting
- Facilitate a spiritual study class for junior youth, teens, or adults
- Participate with a neighborhood association
- Tutor after-school children

Being Creative

- Build or decorate
- Create an art project
- Share family recipes and try out new ones
- Write an article, story, poem, song, or book; participate in a creative writing workshop
- Plant and tend a garden
- Do a jigsaw puzzle

- Refinish furniture
- Make a movie
- Sing songs or play musical instruments; join a chorale group
- Make clothing or jewelry
- Build sand or snow sculptures
- Write letters or emails to each other
- Learn and practice a new language
- Design a website with graphics
- Take photos; frame them; create a screensaver
- Paint a portion of a home

Enjoying Physical Activity/Adventure

- Play cooperative games
- Go for a walk
- Ski cross-country or downhill
- Travel
- Play volleyball or other group sports
- Camp
- Explore caves
- Hike
- Go canoeing or rafting
- Climb hills or mountains
- Play tennis or other racquet sport
- Ride bikes
- Rollerblade or ice skate
- Bowl
- Swim
- Surf
- Ride horses
- Fly kites
- Drive in a road rally or race
- Play football/baseball/soccer/cricket
- Snorkel/scuba dive

Pay close attention to your instincts and feelings as you engage in activities together. If you feel unsafe, overly criticized, or very anxious, do not make excuses for or try to justify your partner's poor behavior (or your own). Are you forcing yourself to participate, and you really do not want to? Are there behavior patterns that the two of you can discuss and change? Do you need outside assistance? Or is the behavior an entrenched pattern and therefore unlikely to change? If so, you need to consider ending the relationship. Your partner may simply be a better fit for someone else.

On the other hand, consistently positive signals, loving feelings, confidence, and a sense of unity with your partner all affirm your choice to continue the relationship.

It is also a great idea to get some outside observations and feedback from close and trusted family, friends, advisors, or others who can be more objective than you, about how you and your partner seem to get along together.

HELPFUL ACTIVITIES

1. Ask a friend to make a movie, slide show, or photo album of you and your partner as a couple. Making this movie or taking these photos might be when you are with family members, during a community service project, at a social event, or while engaged in some other activity. As you look at the pictures, notice whether either of you were practicing identifiable character qualities? Are you happy with how the two of you interact together and with others?
2. Identify a skill that each of you could teach the other. Consider activities such as cooking, gardening, using a particular tool, or whatever fits for the two of you. After teaching each other, discuss the experiences.

~ *Reflection* ~

1. What activities can provide you as a couple with excellent observation opportunities?

OBSERVING INTERACTIONS WITH FAMILY

Since every family situation and dynamic is unique, **wherever possible, it will be good to observe how you and your partner interact with both sets of parents**, or stepparents, foster parents, or other parental surrogates. Not only do you want to learn how your partner and his or her parents interact, but you will **particularly want to observe your partner's interaction with the parent who is the same gender as you are.** This, along with observation of how the parents treat each other, will give you clues as to how your partner will treat you and how your partner will expect to be treated by you. **You may be tempted to assume that because your partner cares so much for you, he or she will never treat you poorly, but this is a risky assumption. A partner who treats his or her parents with respect and courtesy is likely to treat you the same way.**

Here are some specific things to look for when observing your partner's family:
*   Do the family members demonstrate love and mutual support?
*   Do they accept their differences with humor and kindness?
*   Do they struggle for control or compete to an unhealthy extent?
*   Do they fight and put each other down with critical comments?
*   Do they treat each other with respect and equality?

You will likely add more questions to this list out of your own family experiences. Keep in mind that if you are observing a family from another culture or one that speaks a different language, you may need some assistance with translation and interpretation of actions and customs.

One important factor that can determine relationship and marriage success is the capacity you and your partner have to feel and express love that came from childhood experiences. Dr. Molly Barrow puts it this way:

> Someone develops a shorter Relationship Capacity Line if they do not feel loved while growing up, or experience trauma or neglect and fail to learn to give love easily to others. These shorter Lines have less capacity to show love towards a partner, frequently behave in a selfish protective way, and often feel inadequate in relationships. In contrast, a longer Line has greater capacity to give emotionally to a partner, because they clearly felt parental love growing up in a safe environment and learned to share love with others.
>
> You may think you are a Longline in general, compared to all people, however, if your partner's Relationship Capacity Line is longer than yours, then you become the Shortline in that relationship. The power of Matchlines is to illustrate a "relative" relationship between two people—never an absolute judgment about anyone's value as a person. You will benefit from thoroughly assessing your relationships, past and present, to determine your Line Gaps, or differences.[16]

With assistance and skillful handling you may be able to adjust to very different loving capacities, but the greater the difference between you in this, the more likely there will be relationship conflict or imbalance.

Of course, you will also observe the interactions between your partner and your own family. If you trust your parents' ability to discern character in others, observing how they speak to and respond to your partner will be particularly important.

You can also learn from the way both sets of parents act towards you and your partner as a couple and from whatever wisdom or guidance they offer. Since your parents probably know you and your partner better than anyone else does, their input and guidance may be valuable. If your parents or your partner's parents inappropriately attempt to control and interfere in your relationship, you may need to detach somewhat and seek guidance from other elders who respond to you more objectively. Of course, your age and maturity will likely influence your parents' level of involvement.

In some religions or cultures, parents may be very involved in the process of getting to know your partner. All the parents and even some other extended family members may meet with the couple to discuss the viability of the relationship from the beginning, assuming that if the relationship is a good one, it will end in marriage. In the process, parents often provide guidance to the couple about how to maintain their relationship. If you are in this situation, you will benefit from listening to the wisdom of your families. **However, it is also important that you make a free choice of a partner and not let your parents or other relatives coerce the two of you to marry.** If either of you is unwilling, the relationship will probably be unhappy and will not last.

As you, your partner, and your families interact, you will both want to reflect on your own family experiences. Think about the relationship your parents had with each other while you were growing up and how that may have influenced you. It is also important to understand your relationship with each of them now. Your parent-child interactions have resulted in many of your beliefs, fears, and expectations about having a relationship with a partner. What unresolved issues with parents affect you and your partner now? What experiences of disagreement, conflict, or disunity have you and your partner had with your parents in the past, how did you act at the time, and what did you learn from those experiences?

The more resolution and harmony you can achieve with all the parents, the better it will be for you as a couple. Otherwise, you and your partner may tend to project unresolved resentments towards your parents onto each other. There could also be ongoing interference or attempts to disrupt your relationship.

If you need to address family issues, you might seek spiritual or therapeutic counseling, practice forgiveness, make amends, attend workshops, or read books in your quest for healing. Your partner may also help you with identifying patterns between you and your parents of which you were not previously aware, and you may do the same in return. If you are estranged from your parents, healing is more difficult, especially if you are no longer in communication or contact. Perhaps contacting them would open the door of reconnection. If you want to resolve problems that led to your estrangement from your parents, share this with them.

Your parents may not have been able to meet your needs or to model positive relationship skills for you. **If that is the case, you and your partner need to identify what type of relationship you want and intentionally learn appropriate and healthy couple behavior.** For instance, you can learn to give positive acknowledgement to each other, even if you experienced mostly criticism from your parents. Skill building is possible at any age or stage of life. Ask a couple whose relationship you admire and respect to mentor you.

~ *Reflection* ~

1. What dynamics in my family are interesting or unique? In my partner's?
2. How can observations of my partner's parents contribute to my assessment of a partner?
3. What type of relationship do I want to have with my partner's family?
4. What types of interactions between my partner's family members would raise concerns for me?

HELPFUL AND ESSENTIAL ACTIVITIES

Helpful:
1. Invite your partner and his or her parents to a meal you will cook. Do your best to be welcoming, courteous, and hospitable. After everyone leaves, assess what you observed about the interactions among those present. Alternative: Invite other family members, such as siblings, if your parents or your partner's parents are deceased or unavailable.

Essential:
2. Complete Worksheet 6: Learning from Your Parents' Relationship. What aspects of their relationship do you want or not want to have in your relationship with a partner. Use this worksheet to observe your partner's parents as well.

WHEN THERE ARE CHILDREN

If you are a young couple with no children, the subject of having children can probably wait until you know each other very well, and you are beginning to discuss a future together. However, if you already have children, or if you are older and want to have children before it is unlikely to happen smoothly, it makes sense to talk about the subject of children earlier in your relationship. You and your partner may be in different frames of mind on the subject of children or in different life situations. Either or both of you may have children already. One of you may want more children, and the other does not. One of you may see stepparenting as a possibility in the future, and the other is uncertain. All of these are vital to clarify and eventually come to agreement about.

If you already have children, when appropriate, you will introduce them to your partner. It will be a problem if you become involved with someone and then discover that your partner and your children cannot get along at all. It will also be difficult if you find out after you have invested a lot of time in a relationship that your partner has no interest in becoming a stepparent to your children in the future. **It is important to make certain that you share the information about your role as a parent and your expectations for your children's interactions with your partner as soon as possible.** It will not take long to determine if parenthood is an unmovable obstacle in your relationship. In this case, do not hesitate to end it.

It is essential to take your children's feelings, needs, and concerns respectfully into consideration when you are going out socially. If they are young, you will arrange for a responsible caregiver for them. Deciding what you will say to your children about your social life away from the house is something that will take empathy, compassion, fairness, and sensitivity to their needs.

Children raised in a single parent household can respond to you having a partner in a number of ways. They can quickly become attached to any friend or partner that you bring into their lives. Alternatively, they may withhold their involvement until they see if the person will stay around, and therefore may strongly resist building any kind of rapport with your partner. They may see having positive interactions with your partner as disloyalty to their other parent.

If your children become attached to your partner, and your relationship does not work out, they will be hurt. It may be difficult for them to become close to a future partner as a result. You may inadvertently teach them that relationships do not last. A relationship ending can especially reinforce this view if they have already experienced a divorce, the death of a parent, or a parent leaving them.

Because of the complexity of this situation, it is a difficult judgment call whether to find out quickly if everyone gets along, as mentioned above, or choose to be sure your relationship is going well before you introduce your children to your partner. Even though you are not married, you and your partner may find it useful to obtain counseling or information about getting along in stepfamilies. You may also find it beneficial to attend workshops together. [Excellent sources of information are www.stepfamilies.info; www.nancylandrum.com; www.stepfamilyliving.com.]

It will make sense that part of the character exploration you do with your partner includes identifying the qualities that you will want in a potential stepparent for your children. You will also notice the effect your new partner has upon your children and the same in reverse. Does your partner bring out your children's best character qualities? What character qualities do your children bring out in your partner? If you ask them, your children will more than likely be a great source of feedback to you about whether they approve or disapprove of this new person in your life and why.

Interactions between children and partners can be difficult, depending on the attitude of everyone involved. If you have given your children a good reason to feel jealous or abandoned by your new relationship, they may automatically disapprove of it. However, if you have given them reason to feel accepted and included in it, you will find that they are usually faithful observers and supporters of their parent's happiness over time. Courage, courtesy, respect, patience, and love will all aid the process.

If your children are adults, they will be less directly involved in any relationships you have, yet they may be better prepared to offer you feedback than if they were young children. Moreover, it makes sense and is courteous to introduce them to your partner if your relationship becomes serious. Any possible expansion to the family has an emotional impact on all its members, regardless of whether you still live with them or their ages.

~ Reflection ~

1. What are the needs of my children as I participate in a relationship? How can I be sure those needs are met? How will I set priorities if my children's needs seem to conflict with my needs?
2. What considerations do I need to have for a partner's children?
3. What relationship am I willing and able to build with a partner's children?
4. What do I visualize as the relationship a partner will have with my children? How might that relationship be affected by the children's other parent(s)?

HELPFUL ACTIVITY

If you have a partner, plan and carry out an activity that builds unity between you, your partner, and any children you both have. If you do not yet have a partner, choose a good friend who is a parent, and do the activity with them. Use the opportunity to observe character qualities and practice building unity among those participating.

OBSERVING YOUR PARTNER'S INTERACTIONS WITH OTHERS

Consider whether or not your partner chooses friends with excellent character qualities and observe how your partner interacts with them. It may be unwise to pursue a serious relationship with someone who lacks the ability to have friendships with others. Your partner may then be very socially isolated or overly dependent upon you. Also be cautious of a partner who chooses friends with negative or destructive tendencies. Consider these questions:

- Does your partner enjoy long-term, healthy friendships?
- Does your partner stay in touch with friends or generally ignore them?
- How does your partner speak about friends when the friends are not present?
- What type of influence are your partner's friends? Do they encourage unwise activities? How does your partner respond?
- What are your partner's attitudes about continuing "single" activities while in a committed relationship or marriage?

You will also want to observe how your partner treats other people in various situations. Does your partner:

- Adapt to different social situations appropriately?
- Change temporarily and insincerely simply to please people?
- Begin conversations and/or participate in them easily, or have difficulty being with or communicating with others?
- Interact well and show courtesy, confidence, and respect to:
  o Both genders, all ages, friends, professional associates, and new acquaintances?
  o People of a lower socio-economic level?
  o People who provide service to them, such as restaurant servers, hotel cleaning staff, bus drivers, store clerks, trash collectors, administrative clerks, or store employees?
  o People of a higher socio-economic level?
  o People from different cultures or races?
  o People with different spiritual or religious beliefs?
  o People with physical, mental, or emotional disabilities or limitations?
  o Anyone smaller or weaker, such as children or pets?

If your partner treats others poorly, there is a good chance that one day you will be on the receiving end of similar behavior. If your partner demonstrates consistently loving and considerate behavior to others, you can reasonably expect to be treated the same way.

ESSENTIAL ACTIVITY
Arrange an activity with your partner and some mutual friends. Carefully observe their interactions. Arrange a second activity with your partner and his or her friends. Again, carefully observe their interactions and your feelings and reactions.

~ Reflection ~

1. How do I interact with my friends?
2. How do I treat the various types of people listed in this section?
3. How do I feel about my partner's friends?
4. Can I peacefully spend time with my partner's friends? Why or why not?
5. Do we have mutual friends, particularly couples, that we enjoy spending time with together? What could we do to expand our circle of mutual friends?

∽ Encouragement ∾

Effectively observing a partner is a vital but often challenging skill. You now have a far greater understanding both of its importance and how to use this new tool. Be kind to yourself and give yourself time to develop the skill. You will grow to appreciate how effective observation enhances your ability to know your partner well.

It also takes time to be with an expanded circle of people and with a partner enough to accurately observe character in action. You are showing commitment to a healthy and happy future by take the time needed.

REFERENCES FOR CHAPTER 5

1. John Gottman, PhD and Nan Silver, *The Seven Principles for Making Marriage Work*, pp. 19-20

2. Kahlil Gibran, *The Prophet*, p. 59. (1951 Knopf)

3. Agnes Ghaznavi, *Sexuality, Relationships and Spiritual Growth*, p. 26

4. Bill Gothard, *Research in Principles of Life Basic Seminar Textbook*, p. 167

5. Joan Barstow Hernández, *Love, Courtship, and Marriage*, p. 32

6. Ibid., p. 34

7. Gary Chapman, *The Five Love Languages for Singles*, p. 167

8. On behalf of Shoghi Effendi, *Compilation of Compilations, Vol. II*, p. 3

9. Blaine J. Fowers, PhD, *Beyond the Myth of Marital Happiness*, pp. 125, 128

10. United Nations (www.un.org) and the Council of Europe, www.coe.int/t/e/Human_Rights/Equality/)

11. Les Parrott III, *7 Secrets of a Healthy Dating Relationship*, p. 95

12. *More African Proverbs*, p. 49

13. 'Abdu'l-Bahá, *Selections from the Writings of 'Abdu'l-Bahá*, p. 302

14. Agnes Ghaznavi, *Sexuality, Relationships and Spiritual Growth*, p. 20

15. Meditations with Native American Elders" by Don Coyhis (Mohican Nation); copyright 2006; available from White Bison, Inc. at www.whitebison.org

16. Molly Barrow, PhD, "Assessing Your Relationship Capacity" essay in *All-in-One Marriage Prep: 75 Experts Share Tips and Wisdom to Help You Get Ready Now*, p. 228

Chapter 6

Linking Character and Communication

INTRODUCTION

Your character qualities, and of course your partner's, affect your choice of words, your tone of voice, your attitude when listening, and really all aspects of communication. Effective communication is a skill to learn and practice with your partner. The more you both incorporate qualities such as compassion, truthfulness, love, moderation, and respect when you speak to one another, the better.

You and your partner may need to remind each other occasionally, and even more often on bad days, that you are partners, friends, and allies—not opponents, enemies, or adversaries. If you and your partner choose to build your relationship upon unity, friendliness, cooperation, and mutual appreciation, your life together and attitudes towards each other will be happier and more peaceful. In this chapter, you will gain greater insight into how character strengths when misused can cause relationship missteps or dissension and how to turn that around in a positive direction.

Ideally, you and your partner will practice and develop communication skills together. However, your partner may be reluctant to participate, perhaps feeling as if you are forcing the matter. Some people think communication skills training is unnecessary or inappropriate because of cultural or family attitudes.

Many people feel unsure about their communication skills, especially if they have been criticized. The more you learn about communication on your own, the better you can model effective techniques and encourage or influence your partner to try them. Every positive change you make, no matter how small, will affect your partner and your relationship.

Active and Conscious Listening

Effective communication occurs when two people exchange messages and both understand the intended meaning of the messages. **Communication works best in a relationship when you express yourself from your higher nature and use character strengths.** A key aspect of effective mutual communication is attentive listening. Have you ever noticed that if you rearrange the letters of LISTEN they form the word SILENT? **Silence makes it possible to listen fully to your partner with your ears, mind, eyes, and heart, and to see something from your partner's perspective.** "…Everyone should be quick to listen, slow to speak and slow to become angry.…"[1]

By listening fully, you can help your partner feel respected, loved, validated, and appreciated. Your partner will gain confidence and feel more loving towards you. The gift of your full attention encourages your partner to listen well to you in return. Poet and author Oliver Wendell Holmes once wrote, "It is the province of knowledge to speak and it is the privilege of wisdom to listen."[2]

Listening for understanding contributes to effective problem-solving discussions. When you are successful at resolving issues, you reduce or prevent disruption and disunity between you. **Conscious listening enhances trust, love, and unity between you and your partner.** According to spouses Kathlyn Hendricks, PhD, and Gay Hendricks, PhD, conscious listening includes three levels of skill and depth:

> **Level One:** Listen for the words—Give a simple, concise, and accurate summary of what you have heard the speaker say.
> **Level Two:** Listen for the emotions—Hear from your heart the emotions under the words of the speaker.
> **Level Three:** Listen for the wants and needs—Hear beneath the words and the emotions what the speaker is really asking for and needing.[3]

Your openness, empathy, and affirmation of understanding what your partner is saying may encourage your partner to more fully express thoughts, feelings, wants, and needs. Sometimes when you are open and loving with your partner, you can sense what is going on even before words are spoken. Gentle questions or sharing of what you are sensing and hearing can help your partner with clarifying his or her thoughts and emotions. [Note: Excellent information on this process is available in "Habit 5: Seek First to Understand…Then to Be Understood" in Stephen Covey's 7 Habits publications.]

Planning your response while your partner is speaking interferes with your ability to listen completely. When you plan a response, it is usually with the intent to:

- Judge or evaluate
- Criticize
- Influence or control
- Compare
- Fix[4]

In addition, you may focus on defending yourself or emphasizing your own opinion.

At the beginning of a conversation, ask your partner if you should simply listen for understanding. Is your input welcome? Should you suggest solutions? Perhaps your partner simply hopes for some validation, sympathy, or a hug. Maybe he or she wants to offer an apology or straighten out a misunderstanding. **Asking about your role may seem a bit awkward or strange initially, but you will find it tends to reduce misunderstandings and problems between you and your partner.** Having some understanding about where the conversation is going and what role is best for you to play can help you to listen well and both of you to feel less anxious.

While you listen, postpone your natural desire to solve problems, unless your partner requests that. Your partner may not be looking for a solution at all, but just needs to share thoughts and emotions freely to help understand them better. **Listening in the way your partner requests demonstrates that you truly care about his or her feelings and point of view.** If you are distracted and not completely listening, your partner is likely to feel ignored or belittled.

When you are listening at all three levels, show that you receive and clearly understand the message. You might nod your head, make a sympathetic sound or gesture, or ask a clarifying question. Stay focused on your partner and do not try to do other things while your partner is talking. **If your mind wanders, simply acknowledge that you are not sure you heard everything, and ask your partner to please repeat the message. Avoid phone calls, text messages, or any other interrupting media.**

Particularly when the topic is very serious or upsetting, help your partner know you understand by summarizing what you have heard. You might say, "Let me make sure that I understand what you are saying"; "I heard you say…."; or "So, you are saying…." Try to avoid just repeating your partner's exact words. If you have missed a key point, your partner can add to your summary or clarify the communication. Summarizing works best if you do it after each key point your partner makes; otherwise, it will be difficult for you to remember them all. Invite your partner to do the same for you when it is your turn to speak. Summarizing accomplishes the additional purpose of slowing down your interaction when emotions are intense. Consider how this communication tool works for this couple:

> Aliz and Ervin have been in a relationship for about four months. They enjoy volunteering together at the library, watching old movies, and playing computer games.
>
> One afternoon as they rollerblade through their neighborhood park, Ervin stops to chat with three long-time friends. Aliz waits patiently for him to introduce her to his friends, but he doesn't. After the friends depart, Aliz, hurt and upset, becomes quiet and withdraws from Ervin.
>
> "Aliz, is something bothering you?" Ervin asks after a few minutes of silence.
>
> "Yes, there is something I want to talk to you about. When you stopped to talk with your friends earlier, it upset me that you chatted with them for several minutes, but you did not introduce me to them," she says. "I felt really left out of the conversation."
>
> "You felt left out because I didn't introduce you, and that left you feeling ignored and upset," summarizes Ervin.
>
> "Yes, that's exactly how I felt! Can we please agree that you will include me the next time?"
>
> "I'm sorry, Aliz. I was not paying attention. It won't happen again."

Ervin was able to summarize Aliz's concerns successfully because he was listening carefully. He did not become defensive, which would have shifted the focus to him. **When your partner is speaking, remember to stay focused on him or her and take care not to twist the conversation around to make it about you.** Even if what your partner says is about you, you do not have to immediately jump in and defend yourself. Give your partner enough time to communicate fully to be sure you understand. Speaking from your point of view prematurely may interfere with full disclosure of your partner's concern. Your goal is to understand your partner's point of view, not to correct it or manipulate it to agree with your own. When your partner is finished speaking, ask your partner to listen to your thoughts and feelings. As you discover each other's point of view and gain understanding of each other's feelings, you can then work together to resolve the issue.

Your attitude of respect, commitment to equality in your relationship, and practice of patience and other character strengths will enhance your ability to listen. If you feel loving, caring, friendly, and compassionate towards your partner (acting out of your higher nature), you will listen differently than if you are dominating or feeling angry or resentful (out of your lower nature). Remember that you are allies, not adversaries, and that you are responsible for your mental attitude. If you are not ready to listen well, due to hunger, fatigue, distraction, a bad mood, or stress, say so. Suggest a delay in the communication until you are ready to handle it better. If you agree on when and where the discussion will happen, you will be less tempted to avoid it altogether. At times, however, a problem may be so urgent that your partner cannot wait. In that case, proceed and try your best to listen for understanding.

As your relationship grows, you and your partner will increasingly turn to each other to share, listen, and problem-solve. It may take self-discipline to avoid slipping into the unwise habit of just turning to friends and family when you need to talk about important subjects and resolve relationship difficulties. Of course, you will still turn to friends and family under appropriate circumstances, but it is very important to learn the skill of resolving problems together. It is wise to develop confidence in your ability to address concerns if you want your relationship to last.

ESSENTIAL ACTIVITY

Ask your partner to practice the three levels of conscious listening with you. Whoever initially speaks can choose a topic, or you can agree on one together. It may be easier to focus on building your skills if you choose a simple topic with few emotional triggers. Switch roles so that you each practice speaking and listening. Over time you will most likely use this skill for more serious issues and not as likely for smaller ones. You can then both discuss the "Reflection" questions in the box below.

~ *Reflection* ~

1. How do I feel when someone listens attentively to me?
2. What actions, gestures, or responses let others know that I am listening to them? What new ones could I try?
3. How well do I focus on and understand what others say to me? What helps me focus?
4. Can I accurately sense the emotions behind someone's words? If not, am I able to ask the person to verbalize his or her feelings?
5. Can I hear the wants and needs behind a speaker's words? If not, am I able to ask the person to verbalize his or her wants and needs?

THE WAYS YOU SPEAK TO YOUR PARTNER

When you speak, your partner will hear more than just your words. Your tone of voice also reflects your thoughts and feelings and powerfully indicates what is happening behind your words. If you listen carefully, you can usually tell if either of you is feeling upset, happy, angry, excited, or annoyed by the tone used to deliver the words. You will notice that others believe and react to what you say with your tone of voice more than with your actual words. When your words and tone of voice do not match, usually they will believe the tone.

As you speak, you also place emphasis on various syllables or words. Your tone and emphasis convey your emotions and signal to your partner the significance you place on what you are saying.

Before you say something, pause and try to discern what feelings may influence your tone of voice or how you speak. If you are angry, but you attempt to be "nice," the other person will get the mixed message and be confused. If you ask "why?" in a judgmental tone, your partner may feel blamed and become defensive. You can practice saying aloud what you feel and what is on your mind to hear how it sounds before you speak to your partner. You can also record your voice and replay it or say the words to someone who is not involved in the issue, asking for feedback. If you involve someone other than a professional, ensure that you keep your comments vague enough that you do not share personal information that could hurt your partner.

As you listen to your tone of voice, you may conclude that you need to resolve an inner problem or take some calming action before having the conversation with your partner. It is often wise to diffuse the potency of very intense feelings before you speak up so that you do not damage your relationship. At the same time, however, try to identify any feelings you want to communicate clearly and directly so you avoid sending mixed messages, in which your words and tone do not agree.

Unless an issue is so minor that you can simply detach from it, it is best to raise it directly in a purposeful attempt to resolve it, rather than keeping it suppressed. Avoiding direct communication may cause your feelings and concerns to come out through your attitude and tone of voice instead, confusing and hurting your partner.

Once you have communicated your concerns and feelings, ask your partner to summarize what you said. Once you know that your partner understands both your words and your feelings, you can then effectively address and resolve the problem together.

As you increase your understanding of and skill with matching your own tones of voice with your words, you will notice that your trust in each other's words increases. You are also more able to "coach" one another with gentle feedback and communicate effectively about your concerns. As you talk with each other about what your different tones of voice mean, you can explore whether cultural factors and possibly your unique personalities are affecting your tones or interpretations.

Your tone of voice and the emphasis you place on words also reveal information about your character. If you are demonstrating patience, your tone will be calmer than if you are practicing assertiveness. If you are practicing friendliness, your tone will be warm and welcoming. The emphasis you put on certain words and the volume of your voice also communicate how much importance you place on what you are communicating. For example, your forceful expression may indicate that you care about justice in a situation. As you listen to your partner's tone and emphasis, then you learn about his or her character as well.

ESSENTIAL ACTIVITY

This activity will help you understand how tone of voice affects your communications. Say a few of the phrases below to your partner, first in a negative tone of voice and with a negative expression on your face. Then, say the same term with a positive tone of voice and facial expression. Try sending a mixed message where your expression and your tone do not match. Watch your partner's reactions to these various communications. A third person can be an observer who watches both of you and gives feedback. Take turns so that each of you has the opportunity to both speak and listen.

a. Sorry	Fine
b. Excuse me	Thanks
c. Stop it	Come with me
d. Don't touch me	What do you want
e. Will you call me	Why did you do that
f. Whatever you want	Yes, dear
g. All right, I will do it	Can you hear me
h. Sit down	Leave it alone
i. I don't want to talk now	Can you help me
j. How are you	Good morning

Discussion: Which tones of voice did you like and which ones would you prefer *not* to have as part of your partner communications—either giving or receiving? Were any phrases very difficult to say in a positive tone? Did you add "please" automatically to make a phrase sound more positive? Did any cultural differences affect the meaning of any phrase? What did you learn about the tones of voice you frequently use? How do you respond when others use tones of voice that do not match their words?

~ Reflection ~

1. Do I ever use a tone of voice that bothers others? What can I do to remind myself to avoid using it?
2. What tones do I consistently use that are positive and work well?
3. What tones from others do I especially appreciate receiving? Dislike receiving?
4. Do others tend to misinterpret what I say because of my tone or how I speak? What can I do about this pattern?

CHARACTER QUALITY LANGUAGE

It will help you to learn about each other's character when you use *Character Quality Language* to affirm specific qualities in each other. This practice also builds love, appreciation, and happiness between you, particularly when you are specific and sincere. Here are some simple examples:

- "Thank you for being (Helpful, Flexible, Truthful…) when you…."
- "I appreciate your (Courage, Respect, Faithfulness…) when you…."
- "I love how (Accepting, Enthusiastic, Encouraging…) you are!"

Below are two examples of statements that you might say to a partner. The first is a positive statement similar to what you may already comfortably make. The second version uses Character Quality Language instead.

Good Statement:
I am happy that you want to try some new activities with me!
Better Statement Using Character Quality Language:
I really appreciated how Enthusiastic and Courageous you were about going water skiing with me this weekend. I know you have not had much experience with being out on the lake in a boat, and I am happy when you are willing to try something new with me.

The first statement is positive, and your partner will likely feel appreciated. However, the second, more powerful and specific statement acknowledges your partner and encourages continued practice of the character qualities.

Here is another pair of statements:

Good Statement:
Thanks for looking after my daughter when she fell.
Better Statement Using Character Quality Language:
I appreciate how Caring and Helpful you were to Becky when she fell off her bicycle. She was so upset, and your attention and concern helped her to calm down.

Consider these further examples:

- "Your Patience in working with my Dad on the car in the garage yesterday and how Helpful you were to him really touched my heart."
- "It was great watching you be so Enthusiastic at my son's soccer game this morning. Thank you for being so Flexible about the change in starting time."

Using Character Quality Language will help you to strengthen and keep practicing these qualities. Having someone notice your use of a quality encourages your continued use. **It is often easier to criticize than to recognize and appreciate what someone does well. It takes practice to look consciously for someone's positive actions and speak specifically about them, but it is worth the effort and very affirming for everyone involved.** [Refer to your completed Worksheet 4 as a resource and see Part 3 for details about the qualities.]

This practice is also a key tool for parents in helping children learn about and strengthen specific qualities. For example, you can say, "Please be Patient" instead of "Oh, just hold on a minute!" and it helps the child (and you) with learning Patience. Learning the names of the character qualities and highlighting them in your children builds their self-respect. Then you can say, "Thank you for being Caring to your sister today when she was sad" instead of "You were nice to your sister today." If children you already have see you affirming these qualities in each other, this will also give them Confidence in your relationship.

Using Character Quality Language may feel unnatural at first, if it is not how you are used to speaking or hearing others talk. You often speak and hear more negative words than positive ones. However, if you sincerely practice using this language, you will find that it becomes comfortable and easy. Acknowledging your partner's positive attributes encourages ongoing practice and can transform your relationship.

It is difficult to discuss and understand thoughts and experiences for which you and your partner have no common vocabulary. Character Quality Language provides just that, encouraging both of you to learn how to look for and acknowledge character strengths in each other.

Sincere Character Quality Language builds your partner's confidence and self-respect, as well as your own, creating a foundation of positive interactions between the two of you. These positive interactions can help you both to act in accordance with the character qualities, serving as powerful examples for each other and everyone around you.

ESSENTIAL AND HELPFUL ACTIVITIES

Essential:
1. Use Character Quality Language to acknowledge when you see your partner practicing character strengths (see your work on Worksheet 4) or making an effort to strengthen a quality. Start by acknowledging even the smallest display of a quality. Your positive words will likely bring the qualities out even more. Continue using Character Quality Language in your everyday life with other people and assess how they respond. At the same time, begin using Character Quality Language in your inner dialogue when you notice that you are practicing a quality well in your own life.

Helpful:
2. Send a greeting card or create a visual or artistic acknowledgement to show your appreciation of someone's excellent practice of a character quality.

~ Reflection ~

1. How do I respond when someone acknowledges one of my character strengths?
2. Do I ever discount or reject this type of positive comment? Why or why not?
3. How do people respond when I acknowledge their character qualities?
4. What effect might it have on a relationship if my partner and I use Character Quality Language consistently with each other? With any children that we have?

COMMUNICATION CHALLENGES

Of course, you do not usually enter a relationship expecting it to be full of problems. In fact, you probably hope for an abundance of happiness, companionship, and excitement. However, you may discover that you and your partner disagree or argue about many aspects of life and your relationship. Perhaps you do not understand why you have so much disagreement or what is causing it. This section outlines some common communication problems and presents ways to address them skillfully to keep your relationship intact.

Patterns and Methods

Throughout your respective lives, both you and your partner learned and practiced different ways of communicating. Your communications reflect either your higher or your lower nature, prompting you with being positive or negative, praising or attacking, agreeable or argumentative. In addition, your style may be loud, soft, dramatically expressive, or calm. Your communication style probably mirrors some of what you observed in parents, siblings, friends, teachers, coworkers, partners, and others. Some of your interactions are probably healthy and constructive, while others may less beneficial. If you continue learning and practicing, your communication skills will improve.

Expecting your partner to communicate the same way that you learned to communicate while you were growing up will lead to misunderstandings and problems. For instance, one of you may fear that your relationship will fall apart if the two of you seriously disagree about something. The other might feel that a relationship is not healthy or interesting without an occasional loud disagreement. One person may see arguing as healthy debate, while the other sees arguing as a relationship failure. It is important for you to share and discuss your communication expectations and previous experiences with your partner. Doing so will provide an opportunity to determine how your communication styles differ and what is reasonable to expect between you and your partner.

Sensitivity

Communication in a close relationship can be emotionally challenging. You will soon discover what topics are particularly sensitive. Pay careful attention so that you do not unintentionally hurt each other's feelings. If you accidentally—or intentionally—use harmful words that make your partner upset, you might need to assess your motives and use of character qualities. You certainly will want to apologize. You do not want to hurt someone you care about or love.

Although most of what your partner says to you will probably please you, some comments may prompt you to feel sad, angry, or frustrated. You may then wonder whether you should speak up or just stay silent. It is best to say what is on your mind, but with tact and wisdom, as well as continue efforts to develop your communication skills, character qualities, and sensitivity to your partner's needs. *The Tanakh* says, "A gentle response allays wrath; a harsh word provokes anger. ... A healing tongue is a tree of life...."[5]

Sharing and Sabotaging

If you regularly suppress your thoughts and emotions and do not share them with your partner, both of you will likely become very unhappy and frustrated. You may then begin behaving negatively towards each other. If you do not speak up, your partner will have no idea what you are feeling or what is wrong. A buildup of suppressed thoughts and emotions may explode as excessive anger, damaging your relationship. Whenever either of you stops sharing, the other, gently and kindly, can encourage a return to openness and trust.

John M. Gottman, PhD, and his team at the Relationship Research Institute in Seattle, Washington (USA), have discovered a number of indicators that a relationship is beginning to deteriorate. The research focuses on married couples, but the findings can apply to unmarried couples as well. A couple's communication patterns begin to form as soon as their relationship begins. These are the warning signs:

1. Starting interactions negatively and harshly
2. Criticizing your partner's character (character attack)
3. Showing contempt for your partner
4. Reacting defensively with each other (a form of blame)
5. Withdrawing to avoid communication, thereby shutting your partner out (stonewalling)
6. Responding to negativity with strong and overwhelming physical symptoms, such as increased heart rate, elevated blood pressure, or sweating
7. Failing at attempts to repair the relationship
8. Remembering and focusing on bad memories only[6]

You can prevent most of these problems with careful listening, watching your tone of voice, using Character Quality Language, and offering encouragement.

~ Reflection ~

1. What are some of the negative ways I communicate? How do people respond?
2. What was the communication style in my home when I was growing up? What good communication habits did I learn there? What poor habits? What am I doing or going to do to change my poor habits into more effective ones?
3. What physical symptoms occur in me when someone is upset with me or critical? How can I signal to a partner these symptoms are beginning to occur and I need time to recover?

CHARACTER AND COMMUNICATION

If you think about what you have been learning about character throughout this book, you may begin to see how destructive a character attack can be. **Character attacks criticize someone for misusing or lacking character strengths.** Look at these examples:

"You should have paid your bills. You are so **irresponsible**!"
"Where were you? You were late picking me up! I can't **trust** you to do anything right!"

These statements attack a person's responsibility and trustworthiness, inflaming the situation through harsh criticism. It is also very damaging to call your partner names, such as "jerk" or "stupid." Such communications cause estrangement and reduce trust. They make it difficult to share openly and honestly or to feel comfortable around each other. Consider this couple:

Talisha and Drew have been getting to know each other for the last few months after meeting through a matchmaking website. Lately, however, they keep having serious arguments. Drew makes commitments, without discussing them with Talisha, which results in his spending less time with her. She complains loudly each time it happens. Drew yells at Talisha for trying to manage his life. Talisha ends up in tears.

When Drew is together with Talisha, she often interrupts their time together with responding to text messages and calls from friends. Drew gets angry when it happens repeatedly.

They both feel frustrated and unhappy with what is happening, but they are not sure how to change direction.

Because they still value the relationship and do not want to lose it, Talisha and Drew decide to seek help from a relationship coach. He helps them with recognizing that it's often automatic for men to act independently, and guides them with agreeing on when collaboration about plans is needed and when it's not. He reminds them that one of women's strengths is to build the support of female friends, but he also helps Talisha choose the times she interacts with and talks to friends and for how much time. He has them recall and repeat their positive behaviors during happier times when their relationship worked well. With his help, they also learn some new communication knowledge and skills.

Thinking critical thoughts about your partner can also harm your relationship, even without your actually saying anything. Your thoughts influence your attitude and tone of voice, which, in turn, affect your actions or inactions towards your partner.

Instead of attacking your partner's character, you can make a fair-minded complaint or simply raise a concern. Showing appreciation and using Character Quality Language changes the previous negative examples into positive problem-solving communications, which are less likely to put your partner on the defensive and more likely to lead to an apology or attempt to improve.

"Honey, I am concerned that you do not seem to be paying your bills. You are usually so responsible. Is there a problem we can talk through together? Maybe I can help."

"I am tired and upset that I had to wait a long time for you to pick me up. Because you are such a thoughtful person, I know that you wanted to be here on time. What happened?"

These responses invite your partner to share and allow both of you together to determine how to prevent a similar situation from arising again. You will need to use patience and self-discipline so you do not react automatically and attack or respond defensively, and you will enjoy increased harmony and unity.

HELPFUL ACTIVITIES

1. Spend time with a friend or acquaintance with whom it has sometimes been difficult to communicate, focusing on using new skills and improving communications. Pay attention to what you say and do, noticing the results of efforts. What does this experience reveal about the power of your role in communicating with others?
2. Think about a time when you felt angry with someone or someone got angry with you. Analyze which character qualities you were using well and those you were not using effectively. Assess the other person's behavior as well. Does this give you more insight about what caused the problem?

~ *Reflection* ~

1. Do I ever attack the character of others? What words do I tend to use? How do people respond?
2. When has someone attacked my character? How did I respond? Was I able to re-establish unity with the person? How?

MISUSING CHARACTER QUALITIES WITH A PARTNER

In Chapter 1, you began to learn about character strengths and their misuse. Now it is time deepen your understanding of how you may misuse qualities and of the negative effect that can have on a partner and a relationship. Avoiding the misuse of character strengths will increase the harmony in your relationships.

Remember, a character strength misuse occurs when you are strong and effective at practicing a character quality, but at times practice it in one or both of the following ways:

- To excess, and/or
- At the wrong time or place

In both cases your words or actions cause varying degrees of harm to others or yourself and often result in some level of disunity or dissension. When you misuse a character strength, the result is either interpersonal or internal conflict. Here are examples:

Generosity can be used to excess if you buy presents for others when you have no money to spare. Acceptance is practiced in a wrong time and place if you allow someone to abuse you.

If you experience disunity with a partner, look at how you are practicing your qualities. As you expand your understanding of misuses, you greatly increase your ability to identify what is going wrong, either before or during a conflict. You then have the opportunity to take corrective measures to practice your qualities more effectively and rebuild unity. Psychotherapist Erik Blumenthal says, "...nothing can be achieved through conflict and quarrel. Conflict begets further conflict...."[7]

You can resolve misuses by using a "helper quality" to assist you with adjusting your behavior so that the character quality becomes beneficial rather than harmful. Consider moderation first, lessening the excessive practice of the character strength. Moderation can also help you pause and take a step back to see if you are using a quality at the wrong time or place. You will find it useful to think of other helper qualities that can work particularly well for you. When choosing a helper quality, look for those you practice effectively or rarely misuse. If respect is an effective strength for you, it can help you stop misusing other character qualities.

How Misuses Happen

Sometimes misuses stem from self-centeredness or from attempts to control or dominate a partner. Perhaps you practice your strength of friendliness only with those who can help you get ahead in your career, while your partner wants you to be friendlier to your mutual friends. Such matters can cause tension, hurt feelings, or estrangement between you and your partner.

Lower nature feelings, such as pride, anger, insecurity, fear, anxiety, or hate, can lead you to misuse a quality and cause a disruption in your relationship. These negative feelings block you from wisdom. Feeling insecure about your partner's affection can cause you to be too accepting of repeated criticism. Anger or hate can lead you to misuse purposefulness and seek revenge. Both of these situations will cause harm and disunity.

Another example of a misuse is a reaction to something negative that happened in the past. Fearing that the past will repeat itself, you strongly practice a certain quality with a great deal of focused attention, hoping to prevent the negative event or something similar from occurring again. You might behave—often unconsciously—as if practicing the quality will produce an automatically positive result for you. Consider how this happens for Patricia:

A year after her divorce, Patricia still feels angry with her ex-husband for being unfaithful to her. She purposefully goes on with her life, not realizing that being angry causes her to misuse discernment.

Patricia attends an evening college class with other men and women her age. She hopes to meet new friends and maybe even develop a new relationship. After class, many of the attendees go to a nearby restaurant for something to eat. Each time Patricia participates, she is friendly to the women in the group, but she struggles when interacting with the men. She smiles at them, but underneath polite words, as she asks the men questions, her voice sounds angry and judgmental. She determines to discern whether they would be likely to cheat on their wives. Instead of helping her to find men who might be potential partners, this behavior causes the men to avoid her.

The outcome of Patricia's misuse of discernment is alienation from others. Her anger contributes to the misuse, preventing her from developing friendships or relationships with men.

Discernment is an important quality for Patricia to practice as she goes forward. However, her unresolved emotions from the past cause her to use the quality unwisely. Applying moderation would help her be more consistent in her interactions with both women and men. Practicing justice as a helper quality would also assist her to be fair and not to judge people without cause.

Conflict As an Indicator of Misuse

A useful indicator that you are misusing a quality is conflict with your partner. When either of you misuse your character strengths, your interactions may be clumsy and your relationship troubled.

To help you assess and understand a problem between you and a partner, thoughtfully ask yourself the following questions:

- When you feel angry, hurt, or frustrated with each other, what has been going on? Under what circumstances do you express these feelings or does your partner express such feelings to you?
- What problems or conflicts arise between you and people other than your partner? Do the same issues arise each time there are disagreements or misunderstandings? If so, do you know why? What can you learn from these interactions with others to help you relate more smoothly with your partner?
- When an action that you intended to be positive has a negative result instead, what quality were you trying to practice?

For example, you may effectively practice courage in the face of challenges. However, perhaps you have turned this positive quality into harmful, reckless, and risky behavior like sky-diving over treacherous mountainous areas. Your partner is very upset about the risks you are taking with your life and sees your behavior as a misuse of courage. As you reflect on this concern, you begin to understand that it is true.

To resolve the problem, you can then practice moderation, which will guide you to choose a safer landing location than the mountains. You can also turn to helper qualities to assist you, adding care and respect for your partner and others who will be upset if you are badly injured or who will miss you if you die. You can also practice respect for your own physical well-being.

Resolving Misuses with a Partner

Being sensitive to your partner's point of view will prevent problems in your relationship. You will also need to be open and flexible, but without sacrificing your integrity. Discernment will help you see how the dynamics of your character strengths tend to interact with your partner's, giving you the necessary wisdom to identify and resolve misuses.

Once you have identified that you are misusing a quality, apply moderation and other helper qualities to correct your misuse. Moderation helps you use all the other qualities effectively so you do not hurt others or yourself. Visualize a dial that has three positions: left, center, and right. "Left" means you get hurt, "right" means your partner gets hurt, and "center" means you are practicing a quality with appropriate moderation. If you aspire to keep each quality you practice in the center position, you will be practicing moderation, which will benefit both you and your partner. If you experience conflict, disunity, or harmful behavior, then picture this dial and assess which quality is off-center.

Your assessment will shift, depending on the situation. What might appear to be an effective application of moderation at one time, may not be appropriate the next time. Practice discernment and flexibility to change your actions according to your current interactions and circumstances. "Once you make a decision, you are committed to it. Yet, be flexible. Monitor progress, make adjustments along the way when necessary to achieve your goal."[8]

Do not change your beliefs or principles in the process, however. Consider how this couple struggles to determine the appropriate use of character qualities:

> Mei Lu and Shen have been good friends and partners for a few months. Shen recently injured his arm in an accident at work amd is on medical leave for a few weeks while it heals. Mei Lu cares for him by bringing over food and helping him with some of the household tasks he finds difficult, such as cooking, washing the dishes, and doing laundry.
>
> After the cast comes off, Mei Lu visits him, continues taking care of him, insists on lifting and carrying things for him, and does the housework. Because he does not want to hurt her feelings, even though the doctor wants him to resume some activities, Shen tactfully lets her keep helping. This prevents Shen from rebuilding the muscles in his arm appropriately and regaining full use of it. Shen's tactfulness is a problem, and Mei Lu's caring is no longer beneficial. His physical therapist tells Shen he is progressing too slowly. Frustrated by his lack of progress, he finally raises the issue with Mei Lu.

It would have been wise for Mei Lu to realize that it was not appropriate for her to help in the same way throughout Shen's recovery. It would have been more caring to gradually stop doing tasks for him after the cast came off. Shen also misuses tactfulness by keeping silent instead of assertively and kindly expressing what he needs to say.

When applying moderation to various qualities, there are some considerations to keep in mind. **Remember that applying moderation to truthfulness, for instance, does not mean that lying is acceptable.** It does not support your relationship to lie, tell half-truths, or withhold important information. 'Abdu'l-Bahá says, "Truthfulness is the foundation of all human virtues. … When this holy attribute is established in man, all the divine qualities will also be acquired."[9] Adding moderation to truthfulness means that you discern when it is appropriate to tell all of the details you know and when it is not tactful, timely, or wise to do so. Consider how Selim struggles with truthfulness and ends up misusing creativity in the following scenario:

> Peri and Selim have been in a relationship for a few weeks. They agree to save their money so that they can attend a special concert together. Every week, Peri shares what amount she has saved, and she asks Selim how much money he has set aside. He tells her an amount each time. However, he is not really saving the money, because he decides that he will be able to make money quickly by participating in a creative idea a friend has proposed.
>
> Selim does not want Peri to be concerned about how he is actually using the money, so he keeps pretending that he is saving it. However, when it comes time to buy the tickets, his friend's idea has ended badly, and there is no money. Selim admits to Peri that he did not save the money. In his mind, Selim had justified creating a story about saving money and telling it to Peri, because he thought there

would be no harm and that his creative idea to make money would work out fine. Peri is angry and disappointed, and she is not sure whether to trust Selim again.

In this scenario, Selim misused his creativity by hatching a crafty plan that would allow him both to spend his money and to get the tickets without Peri finding out about it. In this situation, Selim practices creativity unwisely. His relationship would have benefited from truthfulness, as well as love and respect for his partner.

When Peri discovers what Selim has done, she could launch a character attack and accuse Selim of being an untrustworthy liar. If, however, Peri values her relationship with Selim and wants to minimize their conflict as well as benefit his character growth, she can address the misuse by speaking to him about his strength. She could say, "I see how you were trying to be creative by finding a way to spend your money and get the tickets at the same time. However, I am very disappointed about not being able to buy the tickets. Can we discuss better ways to use your creativity?" Selim would be less likely to become defensive, and their relationship might be able to move forward.

Shortcoming or Misused Strength?

Sometimes when you assess your words and actions, you may seem to have a shortcoming or to be missing a quality altogether. This is a common and incorrect assumption people typically make when, in truth, they are actually misusing a character strength.

Whenever you or others are unhappy with your words or actions, it makes sense to discern the true cause of your behavior. Is it caused by your weakness or ineffectiveness in practicing a quality or by one that you are misusing? Developing a weak quality, if that is the cause, takes determined effort.

If, however, the root of your behavior is your misuse of a quality, you need simply to determine what it is and then moderate it or use helper qualities to make it effective. If you look closely at the quality of discernment, for example, you see that it empowers you to see clearly and deeply into all matters and make wise decisions based on what you discover. However, if you tend to be critical, you may just make negative comments about what you observe.

When used appropriately, discernment is a powerful force for the good of a relationship, since you can use it to determine and understand the needs of your partner. Used inappropriately, however, as in making critical remarks, discernment can become judgmental and self-righteous. Consider this story:

Eliska is working on her third project of the day one Saturday afternoon at her home. Her partner Ryan has come over to help her move some furniture, but she comments incessantly that he never seems to get the table or couch in just the right place. He begins to get annoyed by her attitude and criticisms. Eliska's negativity and faultfinding causes him to wish he had stayed at his own house or gone to the park to play soccer with some friends instead.

Ryan speaks up assertively, asking her to stop making negative comments. Eliska responds that she is just trying to make her home look nice by pointing out possible improvements. She agrees to think about her comments, however, and how she actually practices discernment. The next few days, as she reflects on her behavior, she realizes that she always looks for what is not going well around her and makes critical remarks about what she sees. She does not usually say something positive when she discerns things going smoothly. She rarely encourages others or expresses appreciation to those who help her.

When Eliska sees Ryan the following weekend, she apologizes for how she treated him. She asks for his help again the next day, promising to behave differently. As he frowns and hesitates, she assures him that she sincerely wants to change and will not criticize his efforts this time. Eliska knows it will be difficult to rebuild Ryan's trust, but she perseveres.

Even when you or your partner misuse a character strength, whether because of not understanding the quality or because of good intentions that go astray, you are still building your capacity to use the quality correctly. In other words, you are exercising the right muscles, but in the wrong way.

Identifying the character qualities you tend to misuse will empower you to accomplish one or more of the following objectives:
- Transform your use of those qualities by practicing moderation along with them
- Determine which other character qualities can help you stop misusing your strengths
- Recognize and build on the strengths you discover that have been hidden by your misuse of them

The more you understand and observe character qualities in others and yourself, the more nuances and layers you will discover. As personal transformation occurs with positive choices, your relationship will benefit. With positive relationship interactions, your harmony and unity as a couple will grow.

~ Reflection ~

1. When have I misused a quality, causing harm to a partner or others?
2. How do I feel when my misuse of character qualities causes harm, conflict, or disunity? How do I resolve such situations?
3. When in particular have I struggled to act with moderation? How would applying moderation in those situations have benefited others and myself?
4. Does my partner appear to misuse any character qualities in ways that affect our relationship? Which qualities? How might I influence a shift in my partner's behavior? Does my partner seem willing to work on practicing qualities in more effective ways?
5. If I identify that I misuse a character quality, causing harm to myself but apparently not harming others, do I need to make a change? Is it possible to harm only myself without harming others?
6. What ways can I build harmony and unity with my partner?

ESSENTIAL ACTIVITIES

1. Think of recent situations that resulted in disunity between you and a partner or another person. Identify what quality you misused and what qualities you might have used to prevent the problem.
2. Complete Worksheet 7: Assessing Your Misuse of Character Qualities. This worksheet will give you experience in identifying both the qualities that you tend to misuse and what could assist you to speak and act more effectively.
3. Complete Worksheet 8: Assessing Character Misuses in Your Relationship Partner to assess your partner's strengths that are misused and ways to encourage improved choices.

❧ Encouragement ❧

You are experiencing vital personal growth and development as you learn constructive ways to communicate. As you strengthen and practice character qualities effectively, your communication patterns will improve. Enjoy the excitement of your progress, and reward yourself for your worthwhile efforts.

REFERENCES FOR CHAPTER 6

1. *The Bible* (New International Version), James 1:19
2. Oliver Wendell Holmes, *The Poet at the Breakfast Table*
3. Summary based on Kathlyn Hendricks, PhD, and Gay Hendricks, Ph.D, *The Conscious Heart*, pp. 267-272
4. Ibid., pp. 265-266
5. *Tanakh*, Mishlei (Proverbs), 15:1, 4
6. Summary based on John Gottman, PhD, and Nan Silver, *The Seven Principles for Making Marriage Work*, Ch. 2
7. Erik Blumenthal, *To Understand and Be Understood*, p. 37
8. Khalil A. Khavari, PhD, *Spiritual Intelligence*, p. 237
9. 'Abdu'l-Bahá, quoted in Shoghi Effendi, *The Advent of Divine Justice*, p. 26

Chapter 7

Connecting Character and Sex

INTRODUCTION

Physical intimacies, including sexual touch and intercourse, have become the norm in dating relationships in many parts of the world for people of all ages. When you care for someone, the pull to be physically intimate can be very strong. Popular media makes having sex very early in a relationship look like positive behavior. It also conveys that it is fine to make very fast decisions about the long-term viability of a relationship based on strong physical attraction.

Of course you *do* want to know that there is a spark of attraction between you and a partner. **However, it is clear that sexual touch alters relationships. Sexual intimacy while you and a partner are getting to know each other, or as a method of getting to know each other, increases the difficulty of objectively assessing a partner's character. It shifts the focus onto physical attraction rather than exploring and developing the other far more important dimensions of your friendship-based relationship.**

As you read the sections that follow, think about the sexual choices that you have made previously, what choices you are committing to today, and what your commitment is to yourself and to a future partner. In a world where sex is so pervasive and prominent, the choices will often not be easy ones for you to make or stay committed to fulfilling. You may feel confused at times, change your commitments, or try new choices. These sections present you with a foundation for whatever you choose to do.

DEFINING SEX AND INTIMACY

Sex is primarily a physical act of intimate touch, but it has mental, emotional, and spiritual components. Some people define sex from a physical standpoint as occurring only when there is sexual intercourse. However, it is actually broader than that, because it includes any intentional contact that arouses a sexual response, whether you are by yourself or with a partner. Therefore, sex also includes actions such as:

- Talking explicitly about sex
- Listening to sexually explicit musical lyrics
- Viewing sexual images (pornography or some television shows and movies)
- Reading books that arouse the desire to have sex
- Fantasizing and masturbating
- Manual sex as a couple
- Oral sex

If you choose not to engage in sex in a relationship, it includes avoiding all of these above actions and more. Even couples who make the choice to have sex will be wise to have respectful limits that eliminate engaging in a number of these activities. As you think about your choices, you will also assess which ones are more likely to expand your lower physical nature rather than develop your higher spiritual one, and therefore reduce your self-respect.

Sex and intimacy are concepts that are often paired together. They can be connected, but they are also quite different. Intimacy is an emotional feeling of familiarity and closeness that is based upon the shared and accumulated experiences between two people. These experiences include every aspect of life. Couples build intimacy by openly and honestly sharing the full range of their thoughts and feelings on a variety of topics. Intimacy includes sharing experiences that build connection and closeness. Some of these experiences can be responding to a challenge together or helping each other with tasks.

~ Reflection ~

1. What is my general attitude towards sex?
2. What does sex mean to me? What are the sources of my information?
3. Do I know enough about sex and its consequences to make informed choices? Where can I gain more information if necessary?
4. What are my understanding, expectations, and needs about intimacy?
5. How can a partner and I develop non-sexual intimacy?

SEX AND CHARACTER

A significant challenge that occurs when you choose to be sexually intimate with someone, particularly early on in a relationship, is that you do not really know the person with whom you are sharing such physical intimacies. Consider this perspective:

> When we feel attracted to someone, it's natural that we want to express that attraction physically, initially through a hug, a kiss, holding hands or physical proximity. However, if these initial, physical expressions of affection become frequent, intensify, and come to play a prominent part in the relationship, they can quickly grow into a force which binds the couple together emotionally and which makes objectivity about one another's qualities difficult to achieve.[1]

Objectivity is challenging to hold onto when you and a partner are having sex. When you have fully "given" yourself to another person physically, you then want confirmation that you have made a good partner choice. As you get to know your partner, you then may minimize serious issues, make excuses for your partner's misbehavior, or not even see problems that are there. Sexual involvement can also make it more difficult to raise concerns or leave a relationship when you do see serious character issues in a partner.

Chelsea and Hunter experienced some of these difficulties:

Chelsea and Hunter meet for the first time when they sit next to each other on a flight from their hometown to another city. He is on his way to visit family, and she has a business meeting to attend. They have a lively conversation throughout the 3-hour flight and feel definite attraction to each other. They are able to meet for dinner at their destination city, and they get together for a date upon their return home. At the end of the date, Chelsea invites Hunter into her apartment. After having some coffee, they begin kissing and touching each other very provocatively. Their passion continues and climaxes with them having sex.

For their next date, Hunter takes Chelsea to the horse racetrack. He keeps excusing himself to go place bets on various horses, most of which lose their races. Hunter becomes increasingly and loudly angry at his streak of bad luck, but Chelsea comforts him. At the end of the night, Hunter has lost hundreds of dollars, but Chelsea reasons to herself that this was probably just a one-time event. She convinces herself that he probably will not get this angry over other things. Chelsea stays the night with him, and she tries to assist him to forget his losses by having sex with him again.

When the couple goes out the next time to a concert, they include Chelsea's sister Charlene and her boyfriend. Chelsea and Charlene talk loudly throughout the concert, making it difficult for anyone around them to focus on the music. Hunter is angry, both at their behavior and at being ignored all night, but he does not want to say anything to Chelsea that might prevent her from staying overnight at his place. He knows Chelsea and Charlene have not seen each other in awhile, and decides to ignore their rudeness.

Very early on in their relationship, Chelsea and Hunter are establishing a pattern of ignoring serious issues, in part to protect their sexual relationship. They are discovering character and behavior problems in each other that may sabotage the relationship, but they are putting their feelings of physical attraction first and not addressing the issues.

Sex without commitment and love becomes meaningless and unsatisfying. When the satisfaction of immediate desires becomes the primary function or focus of a relationship, you may ignore or not communicate your long-term expectations and requirements of each other. This type of uncommitted sexual encounter interferes with getting to know each other mentally, emotionally, and spiritually.

When you physically touch someone, or they touch you, there is an emotional and memory imprint. The more touch there is that feels good, the more you want it to continue. The memory imprint then becomes stronger, as do the ties you will likely feel with the person. **This physical intimacy can set up the illusion in your mind that you and a partner are very close with each other, when you actually are not. One of you may be thinking that having sex means you are in a committed relationship, while the other could be focused only on enjoying the physical experience.** If the relationship then ends, you may still have the desire for more touch that feels good. This desire can set you up to be in an unwise cycle in subsequent relationships of seeking physical contact when you do not know a partner well.

Physical intimacy can be especially tempting when you are in a long-distance relationship, because it can be very difficult to avoid sexual contact when you visit each other. This difficulty is especially the case if you end up staying in the same place together. Your emotions are already high from being together after time apart, and it may feel natural to be physically intimate as a result. You may think that because you do not see each other often, that having sex will make your reunions even better. However, it is already more difficult when you are geographically apart to keep both eyes open so you clearly and accurately observe a partner's character. Having sex is likely to cloud your vision even further and make sex more important than is wise at this stage in your relationship.

~ *Reflection* ~
1. How can having sex affect my ability to know a partner's character?   2. What are my partner's views on sex as a part of dating?
HELPFUL ACTIVITY
Have a discussion with a friend who has had sex with a partner and explore how it affected their relationship.

SAVING SEX FOR MARRIAGE

Ultimately, within marriage, sex is a bonding act of unity between all aspects of two people. The strong love and deep intimacy between the couple make sex more mutually pleasurable, gratifying, and unifying. Consider this perspective from author Justice St. Rain:

Spiritual and emotional intimacy develop in stages. We go from strangers to acquaintances, to activities partners, to friends, to close friends, to intimate friends. "Instant spiritual intimacy" is a fallacy. It is a popular myth because it is very easy to project our fantasies on people rather than wait to see if a person's inner reality matches his or her outer appearance. "We have so much in common...we think so much alike...It was love at first sight." No matter how much we want these things to be true, we can't know that they are until we spend some time together. If they are true, then the time we spend confirming our initial impressions will be a source of great pleasure and fond memories. But if we are mistaken, we will be grateful that we "looked before we leaped." We may tell ourselves we have fallen out of love just in time to avoid a bad relationship, but in fact, we never loved to begin with.

Physical intimacy also develops in stages, and these stages should follow rather than precede their spiritual counterparts. "Instant physical intimacy" is really a form of exposure. There is an adrenaline rush that comes from laying ourselves out naked on the table (emotionally or physically) that has nothing to do with knowing, caring or moving closer, but a great deal to do with our deep longing to be known and accepted. If we do not establish our emotional safety first, then the vulnerability inherent in exposing this longing will only increase our fear and decrease our true intimacy.[2]

There are compelling reasons for you to consider choosing to wait for marriage to have sex. Laura M. Brotherson, a certified family life educator, identifies the following reasons as some of those that relate to saving sex for marriage:

- Indicates trustworthiness
- Provides a profound sense of accomplishment
- Builds confidence and self-respect
- Avoids emotional turmoil and heartache [also known as "relationship drama"]
- Avoids regret
- Develops self-discipline
- Shows maturity
- Provides physical and emotional safety from sexually-transmitted infections or diseases (STIs/STDs) and unwanted pregnancy

Brotherson expands on some of these points with the following focus on one's character [See Part 3 for an explanation of the word "purity"]:

> Those who save sex for marriage may share something in common with those who run a marathon, or who climb Mount Everest—a huge feeling of accomplishment. The enduring satisfaction of having accomplished something difficult, often in the face of great adversity, provides a solid foundation for the soul, and a continuing reservoir of genuine contentment and confidence.
>
> The quick thrill of succumbing to a sexual experience pales in comparison to the permanent thrill of overcoming great odds to maintain sexual purity for marriage. A profound sense of accomplishment can also come from starting over, at any point, to remain sexually pure until marriage.
>
> ...Withstanding the pressures to engage in premarital sexual activity bolsters one's confidence—especially knowing that such an accomplishment can be difficult. The personal thrill of succeeding at something that many say can't be done adds strength to one's confidence and abilities. Confidence in self provides a quiet strength and assurance against the winds of adversity that attempt to blow us over.
>
> Respecting oneself, and others, enough to wait to engage in sexual relations only within marriage also builds self-respect. To respect oneself means to appreciate, to esteem highly, to love. As [people] face life's challenges with resolute determination to save the gift of sexual intimacy for marriage, they develop greater respect for themselves. Self-respect is thus a cause and a result of remaining sexually abstinent before marriage.[3]

For many people, there is also the spiritual significance of sex within marriage to consider. Ideally, marriage includes a strong connection between the hearts and souls of two people. When sexual intimacy includes practicing all of the character qualities, such as confidence, flexibility, patience, generosity, and more, the higher spiritual natures of the couple are part of sexual intimacy.[4] In addition, intercourse becomes an act that affirms the fundamental unity in the marriage.

Many people view all sexual acts as special or sacred between spouses, as described below. Consider this perspective from author Tim Alan Gardner in *Sacred Sex*:

> It is important to acknowledge that God could have arranged the whole re-production thing any way He wanted: a hidden button, a super-secret handshake, or some unique facial exchange that brought about conception. Really, He could have. But instead, He designed sex. He must have had a good reason, but what is it? The answer, in short, is that God wanted sex to be a lot more than just a really fun thing for wives and husbands to do together. And He wanted it to be more than an extremely enjoyable way to populate the planet. He had a far loftier goal in mind. God designed marital sex to be an encounter with the divine. Sexual intimacy... was never intended to be experienced solely in the emotional and physical realms. Rather, it is to be a spiritual, even mystical, experience in which two bodies become one. God is present in a very real way every time this happens.
>
> Sex really is holy. It's a sacred place shared in the intimacy of marriage.[5]

Does the significance of sex between spouses mean that if you have already had sex before marriage, it will be impossible to have a satisfying sex life within marriage? Perhaps not; however, it may be more difficult, take more acceptance, and be more challenging to establish healthy sexual intimacy. These outcomes may especially be the case if you have regrets about not waiting, or if you have had multiple partners. **If you have already had sex, you can also choose a different course for your future. It is never too late.**

You might think that you need to try sex before marriage to ensure that you and your partner are sexually compatible. However, if the two of you have some sexual difficulties together, or the experience does not quite meet either of your expectations, you and your partner may end what could have been a great relationship. A committed married couple is more likely to try options such as discussion, seeking therapy, reading helpful books, praying, and working together to resolve any sexual challenges that arise.

Alternatively, you could experience great sex before marriage, when there is the emotional excitement that often accompanies having an affair, only to discover that this goes away once the relationship becomes more established. The initial thrill evolves into emotions that are more realistic. You may see this change as a sign that the relationship is failing, rather than as a natural process as your love deepens and matures. The best place to explore physical intimacy is within a committed marriage. Otherwise, there is danger in mistaking sexual gratification, and the accompanying emotions of attraction, for the lasting, committed, and more enduring love that is based upon friendship and character.

If you were sexually active in the past, and you are considering making a different choice now, then it may assist you to look back and understand why you made your previous choices. If you find it a challenge understanding the past or making new choices, talk to a close friend or counselor, pray for detachment and self-discipline, meditate, or seek supportive family members or groups.

As you assess what choice to make about sex before marriage, it may assist you to ask yourself some key questions:

- What do I regret from previous sexual choices
- What regrets do I know that others have?
- What do I not want to regret in the future?
- What are my beliefs about sex before marriage?
- What cultural norms, religious scripture, or family values guide my choices?
- What difference will my choices make to my current or future children?

These are not easy questions, so you may need to pause and reflect on them or write in your journal about them. You may also find it beneficial to talk about them with a trusted friend or family member, spiritual advisor, or counselor.

ESSENTIAL ACTIVITIES

1. Complete Worksheet 9: Discerning Your Perceptions and Commitments About Sex to explore your thoughts about sex. It is fine to do this activity on your own. If you already have a partner, then you may wish to involve him/her in completing the worksheet with you. You may also find it helpful to discuss your answers with a trusted friend or relative.

2. Use popular magazines to find and cut out pictures of people projecting love, sex, intimacy, or words that reflect these themes. If you wish, then create a collage by gluing them onto a large sheet of paper or cardboard. Discuss with your partner or a friend the various images in the pictures and the expectations and feelings that arise for you in looking at them. How are your perceptions of sex and intimacy shaped by popular media? By your family? By other sources? Are these positive or negative influences?

   Note: If you are struggling with your sexual responses to magazine photos, please practice discernment and wisdom to determine whether doing this activity will be helpful or harmful for you.

~ *Reflection* ~

1. What do I think, feel, and believe about sex before marriage? About waiting until marriage?
2. Why would I have sex before marriage? If I have sex before marriage, might I regret it later?
3. Why would I wait to have sex until marriage? Are my partner and I willing to practice self-discipline and restraint with touch?
4. If I have already had sex with either a previous or current partner outside of marriage, do I want to make a different choice now? Why or why not?
5. What assumptions and expectations about my future with someone will I make if I have sex with them?
6. If a relationship ends after I have been physically intimate with a partner, how will I feel about my choices and myself?

SUPPORTING THE CHOICE TO WAIT

It is a common myth that people cannot control their sexual impulses and actions. This view has become a widespread misconception. With such a belief, it is little wonder that many give in to sexual temptation. You must believe it is possible to save sex for mar-

riage, in order to be able to do so. Also, it is obviously possible, because there are people who do it successfully. This is when commitment and strength apply. If you believe that you can save this special gift for marriage, and then choose to do so, you will increase your chances of success.

If you choose to wait to have sex until you are married, it will be wise to have a plan to support your choices. One of the main ways to support your commitment is to fill your life with activities that make a positive difference for you, your family, and your community. Spiritual activities and resource people can also provide support and balance for the pull to be sexually involved with someone.

You may have to change some of your habits and routines to avoid temptation. Start by clearly identifying what leads you towards thoughts or actions that involve sex. Then, it will help if you assess your lifestyle and determine where making changes will assist you. These changes may include:

- Minimizing time alone with a close friend or partner
- Choosing to be with different people and in new situations
- Disposing of magazines, books, or movies that lead you to think about sex or to masturbation
- Reading spiritual material together with your partner
- Avoiding going to Internet sites that include sex
- Get involved in activities that keep your thoughts away from a focus on sex
- Minimize or eliminate arousing types of physical touch

Grant knows that he can easily begin to express his attraction to women in physical ways. It has gotten him involved too fast with women at times. He's decided he wants to behave differently in his new relationship with Darlene, because chastity is important to her and he is beginning to think it might be beneficial for him as well. Together they make a commitment to focus on friendship. Each time before he meets her, he visualizes a burner on a gas stove and himself and his desires as the flame. He sees himself turning the flame down very low. When he gets tempted to begin flirting or touching Darlene, he re-visualizes the flame and turns it back down to low.

Your choice requires you to be strong in your convictions and courageous in speaking up about your commitment with a new partner. Dr. Paul Coleman, author of *How to Say It for Couples, Communicating with Tenderness, Openness and Honesty*, recommends that you have specific phrases in mind to say to a partner that you practice ahead of time. Being tentative in your statements will not benefit your relationship, because your partner will be confused about your convictions. Dr. Coleman encourages making the statement clearly and firmly, framed by a positive and reassuring message. For instance, you might say, "You are very important to me and I love you. But I firmly believe it is best that I wait before becoming sexual with you."[6] It is also helpful to have a partner willing to make a similar commitment, so you can both relax and focus on getting to know each other.

You will also think about how to be clear in communicating your new commitment to a current partner, if you have one. Unless your partner is also committed to the same new behavior, your change in perspective will be difficult for him/her to accept. Do your best to be consistent with your message, but also recognize that you may slip backward at times as you learn new behavior. Simply re-commit, forgive yourself, try again, and persevere. It is important to have a partner who has sincere respect for you and your choices.

Part of what will be difficult is that your partner may choose to leave the relationship because you are no longer being a sexual partner. Is it important for you to remain with someone you care about, despite the fact that they are not willing to respect your heart-felt choices? Or will you remain true to yourself and your wise decisions? What can you do to stay strong and handle this choice in a way that respects your integrity?

Be cautious that you do not try to rush prematurely into marriage as a response to this dilemma. Marrying just for the sake of committing to saving sex until marriage will not give you the benefit of practicing your self-discipline, self-respect, courage, and genuine commitment. If you are not ready to be married, making that choice will also not solve your challenge, but will rather compound your difficulties.

~ *Reflection* ~

1. What is my personal commitment about having or not having sex with a partner?
2. What boundaries do I have or want to have for myself related to me touching someone else or allowing a partner to touch me?
3. What changes do I need to make in my life to reduce temptation?
4. How can I communicate my commitment to certain choices about sex to a partner?

ABSTINENCE

Abstinence is a concept that means refraining from indulging any type of appetite. One of the ways it applies is to sexual appetite. In this context, it includes not having sexual intercourse or participating in other types of sexual touch, such as fondling breasts or stroking someone's genitals. Participating in even light sexual touching essentially gives someone permission to touch every part of you. Abstinence is saying "no" to having sexual contact with someone before marriage.

When you feel intensely about someone, you want to try every possible way of being close. Your initial instinct may be to do this through touch. It is better to first develop an emotional, mental, and spiritual bond. This bond provides a strong and lasting connection between two people. If you have not already established love and commitment within your relationship, sex can actually make the painful lack of genuine emotional intimacy more pronounced, frustrating, and upsetting.

Infections and Diseases

One of the important values in choosing abstinence is that it protects your health. Every time you intimately touch someone in a sexual way, from a health and biological perspective, you are not only having sex with them, but you are potentially exposing yourself to anything that their previous partners have had. With each sexual partner you have, concerns such as sexually transmitted infections/diseases (STIs/STDs) increase. Dozens of varieties of STIs/STDs are at epidemic proportions globally, across all ages from teens to seniors, and for both genders.

Some of these conditions can be transmitted through skin or bodily fluid contact other than intercourse. Many do not have obvious symptoms, or the disease could still be in a dormant stage without symptoms. This lack of symptoms can lead to a person becoming infected without even knowing about it. Consequently, they can spread the disease to others without even finding out that they were the cause of the transmission.

Some STIs/STDs are treatable, but some are incurable with treatable symptoms. STIs/STDs can, in some cases, destroy the physical ability to have children in the future, require surgery, or lead to serious illnesses or even death. If you have been sexually active, it is essential to practice responsibility and be tested for these conditions before starting a sexual relationship with a new person or getting married.

Although the following paragraph is from a book addressed to women, it makes points that apply to both genders:

> There are now a bevy of sexually transmitted diseases to worry about from herpes to AIDS. It seems that infected bodily fluids are now classified as a concealed weapon, and you're forced to have an awkward talk before he conceals his weapon inside of you. You need to ask the guy you're thinking of having sex with if he's been tested for AIDS, if he's ever used intravenous drugs, ... and how many sexual partners he's had. ... And if you don't question him at all, it can kill you. As if that's not enough reason to become celibate, there's also the issue of pregnancy to deal with.[7]

The interesting thing about STIs/STDs is that they are of no issue whatsoever to two individuals who are abstinent and then totally monogamous and faithful to each other for a lifetime.

~ Reflection ~

1. What do I think about abstinence?
2. Have I made the commitment to be abstinent? Why or why not?
3. How has being abstinent affected the lives of people I know?

Pregnancy

Along with the questions that arise between couples of whether to "do it" or not on the first date, the second date, or before marriage, comes the possibility of conceiving a child. Pregnancy is sometimes the unavoidable result of sexual intercourse, often due to failing to use birth control or not using it properly. **It is important to uphold the standard of not having sex with anyone with whom you would not want to share the commitment and responsibili-**

ties of lifelong parenthood. If learning the right dance steps with your partner is a challenge, imagine how much more difficult it would be if you were carrying a baby as you learn to dance! The admission price to that dance is costly for everyone involved.

If you had a child without being married to your sexual partner, you may now have a child to raise, have given one up for adoption, or have had an abortion. Depending on the circumstances, how you handled a pregnancy brings up such profound and complex emotional issues; such as, future fertility, guilt, grieving, unwillingness to have children with someone else, how to handle child support, or ongoing contact with the child.

For teens in particular, it is important to remember that any sexual involvement can lead to pregnancy—birth control methods are frequently not effective. It is a myth that you cannot get pregnant the first time you have sex, or that certain times of the month for women are safe. The timing of ovulation is not that predictable. The responsibilities of parenthood can severely disrupt your life, change your plans forever, force you to take on adult responsibilities prematurely, disrupt your education, or leave you economically challenged for many years into the future.

For adults, the risk of pregnancy might still be an issue, and birth control methods can also fail adults, but you may be old enough and more prepared to be a parent if pregnancy does occur. This view of pregnancy may cause you to think that there is no reason to abstain from sex. You may be confident that, if you use contraceptives and lower your risk of pregnancy or disease, there are no other issues to consider. Actually, there are many other serious considerations, particularly if the father chooses not to be involved in the child's life. Raising a child alone is not easy, children do better in a family with two biological and married parents, and it is a lifetime responsibility.[8]

At times, some girls or women deliberately seek sexual intercourse and pregnancy because they believe it will create someone who will love them. This choice is an indicator that the person's self-respect is probably weak, and they will benefit from strengthening their character qualities. Others see pregnancy, consciously or subconsciously, as a way to force their partner to stay with them or to provide them with long-term financial support. Again, this choice does not show respect to either partner, and it can cause long-term harm to the child from having an unwilling parent or from being raised in an unstable home.

~ Reflection ~

1. Am I prepared for the commitment, expense, and emotional and physical demands of being a parent?
2. If I choose to have sex, what will I do to prevent pregnancy?

CHASTITY

Chastity is a less-familiar concept that includes abstinence, but it goes beyond sexual acts outside of marriage. It includes making respectful choices about such aspects of your life as your thoughts, clothing, and entertainment. These choices strengthen your ability to willingly and joyfully wait to have sex until you are married. Buddha says, "Abstain from impurity, and lead a life of chastity."[9] When you choose and commit to chastity, you do not spend your time on sexual activities and preoccupations and instead fill your life with useful activities that fulfill your purpose in life. **The focus on having sex lessens when you balance it with all the rest of your life.**

Chastity is a quality of your higher nature. Author Dawn Eden in *The Thrill of the Chaste* talks about chastity being a vision of your sexual nature as a three-way relationship between you, your husband or future husband, and God. She says, "That means if you have sex without one corner of that triangle in place—with a man who isn't your husband, or with your husband but without faith in God—the act becomes disconnected from its purpose."[10]

Chastity encourages modesty, which can, in part, involve wearing clothing that covers areas of your body normally reserved for sexual experiences. This modesty does not mean that you dress in unattractive ways, but it does mean avoiding dressing in ways that prompt you to act more sexually seductive or that are deliberately provocative to others. Chastity encourages you to avoid actions that prompt sexual thoughts in others.

When practicing chastity, you avoid making comments to someone that include sexual innuendos or suggestions. Your choice of activities also excludes those that prompt sexual thoughts and responses, such as explicit movies or television shows. You also avoid putting alcohol or drugs in your body, which can lower your inhibitions and reduce your ability to make choices that are thoughtful and self-respectful.

At times throughout history, people have believed that chastity applies only to females and that it is impossible for males to practice it. In fact, it is a character quality that applies to and benefits both women and men. **Couples who practice chastity together strengthen their equality.** If you have already been sexually active, but you understand that abstaining and being chaste have value in your life, you can choose to change your behavior. **While you cannot regain your physical virginity once you have lost it, and it is difficult to stop having sex once you start, you can choose to claim abstinence and chastity from this point forward.** However, you may need to spend time becoming clear in your mind about your decision and possibly dealing with feelings about your previous choices.

As with abstinence, chastity includes maintaining faithfulness to your future spouse. You commit to reserve sexual behavior and energy to apply with your marriage partner. Consider this perspective from Rúhíyyih Rabbani in *Prescription for Living*:

> Chastity—one of the rarest of all…gems in the world to-day—means to conserve your personal sex powers, so intimate in nature, capable of conferring so much beauty on your life, for their proper expression which is with your life partner, your mate, the one who with you will share home, children and all the glad and sad burdens of living. The decency, the spiritual cleanliness of marriage, the essential humanness of it, are enhanced a thousandfold by chastity on the part of both men and women, previous to their unions. Their chances of successful marriage are also far greater, for they will then share with each other, in every way, the new life they have embarked upon. Comparisons will not be drawn, over-emphasized appetites on the part of one or the other will not have been cultivated which might mar it, and above all, they will have put sex into its proper place, where instead of stampeding the emotional nature

of the individual (as it does at present to so marked a degree), it will fulfill its natural function in rounding out life and contributing to its normality and healthfulness.[11]

One of the concepts in this quotation is "stampeding the emotional nature of the individual." Often when you are feeling increasingly drawn to another person, your desire for sex with them also increases. As you focus on these feelings, or surround yourself with peers or other influences that promote sex, the feelings grow. Having sex can begin to feel emotionally essential. In a stampede, animals behave impulsively and are out of control, trampling whatever is in their way. If control is an issue for you, the key is to know and do what assists you in maintaining self-discipline.

In reflecting on her struggles with chastity, author Lauren Winner in *Real Sex, The Naked Truth About Chastity*, comments that chastity does not come naturally to her. She says, "In my attempts to live chastely, prayer has been key. It may sound hokey, but I have prayed regularly that God would re-shape my heart and my desires so that I would want the things He wants for me."[12]

You have stronger control over your thoughts and physical needs when you practice chastity. It keeps your mind clear of physical passions that cloud your judgment about a partner or your relationship. "The most challenging part of chastity isn't overcoming temptations. It's gaining the spiritual resources to joyfully face day-to-day life as a cultural outsider."[13]

Part of the gift of practicing chastity is that a "...person who is in control of his sexual impulses is enabled to have profound and enduring friendships with many people, both men and women...."[14] This control liberates people as they stop behaving in ways that prompt jealousy or mistrust.

Chastity, helped by responsibility and purity, also assists you to avoid spending your time on frivolous activities that waste your time. However, it includes choosing to be involved in activities that bring you and a partner genuine happiness, joy, and humor. **Practicing these qualities is not about being perpetually serious about life, but joyfully embracing the best of it. It is about choosing to respect your own higher nature and that of a partner, and not spend time focusing on or developing your lower nature.**

Therapist Agnes Ghaznavi puts chastity in a broader context as she looks forward into a future where more people will choose to practice it:

> Human beings will evolve both individually and collectively: the practice of chastity by both sexes will create a protection for individuals and society as yet never experienced in the history of mankind. It will strengthen people's character, their sense of responsibility for other people's intimate character, feelings and bodily impressions. Nobody will feel the right to transgress another person's intimacy without permission. People will...also be much more conscious in their sensations and enjoyment, and thus will not be carried away by their instincts.....[15]

Just as Ghaznavi does, Mary Baker Eddy, the founder of the Christian Science Church, looks at the greater impact of chastity. She says, "Chastity is the cement of civilization and progress. Without it there is no stability in society...."[16] Stability is increased with healthy, well-functioning families that include faithfulness and monogamy as values.

Like every quality, however, you can misuse it. Chastity only works well when you practice it in a gentle, spiritual context. Without this approach, you can become rigid, self-righteous, and judgmental about both your own and others' sexual choices.

Chastity allows you to make choices that show respect for yourself and others, and allow important aspects of your relationship to blossom.

~ *Reflection* ~
What helps me in being abstinent and practicing chastity when I am in a relationship with someone?
HELPFUL ACTIVITY
Write a poem, a song, or an essay about whatever challenges you face in making choices about abstinence, chastity, and sex.

❦ *Encouragement* ❧

For many people in our global society, both making a commitment to a partner, and the choice to wait to have sex with a partner, are major challenges and accomplishments. This chapter shares choices that may be difficult for you to put into practice, but you can succeed. You may struggle at times with which choices to make, and you will learn from the ones that you do make. With consistent effort and perseverance, you can make the choices that increase your respect for yourself and bring you genuine long-lasting happiness.

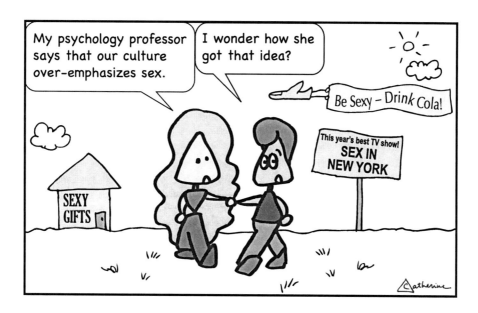

REFERENCES FOR CHAPTER 7

1. Joan Barstow Hernández, *Love, Courtship, and Marriage*, p. 31
2. Justice St. Rain, *Spiritual Guide to Great Sex*, p. 7
3. Laura M. Brotherson, CFLE, *And They Were Not Ashamed—Strengthening Marriage through Sexual Fulfillment* as quoted in "God's Wedding Gift: Why Save Sex for Marriage," p. 14, Meridian Magazine, August 2, 2005, www.ldsmag.com/familyconnections/050802gift.html
4. Susanne M. Alexander with Craig A. Farnsworth and John S. Miller, *Pure Gold: Encouraging Character Qualities in Marriage*, p. 115
5. Tim Alan Gardner, *Sacred Sex: A Spiritual Celebration of Oneness in Marriage*, pp. 4-5
6. Dr. Paul Coleman, *How to Say It for Couples, Communicating with Tenderness, Openness and Honesty*, p. 204
7. Joanne Kimes, *Dating Sucks*, pp. 177-178
8. The National Marriage Project; www.virginia.edu/marriageproject
9. Compiled by Paul Carus, *The Gospel of Buddha*, XLVI:6
10. Dawn Eden, *The Thrill of the Chaste*, pp. 14-15
11. Rúhíyyih Rabbani, *Prescription for Living (Revised Edition)*, pp. 88-89
12. Lauren Winner, *Real Sex, The Naked Truth About Chastity*, p. 23
13. Dawn Eden, *The Thrill of the Chaste*, p. 34
14. On behalf of the Universal House of Justice, *The Compilations of Compilations, Vol. I*, p. 51
15. Agnes Ghaznavi, *Sexuality, Relationships and Spiritual Growth*, p. 36-37
16. Mary Baker Eddy, *Science and Health*, p. 57

PART 2:

WORKSHEETS

Date: _____

Worksheet 1: Understanding Your Character Choices

Purpose: To begin the process of understanding the character choices that you have made and how they have affected your relationships with others.

Instructions:

A) On the first table below, note a few actions that you have taken that had a positive result in any relationship. Consider friends, family, partners, or spouses. Note the effect or outcome of your actions. Then identify a character quality from Chapter 1 or from Part 3 that you demonstrated in that situation.

B) On the second table on the next page, note your actions that have had a negative result and the outcome in those situations. Then identify a character quality that you could have practiced that would have improved the outcome.

Positive Actions (Higher Nature)

Action	Effect/Outcome	Character Qualities That I Practiced
Example: Gave girlfriend a birthday present	She felt appreciated and happy	Thoughtfulness Generosity

Negative Actions (Lower Nature)

Action	Effect/Outcome	Character Qualities I Could Have Practiced
Example: Ignored a friend at a party	He would not speak to me for a week	Friendliness Courtesy

Reflection:

1. What did I learn about my behavior and character growth from completing the tables?

   _____

   _____

   _____

   _____

2. In what improved ways do I want to speak and act in a relationship with a partner?

   _____

   _____

   _____

   _____

Date: _____

Worksheet 2: Assessing Your Character Qualities

Purpose: To gain greater understanding of your own strengths of character and growth areas that need improvement, so you are empowered to prepare to be an excellent partner in a relationship.

Note: See Part 3 for explanations of each of the character qualities listed in the chart below. Go through this content slowly, carefully, and with reflection to accurately increase your knowledge of yourself.

Instructions:

A) Place a number to the right of each character quality in the Rating column (you may wish to use a pencil), using the following assessment scale from 1 to 6:

1 ～ You are very weak at practicing the quality, and your words and actions are resulting in negative outcomes.

2 ～ You are somewhat ineffective at practicing the quality, and your words and actions result in negative outcomes.

3 ～ You are familiar with the quality, know quite well how to practice it, but you sometimes struggle to do so effectively.

4 ～ You are practicing the quality effectively, but not consistently, and your words and actions usually result in positive outcomes.

5 ～ You have the quality as a strength, but you often misuse it and need to moderate it.

6 ～ You are consistently practicing the quality effectively, and your words and actions result in positive outcomes.

B) Put a check mark (✓) next to those qualities on the worksheet that are clearly strengths (rated 4-6).

C) Put an **x** next to the qualities that are too weak to practice effectively in a relationship (rated 1-3).

D) Circle the four qualities that you now want to focus initially on developing in yourself. The qualities that you rated 1s, 2s, or 3s will be good choices for these four qualities, and you will use them to complete your development plan in Worksheet 3.

Character Quality	Rating	✓ or x	Character Quality	Rating	✓ or x
Acceptance			Courtesy		
Assertiveness			Creativity		
Beauty			Detachment		
Caring			Discernment		
Chastity			Encouragement		
Commitment			Enthusiasm		
Compassion			Equality		
Confidence			Excellence		
Contentment			Faithfulness		
Cooperation			Flexibility		
Courage			Forgiveness		
Fortitude			Purity		
Friendliness			Purposefulness		
Generosity			Resilience		
Gentleness			Respect		
Helpfulness			Responsibility		
Honesty			Self-Discipline		
Humility			Service		
Idealism			Sincerity		
Integrity			Spirituality		
Joyfulness			Tactfulness		
Justice			Thankfulness		
Kindness			Thoughtfulness		
Love			Thriftiness		
Loyalty			Trustworthiness		
Mercy			Truthfulness		
Moderation			Unity		
Patience			Wisdom		
Peacefulness			Other:		
Perseverance			Other:		

Reflection:
1. What strong positive character qualities in me will be particular relationship strengths?

    _____
    _____
    _____

2. What character-related concerns do I see in myself?

    _____
    _____
    _____

3. What character strengths and resources will help me with addressing these concerns?

    _____
    _____
    _____

4. What unresolved issues from my past are now visible? (These will be addressed in Chapter 3.)

    _____
    _____
    _____

Date: _____

Worksheet 3: Creating Your Character Development Plan

Purpose: To create a character development plan that will help you to prepare for being a strong, healthy person and partner in a relationship. Developing your character is actually an ongoing endeavor that takes place when you are ready and as you interact with others. However, this activity will increase your awareness of your thoughts and actions and make development of your character qualities a conscious choice.

Instructions:

A) Fill in the form below with your four character-development goals that you circled on Worksheet 2. Note the reasons why the quality and its development are important to you.

B) Write down four specific actions you will take to develop and strengthen each quality (Examples: Patience—wait calmly when my friends are late; Service—wash my mother's car every week). Select target dates for beginning to work on each of them. Then, mark down dates when you will assess your progress and consistency on each action. Write these dates on a calendar or use another system to remind you to revisit this chart.

C) When you are ready to assess your progress, talk to others for their feedback, look over your journal notes, review your behavior, and meditate and reflect on your words and actions. Think carefully about how people responded to you. Then fill in the Signs of Improvement and Lingering Challenges sections. Note any new actions that you now want to take.

Quality to Develop:		
Why?		
Development/Strengthening Actions:	Start Date:	Assess Date:
1.		
2.		
3.		
4.		
Signs of Improvement:		
Lingering Challenges:		
New Actions to Take:		

Quality to Develop:		
Why?		
Development/Strengthening Actions:	Start Date:	Assess Date:
1.		
2.		
3.		
4.		
Signs of Improvement:		
Lingering Challenges:		
New Actions to Take:		

Quality to Develop:		
Why?		
Development/Strengthening Actions:	Start Date:	Assess Date:
1.		
2.		
3.		
4.		
Signs of Improvement:		
Lingering Challenges:		
New Actions to Take:		

Quality to Develop:		
Why?		
Development/Strengthening Actions:	Start Date:	Assess Date:
1.		
2.		
3.		
4.		
Signs of Improvement:		
Lingering Challenges:		
New Actions to Take:		

Reflection:

1. What do family members, friends, or others say about my changed behavior? (Ask them if you do not know.)

   _____
   _____
   _____
   _____

2. Where do I need further improvement?

   _____
   _____
   _____
   _____

3. What other insights did I gain from this activity?

   _____
   _____
   _____
   _____

Date: _____

Bonus Worksheet: Choosing Character Qualities to Look for in a Partner
Excerpted from the eBook *Becoming Relationship Ready*

Purpose: To identify the character qualities you believe are most vital in a partner for you.

Instructions:

A) Read through the entire list of character qualities below and imagine yourself in an excellent relationship. Think about what activities you and your partner might do together and with other people. Imagine the character qualities that help the two of you have positive experiences and interactions. If you are already in a relationship now, try to detach from thinking of your current partner and focus on what is important to you generally.

B) Using the boxes in front of each quality, put the numbers 1-10 **in priority order** for the **10 qualities** that are the most important ones for you to see as strengths in a partner. When you are in a relationship, return to this worksheet to discern whether your partner has these strengths.

	Acceptance		Equality		Love		Thankfulness
	Assertiveness		Excellence		Loyalty		Thoughtfulness
	Beauty		Faithfulness		Mercy		Thriftiness
	Caring		Flexibility		Moderation		Trustworthiness
	Chastity		Forgiveness		Patience		Truthfulness
	Commitment		Fortitude		Peacefulness		Unity
	Compassion		Friendliness		Perseverance		Wisdom
	Confidence		Generosity		Purity		
	Contentment		Gentleness		Purposefulness		
	Cooperation		Helpfulness		Resilience		
	Courage		Honesty		Respect		
	Courtesy		Humility		Responsibility		
	Creativity		Idealism		Self-Discipline		
	Detachment		Integrity		Service		
	Discernment		Joyfulness		Sincerity		
	Encouragement		Justice		Spirituality		
	Enthusiasm		Kindness		Tactfulness		

Questions for Reflection:

1. Why did I choose each of these top 10 qualities?
   1 - _____
   2 - _____
   3 - _____
   4 - _____
   5 - _____
   6 - _____
   7 - _____
   8 - _____
   9 - _____
   10 - _____

2. What connection or overlap is there between my partner's preferred quality strengths and mine?
   _____
   _____
   _____
   _____

3. Would such a partner and I be too much alike? Too different?
   _____
   _____
   _____
   _____

4. What qualities in a partner would balance my qualities or moderate qualities that I sometimes misuse? Do I want to make any changes to my priority list?
   _____
   _____
   _____
   _____

5. What else do I notice?
   _____
   _____
   _____
   _____

Date: _____

Worksheet 4: Assessing Character Strengths in Your Relationship Partner

Purpose: To gain greater understanding of your partner's character strengths and growth areas that need improvement, so you are empowered to make effective relationship choices.

Note: See Part 3 for some explanations of each of the character qualities listed in the chart below. Go through this content slowly, carefully, and with reflection to increase your knowledge of your partner.

Instructions:
A) Place a number to the right of each character quality in the Rating column (you may wish to use a pencil), using the following assessment scale from 1 to 5:
  1 ~ Your partner is very weak at practicing the quality, and words and actions are resulting in negative outcomes.
  2 ~ Your partner is somewhat ineffective at practicing the quality, and words and actions result in negative outcomes.
  3 ~ Your partner is familiar with the quality, knows quite well how to practice it, but sometimes struggles to do so effectively.
  4 ~ Your partner is practicing the quality effectively, but not consistently, and words and actions usually result in positive outcomes.
  5 ~ Your partner is consistently practicing the quality effectively, and words and actions result in positive outcomes.
B) Put a check mark (✓) next to those qualities on the worksheet that are clearly strengths (4-5).
C) Put an ✗ next to the qualities that are too weak to practice effectively in a relationship (1-3).
D) Answer Reflection questions.

Character Quality	Rating	✓ or ✗	Character Quality	Rating	✓ or ✗
Acceptance			Excellence		
Assertiveness			Faithfulness		
Beauty			Flexibility		
Caring			Forgiveness		
Chastity			Fortitude		
Commitment			Friendliness		
Compassion			Generosity		
Confidence			Gentleness		
Contentment			Helpfulness		
Cooperation			Honesty		
Courage			Humility		
Courtesy			Idealism		

Creativity			Integrity		
Detachment			Joyfulness		
Discernment			Justice		
Encouragement			Kindness		
Enthusiasm			Love		
Equality			Loyalty		
Mercy			Service		
Moderation			Sincerity		
Patience			Spirituality		
Peacefulness			Tactfulness		
Perseverance			Thankfulness		
Purity			Thoughtfulness		
Purposefulness			Thriftiness		
Resilience			Trustworthiness		
Respect			Truthfulness		
Responsibility			Unity		
Self-Discipline			Wisdom		

Reflection:

1. What strong positive character qualities in my partner will be particular relationship strengths?

_____
_____
_____
_____

2. What character-related concerns do I see in my partner?

_____
_____
_____
_____

3. What qualities that I want as strengths in a partner are actually weak in this person?

_____
_____
_____
_____

4. What character strengths and resources will help me to address these concerns?

_____

_____

_____

_____

Date: _____

Worksheet 5: Practicing Observation Skills

Purpose: To improve your ability to observe others effectively. Choose your partner (preferable) or someone else to observe for a few days. Consider letting the person know about your observation plan and obtaining agreement to proceed.

Instructions:

A) Make specific notes of your observations in the table below. In the first column, note the person's words, gestures, and actions.

B) In the second column, note any character strengths you think the person demonstrated.

C) In the third column, note your appreciation for, concerns about, or interpretations of what you observed.

Words, Gestures, Attitudes, or Actions	Character Qualities	Observation Notes

Words, Gestures, Attitudes, or Actions	Character Qualities	Observation Notes

Reflection:
1. How did I feel while doing this observation? How did I overcome any hesitancy I felt?

_____

_____

_____

2. What did I learn about the other person?

_____

_____

_____

3. What did I learn about myself?

_____

_____

_____

4. In what ways did this experience strengthen my observation skills?

_____

_____

_____

Date: _____

Worksheet 6: Learning from Your Parents' Relationship

Purpose: To observe your own parents and learn more about how they and their relationship affect your attitudes and relationships. You can use this worksheet as a discussion guide to learn about your partner's parents as well.

Instructions:

A) Answer the questions that follow about your parents' relationship. If you did not grow up with them, answer the questions according to the primary marriage or relationship you observed while growing up. If you grew up with more than one parental-type relationship, then use a separate piece of paper or page in your journal to complete the worksheet content for each.

1. What words describe my parents' relationship?

a. _____	d. _____
b. _____	e. _____
c. _____	f. _____

Other comment: _____

2. What have I observed in my parents' relationship that I *want* to see in my own?

a. _____	d. _____
b. _____	e. _____
c. _____	f. _____

Other comment: _____

3. What have I observed in my parents' relationship that I do not want to see in my own?

a. _____	d. _____
b. _____	e. _____
c. _____	f. _____

Other comment: _____

4. What positive aspects of my parents' behavior towards each other do I repeat with my partner?

a. _____	d. _____
b. _____	e. _____
c. _____	f. _____

Other comment: _____

5. What negative aspects of my parents' behavior towards each other do I repeat with my partner?

a. _____	d. _____
b. _____	e. _____
c. _____	f. _____

Other comment: _____

6. What character qualities did I regularly see my parents practice?

_____
_____
_____
_____

7. What have I observed about the interactions between my partner and my parents?

_____
_____
_____
_____

8. What other observations about my parents would be useful for me to consider in my relationship with my partner?

_____
_____
_____
_____
_____

Date: _____

Worksheet 7: Assessing Your Misuse of Character Qualities

Purpose: To clarify the character strengths you misuse, the consequences, and effective strategies to practice them effectively instead. (Note: You may have begun this assessment work on Worksheet 1.)

Instructions:

A) Review the character qualities in Part 3 and identify three quality strengths you misuse at times, thereby hurting others and causing dissension or disunity. Focus on your interactions with your partner.

B) Identify helper qualities for you to practice, and consider how these may affect your words and actions.

1. First quality strength that I sometimes misuse: _____
    Negative outcomes: _____
    Helper qualities that might assist me to use this quality effectively:
    _____Moderation _____   _____

    _____   _____

    What new ways can I speak and act when using these helper qualities?

    _____

    _____

2. Second quality strength that I sometimes misuse: _____
    Negative outcomes: _____
    Helper qualities that might assist me to use this quality effectively:
    _____Moderation_____   _____

    _____   _____

    What new ways can I speak and act when using these helper qualities?

    _____

    _____

3. Third quality strength that I sometimes misuse: _____
    Negative outcomes: _____
    Helper qualities that might assist me to use this quality effectively:
    _____Moderation_____   _____

    _____   _____

    What new ways can I speak and act when using these helper qualities?

    _____

    _____

Date: _____

Worksheet 8: Assessing Character Misuses in Your Relationship Partner

Purpose: To assess a partner's character strengths that are sometimes misused.

Instructions:

A) On the list below, put an "x" next to the qualities that you observe your partner has as strengths but sometimes or often misuses, and make a brief note of what occurs. Use the detailed descriptions about character in Part 3 to help you.

Misuses?	Character Quality	Misuses?	Character Quality	Misuses?	Character Quality
	Acceptance		Flexibility		Perseverance
	Assertiveness		Forgiveness		Purity
	Beauty		Fortitude		Purposefulness
	Caring		Friendliness		Resilience
	Chastity		Generosity		Respect
	Commitment		Gentleness		Responsibility
	Compassion		Helpfulness		Self-Discipline
	Confidence		Honesty		Service
	Contentment		Humility		Sincerity
	Cooperation		Idealism		Spirituality
	Courage		Integrity		Tactfulness
	Courtesy		Joyfulness		Thankfulness
	Creativity		Justice		Thoughtfulness
	Detachment		Kindness		Thriftiness
	Discernment		Love		Trustworthiness
	Encouragement		Loyalty		Truthfulness
	Enthusiasm		Mercy		Unity
	Equality		Moderation		Wisdom
	Excellence		Patience		
	Faithfulness		Peacefulness		

B) Choose two misused qualities from above. Note if you see any particular circumstances or issues that trigger the misuse to occur. Identify the helper qualities that may assist your partner to moderate the use of the qualities. In addition, identify some ways you can encourage your partner to stop the misuses.

Misused Quality: _____
Triggering Circumstances: _____

_____

Helper Qualities: _____
Encouraging Statements to Offer:

_____

_____

_____

Misused Quality: _____
Triggering Circumstances: _____

_____

Helper Qualities: _____
Encouraging Statements to Offer:

_____

_____

_____

Date: _____

Worksheet 9: Discerning Your Perceptions and Commitments About Sex

Purpose: To understand many of the different associations you have related to sex. This process will also help you with making commitments about what sexual activities you will choose not to participate in prior to marriage.

Instructions:
A) Reflect, and then complete the first list with all the words that you can think of that relate to sex and sexual experiences.
B) Reflect, and then complete the second section with the activities you will do your best not to engage in before marriage.

Words Related to Sex:

_____   _____
_____   _____
_____   _____
_____   _____
_____   _____

Sexual Activities You Are Committed to Not Do Before Marriage:

_____   _____
_____   _____
_____   _____

Reflection:
1. What insights did I gain, or what did I learn about my attitudes and experiences related to sex?
_____
_____

2. Why am I committed to not participate in the sexual activities that I wrote down?
_____
_____

3. What actions or strategies will help me with practicing abstinence and chastity?
_____
_____

PART 3:

POWERFUL
CHARACTER
QUALITIES

๛ Character Qualities ๏

1. Acceptance
2. Assertiveness
3. Beauty
4. Caring
5. Chastity
6. Commitment
7. Compassion
8. Confidence
9. Contentment
10. Cooperation
11. Courage
12. Courtesy
13. Creativity
14. Detachment
15. Discernment
16. Encouragement
17. Enthusiasm
18. Equality
19. Excellence
20. Faithfulness
21. Flexibility
22. Forgiveness
23. Fortitude
24. Friendliness
25. Generosity
26. Gentleness
27. Helpfulness
28. Honesty
29. Humility
30. Idealism
31. Integrity
32. Joyfulness
33. Justice
34. Kindness
35. Love
36. Loyalty
37. Mercy
38. Moderation
39. Patience
40. Peacefulness
41. Perseverance
42. Purity
43. Purposefulness
44. Resilience
45. Respect
46. Responsibility
47. Self-Discipline
48. Service
49. Sincerity
50. Spirituality
51. Tactfulness
52. Thankfulness
53. Thoughtfulness
54. Thriftiness
55. Trustworthiness
56. Truthfulness
57. Unity
58. Wisdom

◅ 1 ~ Acceptance ▻

Acceptance is a deep, meaningful embracing of who someone is, as well as acknowledging that people and events are as they are or were as they were, rather than wasting time and energy trying to change people, regret the past, or influence events when it is unwise or there is no possibility of success.

Someone practices Acceptance effectively when he/she:

- Acknowledges and respects the thoughts, opinions, and actions of others while striving to understand them more deeply
- Stays calm and composed when people or circumstances cause plans to alter
- Builds friendships with people who are different from him/her in personality, culture, religion, race, or some other way
- Avoids resisting or trying to change what is unchangeable about circumstances or people
- Frees others to grow and choose to make the changes they want to
- Sees and responds to reality as it is, even when it is unpleasant
- Understands and appreciates other people, giving them the freedom to be just as they are, including their limitations, frailties, weaknesses, struggles, and experiences
- Knows himself/herself thoroughly and that his/her development is a work in progress

Someone needs to strengthen Acceptance when he/she:

- Loses composure, gets agitated, and becomes critical when people or events do not meet expectations and there is no way to alter the situation
- Tries to change people or sees their words and actions as invalid
- Criticizes others for not doing things his/her way
- Criticizes himself/herself destructively or considers aspects of himself/herself unworthy
- Resists or complains about the direction and circumstances of his/her life and that of others, as well as daydreaming and wishing things were different
- Decides who to associate with or have a relationship with based on prejudice

Someone misuses the strength of Acceptance when he/she:

- Goes along with negative situations or lets others treat him/her poorly
- Doesn't speak up in dangerous, harmful, illegal, or dishonest situations
- Fails to exercise influence or control to prevent or improve a negative situation
- Seeks opinions and feedback exclusively from people who will agree with him/her or ignores or reacts poorly to appropriate feedback or guidance from respected sources that indicate it would be wise to make changes in himself/herself

⁓ 2 ~ Assertiveness ⁓

Assertiveness is speaking up or acting decisively to improve a situation for the benefit of others and oneself.

Someone practices Assertiveness effectively when he/she:

- Thinks and acts for himself/herself, defending words and actions when appropriate
- Steps forward into appropriate participation or leadership roles
- Believes he/she is a worthy person and takes actions to make his/her true self known, including thoughts, ideas, opinions, feelings, boundaries, limitations, intentions, plans, or beliefs
- Asks someone to meet a need of others or his/hers in a direct and respectful way
- Acts to resolve a problem when appropriate
- Requests or insists upon respectful treatment for himself/herself or others

Someone needs to strengthen Assertiveness when he/she:

- Allows others to treat him/her with disrespect or act on his/her behalf without consent or input
- Remains quiet, instead of speaking up to give valuable input or to defend a cause that he/she believes in
- Fails to set personal standards or healthy boundaries for appropriate behavior for himself/herself or others and changing them regularly

Someone misuses the strength of Assertiveness when he/she:

- Behaves in an aggressive, angry, violent, bossy, or pushy way without considering the rights or viewpoints of others
- Uses offensive or rude words or an overly directive tone of voice to dominate others or to get his/her own way, often monopolizing conversations
- Steps forward into action when not asked or at an appropriate time for leadership
- Sees his/her leadership style as the only right one

❧ 3 ~ Beauty ❧

Beauty is expressing the best of one's inner spirit and demonstrating, seeing, and creating attractiveness, loveliness, or order wherever possible.

Someone practices Beauty effectively when he/she:

- Sees much that is wonderful and awe-inspiring in the world and in himself/herself and maintains a positive attitude and good humor
- Grooms and dresses himself/herself in an attractive way
- Takes care of his/her home, property, and workplace, keeping it clean, orderly, welcoming, and harmonious
- Smiles sincerely and does his/her best to radiate happiness and relaxation
- Encourages and takes action to accomplish mental, spiritual, and physical well-being and growth in himself/herself and others
- Develops or creates things pleasing to the body, mind, heart, and soul
- Enriches his/her life with music, art, literature, dance, science, nature, colors, textures, flavors, and architecture, as well as positive friends, words, and activities
- Expresses appreciation for the attractive attributes and qualities of others, such as kindness, gentleness, and respect

Someone needs to strengthen Beauty when he/she:

- Neglects his/her own appearance and well-being
- Allows his/her home or work environment to deteriorate
- Reduces his/her attractiveness by frowning or looking at others with hostility or disrespect or often whining and complaining
- Avoids positive or inspirational sources of upliftment
- Exhibits unattractive and unhealthy negative behaviors; such as, putting others down, criticizing, humiliating another, shouting, swearing, or acting harmfully, possibly under the influence of alcohol or drugs

Someone misuses the strength of Beauty when he/she:

- Boasts about his/her appearance or behaves in a vain and arrogant manner
- Feels or demonstrates intolerance for mental, emotional, spiritual, and physical imperfections in others or himself/herself
- Idolizes people whose appearance is a certain way
- Wears extreme or provocative clothing, too much jewelry or tattoos, or excessively decorates his/her body in a culturally inappropriate way
- Treats someone as a sex object or views and values pornography (defined as sexually explicit material with the primary purpose of causing sexual arousal)

∾ 4 ~ Caring ∾

Caring is giving sincere love, attention, consideration, and assistance to others and responding to needy situations in timely and appropriate ways.

Someone practices Caring effectively when he/she:
- Notices when others are going through difficult times and meets their needs for relief, comfort, and assistance with consideration and empathy
- Listens attentively and compassionately
- Pays attention to personal feedback from others and adjusts words, attitudes, and actions as appropriate in response
- Gives his/her best effort to complete tasks with consistent and thorough attention to details
- Shares his/her time with others and shows interest in them
- Looks after his/her own well-being and that of others in appropriate ways
- Acts with wise restraint and appropriate caution in potentially unsafe circumstances
- Maintains a good understanding of local and world events

Someone needs to strengthen Caring when he/she:
- Regularly ignores the needs, wishes, requests, boundaries, and concerns of others or responds negatively or harshly to them
- Refuses to be proactive in reaching out to others with assistance
- Communicates to others that they are less capable than he/she is
- Mistreats others or their possessions
- Chooses to be with hurtful people or in harmful circumstances
- Ignores or minimizes the importance of community or global issues

Someone misuses the strength of Caring when he/she:
- Meddles in, or attempts to manage, others' lives or situations without their need or invitation, doing what he/she thinks is needed instead of asking
- Becomes over-protective or allows others to become unnecessarily or unhealthily dependent upon him/her
- Makes excessive efforts to meet the perceived needs of others
- Justifies unwise actions with expressions of affection

∽ 5 ~ Chastity ∾

Chastity is maintaining sexual purity and reserving sexual attraction, responses, and intimacy as a special and respectful gift to share with a marriage partner.

Someone practices Chastity effectively when he/she:

- Moderates and restrains the power of attraction to others, channeling it moderately and appropriately only with a chosen partner; avoids inappropriate flirting or contact in person or through electronic media
- Regards sexual intercourse as a spiritual act of unity that is only consummated within marriage
- Releases passion appropriately with his/her spouse, understanding what is sexually pleasurable to him/her and meeting his/her needs as much as possible as well as his/her own
- Abstains from sexually and physically arousing and intimate acts before marriage or outside of marriage with someone other than his/her spouse
- Speaks, dresses, and moves modestly to avoid inviting inappropriate attention, touch, and sexual attraction; respects appropriate privacy
- Strives to keep his/her mind from holding onto sexual thoughts and also to control his/her sexual desires and impulses, other than appropriate ones related to his/her spouse
- Avoids substances such as alcohol or drugs, or being in certain situations, because they may reduce his/her sexual inhibitions
- Chooses respectful entertainment and activities for others and himself/herself; avoids telling or listening to jokes or stories with sexual content
- Builds and maintains strong platonic friendships with both men and women, keeping appropriate boundaries and avoiding sexual innuendos, domination, or seduction
- Treats the bodies, minds, hearts, and souls of others with equality, respect, and gentleness
- Fills his/her life with worthwhile purposes and service, placing less focus, emphasis, and importance on sex, especially prior to marriage

Someone needs to strengthen Chastity when he/she:

- Has sex outside of marriage, which can threaten health, well-being, jobs, or family unity
- Sees sex as the primary way to achieve happiness or to have a relationship
- Acts in a sexually seductive manner or engages in arousing or sexual touch outside of marriage
- Values a partner's physical attributes more than his or her character qualities; views anyone as a sex object instead of as a whole person
- Views sex as a game, spectator sport, diversion, opportunity for conquest, imposition of power, something to brag about, way to become acquainted, or as a means of self-centered relaxation
- Pursues pleasure through sexually stimulating entertainment or activities with others besides a spouse (in person or through electronic media)
- Engages in excessive sexual fantasies, particularly about a non-marriage partner; views or participates in pornography; excessively masturbates; or becomes addicted to sexual pleasure
- Abuses others sexually by forceful or manipulative behavior, threats, or violence

Someone misuses the strength of Chastity when he/she:

- Rejects or disparages his/her own natural sexuality and sensuality or that of others, acting as if sex is something dirty or wrong rather than a spiritual gift contributing to the unique bond that unites a married couple
- Fails to communicate affectionate feelings to a partner/spouse both verbally and physically
- Judges, condemns, gossips, or backbites about the sexual activities of others or himself/herself

≈ 6 ~ *Commitment* ≈

Commitment is making and keeping a reasonable promise or binding agreement to others or to oneself, including setting and meeting certain goals, standards, or expectations, as well as completing tasks to which one has agreed.

Someone practices Commitment effectively when he/she:

- Meets agreed-upon expectations and keeps his/her word and promises, following through by doing what he/she says he/she will do
- Accepts and fulfills the responsibilities that accompany an agreement or decision
- Keeps pursuing a planned or agreed course of action or works to improve himself/herself or a situation, even when it becomes difficult to do so
- Makes appropriate choices to move forward in healthy relationships or situations even when feeling some fear or anxiety based on previous experiences or the experiences of others

Someone needs to strengthen Commitment when he/she:

- Breaks promises, failing to honor his/her word or stated intentions
- Fails to make or to follow through on agreements or resolutions
- States agreements in such a vague way that there is no accountability
- Ignores the responsibilities necessary to fulfill an agreement
- Regards relationships or situations as short-term conquests without looking at the long-term consequences or larger picture
- Sabotages relationships, plans, or situations
- Refuses to engage in constructive problem solving when issues challenge a relationship

Someone misuses the strength of Commitment when he/she:

- Behaves in an inflexible, rigid, close-minded, or stubborn manner
- Refuses to renegotiate promises or situations even when there is good reason to do so
- Keeps commitments unwisely even when they clearly endanger health, safety, or relationships

∽ 7 ~ Compassion ∾

Compassion is feeling genuine concern for others and oneself, empathizing with the pain and suffering of those in difficult situations, and seeking ways to relieve their pain and ease their suffering.

Someone practices Compassion effectively when he/she:

- Listens actively with an open heart and mind to understand the burdens, problems, and pain others carry in their bodies, minds, hearts, or souls
- Assists and comforts those who are ill, injured, or in trouble, or who are suffering from mistakes they made
- Comforts a grieving person
- Strengthens or empowers others to ease their own suffering through their own efforts
- Pays attention to his/her own pain and struggles and gently allows himself/herself time to grieve and heal

Someone needs to strengthen Compassion when he/she:

- Keeps a cold or uncaring distance between himself/herself and others or refuses to communicate in a meaningful way to solve a problem
- Ignores, minimizes, or fails to notice others' problems, feelings, or issues
- Judges others as too weak or incompetent to handle their own lives and problems
- Perceives grieving or needing healing time as signs of weakness
- Harms someone mentally, emotionally, physically, or spiritually

Someone misuses the strength of Compassion when he/she:

- Overly involves himself/herself in feeling or relieving the pain or responding to the needs of others, while neglecting his/her own primary responsibilities
- Reacts to reduce someone's pain too quickly without knowing all the facts, which may cause more harm
- Quickly defends someone against a perceived oppressor without fully understanding the situation

∽ 8 ~ *Confidence* ∾

Confidence is trusting one's inner value, worthy intentions, capacity to think and act effectively, and ability to accomplish stated goals of oneself and of others.

Someone practices Confidence effectively when he/she:

- Demonstrates belief in himself/herself and the worth of his/her actions, trusting that he/she can handle whatever problems or circumstances arise and maintaining the same belief and trust in others
- Uses his/her talents and abilities to benefit others and himself/herself
- Knows his/her principles, opinions, and beliefs and acts on them consistently and courteously
- Assertively makes thoughtful decisions and initiates action as appropriate, while being aware of the wisdom of consulting and collaborating with others and making unified decisions
- Pursues worthy goals individually and with others
- Tries something new, trusting that he/she will learn from the experience or succeed at accomplishing a goal
- Uses body language to convey self-respect; such as, sitting, standing, or walking with appropriate posture, dignity, and speed; maintaining cleanliness; or dressing appropriately for the circumstances
- Seeks to overcome personal and group challenges
- Attempts to understand and overcome doubts and fears, recognizing when they are invalid or excessive, and thinking positive and constructive thoughts instead

Someone needs to strengthen Confidence when he/she:

- Is indecisive and overwhelms himself/herself with doubts, anxieties, and fears
- Wastes energy thinking about why he/she cannot do some activity or task instead of using his/her resources to attempt it
- Criticizes himself/herself or others
- Withdraws from activities or other people
- Believes or acts as if he/she is less capable or competent than someone else when untrue
- Participates in easy activities often or sets unchallenging goals, avoiding positions of leadership or service to others that he/she has the ability to fulfill
- Sabotages relationships or situations by not believing himself/herself capable of being successful

Someone misuses the strength of Confidence when he/she:

- Acts self-centered or conceited
- Brags about his/her accomplishments or acts as if he/she is more capable than others
- Behaves in an overbearing, dominant, and bossy manner towards others
- Insists that his/her ways and plans are best and that those of others are wrong, closing his/her mind to other options

❧ 9 ~ Contentment ❧

Contentment is maintaining happiness and tranquility in body, mind, heart, and soul, with calm, accepting feelings and actions towards relationships, employment, surroundings, situations, and life in general.

Someone practices Contentment effectively when he/she:
- Calmly accepts the natural flow of changes in his/her body and life and those of others
- Appreciates the fulfillment of his/her purposes, profession, and activities, especially when they make the best use of his/her talents and abilities
- Enjoys the people and blessings in his/her life
- Pauses to breathe, slow down, relax, and enjoy the moment or the pace of circumstances
- Accepts the outcome of an activity, event, or project, detaching from any upset feelings
- Stops trying to fix something or to make things turn out the way that he/she thinks they should
- Appreciates what he/she has instead of constantly focusing on his/her wants and attempting to acquire more

Someone needs to strengthen Contentment when he/she:
- Compares his/her life to the lives of others and finds it lacking, resulting in envy or jealousy
- Complains to or pressures the people in his/her life to change to make him/her happy
- Feels unsettled, anxious, or fearful about the present or future
- Wants what others have or idealizes the relationships or circumstances of others

Someone misuses the strength of Contentment when he/she:
- Accepts the inappropriate actions of others or does not remove himself/herself from harmful situations
- Avoids engaging in solving problems and relies on others to do the work to resolve a situation for him/her or others
- Passively lets his/her life and mind stagnate or decline, not seeing any need for change or attempting to maintain or reach his/her full potential
- Proudly or stubbornly resists fresh ideas, the influence of others, and change
- Determines to remain the same without improving himself/herself or his/her life

❧ 10 ~ Cooperation ❧

Cooperation is working with others in harmony to create or accomplish something that would be more difficult or impossible to accomplish by one person working alone.

Someone practices Cooperation effectively when he/she:

- Shares thoughts, ideas, and time while working in partnership with others to accomplish worthwhile tasks and goals
- Seeks out and utilizes the talents, abilities, specialties, and strengths of others, while sharing his/her own as well
- Regards others as partners in creating new ideas and solving problems
- Works in harmony with leaders who need others to help accomplish something
- Adjusts his/her ideas, wishes, and expectations while building a reasonable consensus with others
- Supports fully any decisions that are made in unity by or with others
- Participates well in making and executing plans for activities or events with others
- Practices teamwork, appropriate leadership, and good sportsmanship
- Offers time, energy, and resources and accepts assistance from others

Someone needs to strengthen Cooperation when he/she:

- Avoids participating in relationship-building or group activities, acting as a partner or team member, or interacting as a peer with others; participates begrudgingly or with a poor attitude
- Causes conflict and disharmony between others or between others and himself/herself
- Resists assistance from others or participation with them and tries to do most things independently
- Regards others as incapable of participating positively in an activity
- Undermines or refuses to follow decisions made in unity by or with others

Someone misuses the strength of Cooperation when he/she:

- Sacrifices his/her values or principles to participate in unwise or harmful activities with others
- Keeps silent about important concerns that need to be addressed to avoid upsetting people or drawing attention to himself/herself
- Works with others only to gain something from them

~ 11 ~ Courage ~

Courage is taking brave and bold action voluntarily, defending what is right, or facing and completing a worthwhile challenge, even when experiencing fear, resistance, uncertainty, opposition, hardship, or possible danger.

Someone practices Courage effectively when he/she:

- Faces danger, risk, loss, potential injury, or a difficult situation; assesses the risks and consequences; prioritizes; and takes effective action in spite of feeling fear or other uncomfortable feelings
- Maintains self-control, staying confident, selfless, resolute, and brave when facing difficult situations or vital tasks
- Tries new activities, enters new situations, and changes plans as needed
- Initiates and builds friendships and relationships without holding back important parts of himself/herself after trust has been established and risks assessed and considered
- Resumes life vigorously after a difficult loss or error
- Speaks appropriately and constructively what is on his/her mind and heart, even when it is difficult for others to hear what he/she needs to say
- Makes necessary positive changes in his/her self or life, even when others object

Someone needs to strengthen Courage when he/she:

- Gives priority to his/her doubts and fears of failure and avoids acting or taking necessary risks
- Avoids sharing his/her thoughts and feelings appropriately with others
- Allows others to dominate, use, or abuse him/her in any way
- Ignores or denies his/her own values, allowing the unwise actions of others to continue

Someone misuses the strength of Courage when he/she:

- Speaks brazenly or acts recklessly without regard for the feelings or welfare of others or taking into consideration the larger situation or potential negative consequences
- Behaves too boldly or quickly, or in excess of personal limitations, causing negative consequences or conflict

∽ 12 ~ Courtesy ∾

Courtesy is showing gracious and warm consideration for others by interacting with polite manners, respectful gestures, thoughtful actions, and kind language.

Someone practices Courtesy effectively when he/she:

- Notices and interacts with others with genuine sensitivity, choosing the appropriate timing, words, and gestures with care
- Shows thoughtful consideration for the needs of others through words and actions
- Assists others politely as a gesture of respect, even with actions they could do for themselves, such as opening a door, making a phone call, or carrying something
- Uses respectful speech when interacting or making requests
- Uses manners and speaks politely, freely saying "please" and "thank you"
- Provides gracious and attentive hospitality or arrangements for others
- Acknowledges gifts from and thoughtful actions of others
- Conveys necessary messages and communications in a clear, polite way

Someone needs to strengthen Courtesy when he/she:

- Puts himself/herself first selfishly, acting as though he/she is more important than others
- Behaves abruptly or rudely, or is short-tempered with others
- Gives orders to or makes demands of others inappropriately for his/her role, the role of others, or the circumstances
- Fails to communicate about timing, plans, or issues that affect others
- Expresses judgment of others or excludes others from activities and events

Someone misuses the strength of Courtesy when he/she:

- Worries self-consciously about how others view his/her actions
- Uses a level of stiff formality inappropriate for the situation
- Speaks or acts insincerely without really caring about the true needs of others, typically to manipulate them or to have his/her own way
- Acts politely only towards people he/she thinks deserve to be treated well

❧ 13 ~ Creativity ❧

Creativity is drawing on ideas, inspiration, or imagination to develop or produce something new, including contributions and solutions that benefit others or oneself.

Someone practices Creativity effectively when he/she:

- Tries new activities, adventures, and experiences alone or with others, responding positively to encouragement and enthusiasm
- Develops new approaches, systems, and solutions to problems and seeks ways to fulfill the potential of excellent ideas, producing positive outcomes in his/her life, relationships, community service projects, and employment
- Discovers and develops his/her talents for artistic activities or crafts; such as, painting, poetry, writing, drawing, woodworking, gardening, cooking, dancing, or music and encourages others to do the same
- Conducts experiments, open-mindedly testing new hypotheses or developing new theories, approaches, or ways of thinking, speaking, or acting
- Uses a variety of ways to seek inspiration for artistic expressions; to develop something new, surprising, or unusual; or to solve problems; possibilities could include dreaming, group discussion, trying new experiences, physical activity, time out in nature, prayer, or meditation
- Identifies and utilizes all possible resources and people to achieve the best outcome
- Makes uplifting and attractive changes in his/her home or work environment
- Tries, finds, or prepares new and interesting foods and combinations of foods

Someone needs to strengthen Creativity when he/she:

- Focuses narrowly on the presumed facts of a situation and closes himself/herself off from new possibilities
- Does something repeatedly, even when it does not work well, such as behaving in the same way in a new relationship or situation as he/she has in previous ones or previously in a current one
- Blocks, discounts, or withholds his/her gifts or capacity for personal expressions of any type or shows a lack of confidence in them
- Becomes bored or stays stuck in boring routines, habits, jobs, relationships, or circumstances

Someone misuses the strength of Creativity when he/she:

- Devises plans that manipulate, hurt, injure, belittle, or insult others
- Desires something so strongly that he/she finds dishonest or immoral ways to achieve or obtain it
- Becomes so focused on thoughts, ideas, and inspirations that positive and healthy relationships and responsibilities are neglected or jeopardized
- Makes up stories to conceal or justify misbehavior or exaggerates his/her behavior to avoid responding appropriately to reality
- Makes interesting but disruptive changes without a good reason for doing so

⊰ 14 ~ Detachment ⊱

Detachment is stepping back to gain a different perspective on what is happening and placing less importance on worldly concerns, while selflessly letting go of one's feelings, hopes, desires, attachments, and need to be in control.

Someone practices Detachment effectively when he/she:

- Empathizes with others without making their feelings his/her own or suffering because of the actions or reactions of others
- Thinks rationally and clearly with some emotional distance; responding according to the known facts without exhibiting personal bias, strong emotions, or preconceived expectations
- Gathers information, seeks input from others, and examines the facts related to a project, situation, or person without premature judgment or participating in backbiting or gossip
- Seeks spiritual solutions to issues
- Releases desires or dreams that are unrealistic or unattainable, grieving as needed and then letting go of the loss
- Accepts a present situation with equanimity, even if it is difficult, uncomfortable, or not what he/she would have chosen
- Frees himself/herself from unhealthy or unwise attachment to people, incidents from the past, physical objects, and desires
- Lets go of overly strong fears of losing something or someone
- Bases choices on current circumstances rather than solely on previous experiences
- Understands and accepts the limitations of others and his/her own; lets go of unreasonable expectations
- Gives away or disposes of unnecessary items in his/her home or workplace, or sacrifices holding onto items when someone else has a greater need for them

Someone needs to strengthen Detachment when he/she:

- Reacts emotionally and speculates about possible outcomes or explanations; jumps to conclusions rather than pausing to determine the facts of the matter accurately
- Attaches himself/herself emotionally to someone or something so strongly that he/she abandons good judgment or uses that person to reinforce his/her unwise conclusions
- Takes over so that others do not have to handle basic responsibilities such as eating, going to bed, getting up, going to work, or paying bills
- Depends excessively upon others in ways that negatively affect their well-being or his/her own
- Jumps in to prevent a problem or crisis so quickly that it prevents learning experiences for others
- Holds onto objects, paperwork, situations, and people even when doing so interferes with effective functioning or achieving one's higher goals in life
- Focuses on material possessions and actions while ignoring spiritual principles or choices

Someone misuses the strength of Detachment when he/she:

- Fails to consider with sensitivity the well-being of others
- Isolates himself/herself from others, treating them in a cool, distant, and unloving way
- Acts as if he/she has no opinions or needs
- Disposes of belongings, objects, or property without regard for value, sentiment, or usefulness to others or himself/herself
- Neglects personal responsibilities or denies involvement in situations

∽ 15 ~ Discernment ∾

Discernment is perceiving and understanding oneself, others, and situations accurately, deeply, and objectively, including discriminating between what is beneficial and what is harmful, without prejudice or bias.

Someone practices Discernment effectively when he/she:
- Considers a variety of perspectives, feelings, and facts and responds appropriately, honestly, and fairly to what is true and useful, avoiding prejudice, biases, or stereotypes
- Makes effective choices between right and wrong, understanding the factors that influence his/her choices
- Understands his/her own character, motives, intentions, expectations, and reactions, as well as those of others, including whether biases, prejudices, or incidents from the past are factors
- Observes, analyzes, and determines needs and priorities in various areas of his/her life, relationships, home, work, and community
- Observes the practice of character qualities in others carefully, assessing their relative strengths and weaknesses, and determines appropriate responses
- Distinguishes whether an observation is significant, minor, or irrelevant and how to respond to it; respects confidentiality and others' privacy appropriately
- Bases his/her choices and beliefs upon the best and most factual input, while still respecting his/her intuition and inspiration; adjusts when new information is presented

Someone needs to strengthen Discernment when he/she:
- Jumps to conclusions
- Fails to listen carefully to others
- Lets himself/herself be fooled into giving or accepting false information
- Makes choices carelessly without considering his/her morals, values, beliefs, or principles; uses his/her beliefs to justify lying, stealing, or other negative or harmful behavior
- Fails to weigh the consequences of his/her words and actions before speaking or acting
- Takes the words or actions of others too seriously or not seriously enough
- Overlooks or denies important aspects of a person or situation and fails to respond appropriately

Someone misuses the strength of Discernment when he/she:
- Pries into the private concerns or lives of others
- Judges a current relationship or situation by the results of previous ones without looking at the real facts of the current relationship or situation
- Idolizes others
- Looks critically and judgmentally only for the flaws of others and overlooks their positive qualities; focuses only on the positive qualities of a partner when considering marrying and ignores serious issues

❧ 16 ~ Encouragement ❧

Encouragement is offering sincere, uplifting acknowledgment of the character strengths, effective actions, or good intentions of others and oneself; inspiring or assisting others and oneself to start, continue, or stop doing something; and fostering personal growth and development.

Someone practices Encouragement effectively when he/she:

- Assists people who are discouraged, especially when they try hard or attempt something new
- Accompanies others when they are attempting new tasks, providing demonstrations of new behavior as needed
- Expresses confidence in the ability of others to succeed
- Inspires others to act with courage when they struggle with fear or uncertainty
- Notices the choices and plans others make or want to make, offering them his/her sincere support
- Acknowledges the best in others and in their words and actions

Someone needs to strengthen Encouragement when he/she:

- Criticizes, ridicules, belittles, jokes about, or devalues the attempts, abilities, or character of others
- Ignores what is important to the people in his/her life
- Takes for granted the efforts of others close to him/her, failing to show appreciation
- Compares those close to him/her to others unfavorably

Someone misuses the strength of Encouragement when he/she:

- Pushes or manipulates others to do something
- Tries to get someone to do something that is harmful, unwise, or that they do not want to do of their own volition
- Uses insincere praise or flattery to get his/her own way with others

❧ 17 ~ Enthusiasm ❧

Enthusiasm is expressing genuine positive and joyful feelings, often in a high-spirited way, about an occasion, activity, important occurrence, goal, person, or extraordinary situation.

Someone practices Enthusiasm effectively when he/she:

- Expresses pleasure and excitement about something that happens or could happen
- Looks for the best in people and situations and shares that perspective with others
- Approaches tasks or adventures wholeheartedly and energetically
- Appreciates the positive aspects of a task that could otherwise be seen as tedious, boring, or difficult
- Enjoys what he/she is doing
- Expresses gratitude to God and participates joyfully in spiritual or positive practices and activities

Someone needs to strengthen Enthusiasm when he/she:

- Regards everything as the same and nothing as great, extraordinary, or inspiring
- Acts discouraged, resigned, negative, bored, or cynical
- Criticizes the ideas of others
- Holds and expresses negative expectations for current and future events
- Grumbles, whines, or complains about many areas of his/her life

Someone misuses the strength of Enthusiasm when he/she:

- Jumps impulsively into a belief, project, relationship, job, or idea without adequately assessing its substance, long-term benefits, or value
- Raves excessively about something and insists that others should be as excited as he/she is
- Presents incomplete or inaccurate information to people to get them to see a situation his/her way
- Fakes excitement for his/her own gain or to mislead people

❦ 18 ~ Equality ❧

Equality is creating a balanced partnership between people who work together as a team, especially a woman and man in a relationship or marriage, respecting each person as a worthy and noble human being.

Someone practices Equality effectively when he/she:
- Communicates his/her thoughts and feelings and encourages others to do the same
- Listens carefully to others and respects their points of view
- Honors the participation of others in a relationship, education, work project, community event, or other situation
- Regards both others and himself/herself as valuable human beings with diverse, valuable contributions to make
- Determines with others in a fair and equitable manner their roles and how they will handle joint responsibilities
- Discusses issues and makes decisions in partnership with others as appropriate and whenever possible
- Learns new skills to increase balance between others and himself/herself

Someone needs to strengthen Equality when he/she:
- Gives orders to, makes demands of, or tries to dominate or control others
- Acts as if he/she is superior or inferior to another or bases interactions on bias, prejudice, or stereotypes
- Expects others to do his/her fair share of tasks for him/her
- Insists that everyone's roles and responsibilities be identical or divided according to unexamined traditional roles
- Holds back important information, thoughts, or feelings related to a discussion or decision, perhaps devaluing them and thinking they are not really valuable or legitimate or that others are not capable of understanding

Someone misuses the strength of Equality when he/she:
- Changes his/her expectations or opinions in an inconsistent way about roles or what responsibilities should be
- Changes himself/herself inappropriately or tries to change others in an effort to establish balance
- Ignores, belittles, devalues, does not see, or hesitates to point out authentic individual or gender differences
- Demands a trade in exchange for an action of another person

❧ 19 ~ Excellence ❧

Excellence is striving to achieve high standards and a superior quality of work and effort, as well as fulfilling one's potential for character growth and development.

Someone practices Excellence effectively when he/she:

- Goes beyond the minimum required and gives his/her best in every effort, selflessly paying attention to the details that make a difference to others, enhance their experience, and achieve superior results and outcomes
- Gains the necessary knowledge and then practices tasks, skills, talents, character qualities, and positive behaviors until performing them consistently and effectively
- Welcomes opportunities for continual improvement
- Creates beneficial outcomes that endure or that others can sustain long-term
- Achieves outstanding success through working cooperatively with others
- Approaches tasks in a productive and effective way
- Works to fulfill positive purposes in life

Someone needs to strengthen Excellence when he/she:

- Treats responsibilities carelessly
- Performs work in a sloppy way
- Neglects relationships with others
- Avoids developing his/her mind, character qualities, talents, and capacities
- Settles for mediocrity, adopts society's minimum standards, or sets such low standards of achievement that he/she fails to fulfill his/her potential or be of effective service to others

Someone misuses the strength of Excellence when he/she:

- Approaches tasks in an overly meticulous and time-consuming way with a focus on perfection
- Places a higher emphasis on making things perfect than on treating others with courtesy and kindness
- Treats others and himself/herself inflexibly and impatiently, ignoring personal limitations
- Holds an attitude of superiority towards others
- Reacts intolerantly to someone or something that does not meet his/her standards
- Allows competition with others to be the primary motivation for achievement

20 ~ Faithfulness

Faithfulness is being steadfast and maintaining commitments to others, to a set of beliefs, or to an organization.

Someone practices Faithfulness effectively when he/she:
- Demonstrates appropriate loyalty and trustworthiness in thoughts, words, and actions
- Respects the bond he/she has with others and carries out appropriate choices that maintain the happiness, unity, and integrity of their relationship
- Maintains a sexual relationship only with his/her marriage partner
- Practices and stays firm in his/her beliefs and core values in an honest, sincere, and forthright manner

Someone needs to strengthen Faithfulness when he/she:
- Shares or connects his/her time, money, work, emotions, body, mind, heart, or soul inappropriately with someone when he/she is already committed to another person or situation
- Acts or speaks in a manner contrary to his/her values and beliefs
- Tries to undermine the reasonable beliefs and faith of others
- Focuses more on superficial relationships than on committed relationships with others; such as, a partner/spouse, family, or work colleague

Someone misuses the strength of Faithfulness when he/she:
- Follows directions, beliefs, or positions on issues unquestioningly without conscious thought, choice, or investigation of their truth, often in spite of valid reasons to reconsider them
- Shows unwavering support for or gives blind obedience to a harmful, disloyal, or dishonest relationship or organization

~ 21 ~ Flexibility ~

Flexibility is adjusting to life as it happens and embracing changes as needed, while remaining true to one's core values, beliefs, and appropriate priorities.

Someone practices Flexibility effectively when he/she:

- Detaches from plans, situations, or outcomes as needed
- Appreciates the joys and benefits of unplanned and unexpected happenings
- Participates enthusiastically in a spontaneous activity
- Stays open to new ideas, creative options, innovative approaches, and alternative perspectives
- Adjusts his/her thoughts, attitudes, and actions as needed to respond to new information, difficulties, or surprises
- Adapts gently to changes in people and circumstances without resistance, anxiety, fear, anger, or upset feelings
- Stays open to learning about and changing himself/herself and engaging in character growth
- Bends to follow the Will of God

Someone needs to strengthen Flexibility when he/she:

- Insists stubbornly that nothing should ever change, rules are meant to be rigidly followed, or that her/his way is the only right way
- Resists changing schedules, plans, structures, or goals
- Refuses to change himself/herself, beliefs, relationships, patterns of living, living location, education, or employment, even when there are compelling reasons to do so
- Discounts the views or practices of others, refusing to consider them in an open and discerning manner
- Becomes unreasonably upset by unforeseen circumstances or changes in plans

Someone misuses the strength of Flexibility when he/she:

- Abandons or ignores his/her principles and good judgment to respond to the requests of others or to give in to peer, spouse, or family pressure when the choice is against his/her core values
- Changes his/her mind frequently or quickly for no good reason
- Avoids making choices, decisions, schedules, plans, structures, or goals

∾ 22 ~ Forgiveness ⌒

Forgiveness is pardoning someone for saying or doing something hurtful or harmful, giving up a desire for revenge, and letting go of anger and resentment.

Someone practices Forgiveness effectively when he/she:

- Examines what happened with discernment and compassion, tries to understand it and the person, accepts it as unchangeable, grieves sufficiently, and lets go of his/her feelings of anger, resentment, pain, or bitterness
- Gives others and himself/herself the opportunity to restore a relationship after a hurtful experience, speaking and acting as needed to express remorse, apologize, change, make amends, resolve issues, reconcile, and start over anew
- Seeks to understand the values, culture, and viewpoints of others
- Resists focusing excessively on the faults and mistakes of others and himself/herself, releasing grudges or hurts about words or actions as promptly as possible
- Values inner harmony and unity with others enough to let go of negative feelings about what happened
- Pardons a wrongdoer, including himself/herself, with sincerity and courage

Someone needs to strengthen Forgiveness when he/she:

- Keeps replaying the incident in his/her mind, feels like a victim, and holds onto bitterness and anger
- Seeks revenge against those who have hurt or betrayed him/her
- Refuses to accept an apology/amends when someone else has made a mistake or done something hurtful, or to make an apology and amends when he/she is at fault
- Holds grudges and resentment
- Raises a problem or former error repeatedly
- Withholds acceptance and pardon until the other person specifically asks for it
- Criticizes the words or actions of others or himself/herself repeatedly and often harshly

Someone misuses the strength of Forgiveness when he/she:

- Accepts unjust, abusive, or harmful actions from someone without resolution
- Avoids holding others or himself/herself accountable for words or actions
- Behaves poorly without restraint because he/she presumes automatic pardon
- Equates pardon with forgetting what happened
- Thinks that having an explanation for an action should equate with receiving pardon
- Bargains giving pardon in exchange for something

❧ 23 ~ Fortitude ❧

Fortitude is staying brave, resolute, steadfast, and strong mentally, emotionally, physically, and spiritually when facing challenges, difficulties, adversity, danger, pain, or temptation.

Someone practices Fortitude effectively when he/she:

- Accepts a difficult situation and persists with responding to it, managing it, and helping others through it; learns and grows through the process
- Develops and practices his/her character qualities so that strengths consistently and effectively guide his/her choices when facing difficult situations
- Stands firm in his/her beliefs, values, and convictions, making the best choices possible, even when they are difficult or unpopular
- Enhances and reinforces his/her healthy emotional bonds with a partner/spouse, family, friends, employer, and organizations so that these relationships are durable and long-term
- Draws on appropriate resources to complete tasks and resolve difficulties; such as, prayer, meditation, friends, family members, counseling, support groups, and thankfulness for blessings

Someone needs to strengthen Fortitude when he/she:

- Gives up easily when faced with difficult or challenging tasks
- Lets destructive fears and weaknesses hold him/her back from or interfere with fully participating in relationships and life experiences
- Abandons solid and healthy friendships, relationships, and situations without first sincerely and persistently attempting to work through problems and find solutions
- Wallows in self-pity, complains, denies, runs away from, or overreacts when facing serious issues and problems
- Gives in to harmful temptation
- Ignores or behaves in ways that are contrary to his/her values or beliefs

Someone misuses the strength of Fortitude when he/she:

- Approaches tasks or people in a rigid way
- Bullies others who are weaker than he/she is
- Refuses stubbornly to consider changing plans; insists that he/she is right about how to handle whatever problems arise
- Refuses to consider or discounts the advice or input of others
- Withholds communication, contact, and/or love in a stubborn and willful way

24 ~ Friendliness

Friendliness is demonstrating an outgoing and positive social attitude and reaching out to connect with and build relationships with people.

Someone practices Friendliness effectively when he/she:
- Greets and includes others in a warm, pleasant, and inviting way, remembering and using people's names and recalling important details about their lives or circumstances
- Smiles at others and shares thoughts, ideas, and laughter with them
- Spends time with, shares experiences and celebrations with, uplifts, and helps people during both good and difficult times
- Takes an interest in others and listens carefully to them, acknowledging and validating what they say or do, and keeping private any personal information they share
- Gets to know others, their circumstances, and their needs through asking appropriate questions, sharing information, and spending time with them
- Offers welcoming and courteous hospitality at his/her home and workplace or as a host in a public place

Someone needs to strengthen Friendliness when he/she:
- Behaves in a cool, distant, or overly reserved way towards others
- Frowns at or greets others coolly
- Fails to recognize when questions or comments are intrusive or when sharing personal information or comments is unwise, unwanted, or burdensome
- Avoids extending hospitality or neglects to prepare the environment or refreshments so that he/she can minimize social interaction with others
- Isolates himself/herself from others or waits for others to be friendly first
- Gossips, backbites, or spreads slander about others

Someone misuses the strength of Friendliness when he/she:
- Connects only with those who can increase his/her status and importance
- Spends an excessive amount of time with friends, allowing them to be overly influential
- Neglects his/her responsibilities, family, or work to spend time with friends
- Succumbs to inappropriate intimacy or sexually seductive behavior with someone because of an inflated and unrealistic view of their friendship
- Pushes others persistently for social invitations or to plan social occasions
- Ignores boundaries and the personal space of others, taking action to receive attention

❧ 25 ~ Generosity ❧

Generosity is giving away or sharing what one has, such as affection, money, time, appreciation, encouragement, gifts, celebrations, positive feedback, resources, knowledge, wisdom, possessions, physical abilities, personal energy, ideas, or resources with open mind, heart, and hands.

Someone practices Generosity effectively when he/she:

- Gives joyfully, willingly, or sacrificially without expecting to receive praise, gratitude, or any reward in return
- Notices and gives what others truly need, want, and appreciate in respectful ways, not just what is convenient
- Acknowledges the best in others openly and shares his/her best self with them
- Shares words and emotions, especially love, from his/her heart
- Acknowledges the abundance of gifts in his/her life and shares them with others
- Welcomes gifts from others

Someone needs to strengthen Generosity when he/she:

- Hoards what he/she has or is miserly or stingy with his/her heart, time, talents, money, or possessions, not sharing them even when there is an abundance
- Acts hesitant or reluctant to share what he/she has with others
- Loans, but never gives to others
- Withholds love, encouragement, praise, important feelings, or vital information from those close to him/her
- Lives and acts as if everything is scarce or unavailable
- Fails to acknowledge gifts from others

Someone misuses the strength of Generosity when he/she:

- Gives to the extent that he/she neglects his/her own future or responsibilities to others
- Lives extravagantly or wastefully
- Gambles with his/her resources, putting important aspects of his/her health or life at risk
- Gives only to gain positive regard or rewards from others

26 ~ Gentleness

Gentleness is expressing consideration from the heart, honoring the feelings of others and oneself, and using soft and careful physical touch, movement, and words.

Someone practices Gentleness effectively when he/she:
- Uses self-awareness and self-discipline to moderate and control his/her words and actions, expressing sensitivity to the feelings and situations of others or himself/herself
- Touches animals or people in ways that express affection and tenderness
- Acts in ways that promote feelings of safety and security for others
- Moves at a relaxed or easy pace
- Protects things from breaking and shields people, animals, and the environment from harm or injury
- Thinks positive thoughts instead of critical ones
- Moderates the volume of his/her voice and minimizes unnecessary loud noises and frantic or rough activity

Someone needs to strengthen Gentleness when he/she:
- Treats something or someone roughly or cruelly
- Yells loudly or speaks harshly, forcefully, or sarcastically
- Dominates or monopolizes conversations
- Enjoys seeing violent or sexually demeaning action in television shows, movies, video games, or other entertainment
- Becomes angry with others or himself/herself and reacts in ways that cause harm
- Moves in overly fast, uncoordinated, or highly stressed ways that disturb others

Someone misuses the strength of Gentleness when he/she:
- Avoids taking action, commenting, or firmly responding to someone else's harsh words or violent actions
- Acts in an overly submissive, unassertive, docile way, allowing others to manipulate or take advantage of him/her or for him/her to manipulate others
- Uses soft touch and speech to ingratiate himself/herself to others or to gain inappropriate liberties with others

∽ 27 ~ Helpfulness ∾

Helpfulness is taking appropriate action to address the needs or participate in solving the problems of others or oneself.

Someone practices Helpfulness effectively when he/she:

- Assists others as needed or requested to make life easier or less stressful for them or to nurture their growth
- Performs tasks for others that they cannot do or find difficult to do for themselves
- Observes his/her surroundings and interactions in a conscious way and listens to people to understand what needs to be done
- Creates solutions for problems and promptly takes action to improve situations
- Discerns before acting whether his/her actions are needed, wanted, and likely to produce a positive outcome
- Asks for the assistance of others as appropriate; gracefully and thankfully accepts assistance
- Assists situations, interactions, and relationships by taking needed actions to improve his/her own character and behavior

Someone needs to strengthen Helpfulness when he/she:

- Focuses mostly on his/her own needs, while being unaware or neglectful of the needs of others
- Avoids taking positive action even when it is obvious that someone wants, needs, or is asking for assistance
- Holds an unwilling, begrudging, or selfish attitude about assisting others
- Refuses to ask for or accept necessary or wise assistance from others
- Sees accepting assistance from others as being weak or as a negative statement about his/her competence or worth as a human being
- Criticizes others for their ways of providing assistance, expressing frustration rather than appreciation or gratitude

Someone misuses the strength of Helpfulness when he/she:

- Ignores his/her own values or principles to assist someone
- Aids only those who may benefit him/her
- Assists others in ways that enable them to avoid their responsibilities or escape the consequences for their actions
- Stays so busy aiding others that he/she neglects personal responsibilities, including taking care of his/her well-being
- Fails to think through the assistance that he/she offers to others to make certain the outcome will be positive and will truly meet their needs
- Hovers over others, interfering with rather than assisting them

❦ 28 ~ Honesty ❧

Honesty is acting and speaking consistently with high and incorruptible moral, ethical, and legal standards.

Someone practices Honesty effectively when he/she:
- Acts according to laws, high standards, and strong values when handling money, property, and matters affecting others
- Learns about himself/herself and speaks clearly and directly with others about who he/she is and what is important, sharing feelings, thoughts, and other personal information as appropriate
- Provides a safe, confidential environment for others to share who they are and what they are doing or have done, including their feelings, thoughts, and other important personal information as appropriate
- Bases words, actions, and choices upon beliefs and principles; says what he/she means, means what he/she says, and does what he/she promises
- Assesses motives, words, and actions regularly and listens to and responds effectively to appropriate feedback from others
- Apologizes, expresses genuine remorse, handles the consequences appropriately, and makes amends after doing or saying something hurtful, inappropriate, immoral, unethical, or illegal

Someone needs to strengthen Honesty when he/she:
- Withholds important information about himself/herself and his/her actions, life, or particular situations; keeps secrets inappropriately
- Presents aspects of himself/herself inaccurately; such as, temporarily changing his/her appearance to deliberately create a false impression, or by putting inaccurate information on a resume or personal profile; allowing others to believe something that is exaggerated or untrue
- Conceals his/her behavior from those who have a legitimate interest in it
- Uses the resources, possessions, or work time of a company or organization for unauthorized personal purposes
- Cheats, steals, takes credit for the work of others, defrauds people, or makes false promises; acts in a corrupt way with responsibilities, using questionable practices such as taking or giving bribes
- Gives into temptation or pressure to act improperly
- Hides his/her true intentions and reasons for actions or participation
- Compromises or hides his/her beliefs and principles
- Acts in ways that differ from his/her words and professed beliefs

Someone misuses the strength of Honesty when he/she:
- Speaks or acts forthrightly but without discretion, wisdom, or consideration of timing; shares confidential information inappropriately with others
- Backbites, gossips, or spreads slander about the character of another person
- Speaks in a blunt, harsh, or cruel way that upsets or hurts others
- Brags about his/her good deeds

᪥ 29 ~ Humility ᪥

Humility is seeing the strengths, imperfections, abilities, accomplishments, failures, and all other aspects of oneself and others in realistic perspective; acting consistently according to principles, morals, and values rather than ego; and acknowledging the greatness of God.

Someone practices Humility effectively when he/she:

- Prays and maintains a relationship with God
- Accepts having a dual nature that leads him/her to engage in both positive and harmful behavior
- Assesses accurately his/her own abilities and achievements and quietly accepts praise from others
- Keeps his/her ego in check and modestly avoids pride or boasting about his/her service and accomplishments or emphasizing his/her failures; name, fame, and rank are not important
- Shares his/her human errors and weaknesses in appropriate circumstances when it will benefit others
- Gives respect and high regard to others and their needs, sharing credit for accomplishments
- Acts according to principles and puts them ahead of himself/herself
- Serves others to the best of his/her ability
- Admits his/her mistakes to those he/she harms, learns from those experiences, and makes apologies, amends, and behavior changes as appropriate
- Acknowledges and is patient with his/her own limitations and imperfections, willingly accepts and acknowledges feedback and assistance from others, and requests help when needed

Someone needs to strengthen Humility when he/she:

- Treats others as inferior through attitudes, voice intonations, or actions and maintains a superior attitude as if he/she has all the answers
- Brags and boasts about his/her accomplishments and ideas, favorably comparing them to those of others
- Refuses to delegate or involve others, thinking that he/she does things better than them; re-does what others have done because he/she thinks it can be done better
- Believes that he/she is usually right and others are usually wrong
- Criticizes others and himself/herself for mistakes and shortcomings
- Engages in overly intense and inappropriate competition and power plays with others
- Puts his/her own needs before the needs of others consistently

Someone misuses the strength of Humility when he/she:

- Accepts poor treatment from others, believing that he/she is unworthy of respect
- Focuses his/her attention excessively on himself/herself
- Demonstrates a lack of self-confidence and excessively criticizes himself/herself
- Acts in ways that assist others to feel excessively self-important
- Confuses humility with humiliation by degrading and shaming others or himself/herself

30 ~ Idealism

Idealism is envisioning what is possible, thinking beyond what currently exists, and taking action towards or advocating for beneficial change.

Someone practices Idealism effectively when he/she:
- Creates a vision for what he/she wants in a future situation; such as, a relationship, marriage, family, career, finances, company, community, or experience
- Seeks effective and sustainable solutions to the problems and injustices of the family, the workplace, the neighborhood, the country, and the world
- Works towards solutions that benefit as many as possible
- Holds an optimistic vision of a better world in the future and works to realize that vision now
- Takes action where possible to transform situations from negative into positive
- Seeks sources of inspiration about making a positive difference for others

Someone needs to strengthen Idealism when he/she:
- Fails to see what needs improvement in his/her character, life, and in the world
- Holds a pessimistic, sad, or hopeless attitude about the state of the world, his/her community, his/her family, or himself/herself
- Settles for poor circumstances or complains, rather than taking action to improve a situation or requesting help from others to carry out change

Someone misuses the strength of Idealism when he/she:
- Holds such high ideals that he/she becomes intolerant of shortcomings in anyone or in any aspect of life
- Neglects his/her current responsibilities while dreaming of what could have been or should be
- Becomes obsessive about fixing every little detail in life
- Rushes into overly ambitious plans without enough realistic planning, preparation, and securing of resources

᷈ 31 ~ *Integrity* ᷉

Integrity is achieving a state of balance and wholeness in life and character, by acting in accord with civil laws and deepest beliefs, highest values and principles, and stated word.

Someone practices Integrity effectively when he/she:
- Acts and speaks in harmony with his/her ideals, beliefs, and intentions
- Stays true to his/her word, keeping his/her promises and fulfilling his/her commitments
- Acts reliably, showing others that they can count on his/her consistent behavior
- Practices a high moral and ethical standard in personal behavior and encourages others to also follow a high code of ethics in education, the workplace, and service commitments
- Uses his/her character strengths consistently with others and in service to others
- Handles responsibilities in a timely manner

Someone needs to strengthen Integrity when he/she:
- Breaks agreements and promises and fails to honor his/her word
- Accepts and maintains a low standard of behavior for himself/herself and makes little or no effort to improve
- Acts immorally, unethically, or illegally
- Attempts to escape the natural consequences of his/her harmful actions
- Takes no action to restore wholeness in a situation and right a difficult or harmful situation or relationship
- Acts in a hypocritical way, different from his/her stated beliefs

Someone misuses the strength of Integrity when he/she:
- Acts quickly with poorly thought-out motives
- Places trust in others inappropriately, allowing himself/herself to be easily fooled or led astray
- Becomes overly fussy, critical, and insists on perfection

∽ 32 ~ Joyfulness ∾

Joyfulness is being in a state of high-spirited and ecstatic delight, gladness, blissfulness, great happiness, and jubilation.

Someone practices Joyfulness effectively when he/she:
- Celebrates the wonders of life
- Smiles, laughs, and vibrantly enjoys life, even during difficult or sad times and experiences that include grief or anger
- Enjoys and shares humor, laughter, and light-hearted fun appropriately in his/her life and with others
- Immerses himself/herself in happy and healthy worship, prayer, and meditation, experiencing spiritual inspiration, upliftment, and radiance
- Shares new knowledge and insights with others in an excited way
- Experiences the pleasure of knowing he/she has done his/her best and made wise choices
- Looks optimistically for the best in life and others
- Transforms difficult or negative experiences into opportunities for growth and gratitude

Someone needs to strengthen Joyfulness when he/she:
- Grumbles, whines, or complains about his/her life, acting very immersed in self
- Looks at life and experiences with pessimism, expressing his/her expectation of negative outcomes
- Uses a falsely positive expression to mask underlying feelings of depression, inadequacy, or pain
- Fails to rejoice in the blessings others receive or in those that come into his/her life, or acts with envy or jealously about what is positive in the lives of others
- Avoids happy and enjoyable people, places, and experiences because of his/her negative attitude

Someone misuses the strength of Joyfulness when he/she:
- Responds without sensitivity to a sorrowful situation, invalidating the sad feelings of others
- Delights in getting his/her own way through flattery, manipulation, or enticement
- Exults in or laughs at the suffering of others
- Demonstrates exaggerated or excessively high moods
- Rejoices excessively over minor events

❧ 33 ~ Justice ❧

Justice is making a fair decision or taking fair action free of any bias or prejudice after carefully assessing all the facts, feelings, people, principles, laws, risks, and consequences related to a situation.

Someone practices Justice effectively when he/she:

- Maintains balance in his/her relationships and agreements, so that most involved feel the balance and give and take between them is fair over time
- Searches for truth and forms his/her opinions and conclusions based on objective facts
- Treats others fairly, searching for equitable solutions and reaching impartial decisions
- Responds when moved or angered by the suffering of others and gives aid, comfort, and/ or assistance to those who have been neglected, abused, or mistreated or who lack the resources to help themselves
- Acknowledges, honors, and stands up for his/her own rights and the rights of others, seeking to prevent harm or mistreatment to people, animals, or property
- Works to restore integrity where there has been unwise, unlawful, or unfair activity, ensuring that the wishes and rights of those harmed are taken into consideration
- Rejects as unacceptable and against moral and ethical principles the harmful misbehavior of others or himself/herself, such as lying, cheating, stealing, abusiveness, or violence, and works for conflict resolution, reparations, and the best possible outcomes in those situations

Someone needs to strengthen Justice when he/she:

- Assumes others will accommodate his/her needs without communicating what they are and including him/her accommodating theirs as well
- Becomes aware of unfairness within the community or in the world without taking even the smallest of steps to try to better the situation
- Complains to people who can do nothing to solve a problem
- Acts to address issues without the agreement or permission of those involved
- Acts unfairly or unlawfully, disrespectfully trampling on the rights of others
- Mistreats, threatens, manipulates, abuses, harms, or injures others
- Makes decisions based on bias or prejudice or without careful thought
- Fails to look for or discern the facts of a situation
- Dominates or oppresses others, using his/her strength, words, or actions to hurt or overcome them
- Behaves with excessive mercy when fairness is called for instead

Someone misuses the strength of Justice when he/she:

- Tries so hard to be fair that he/she becomes indecisive or insensitive to the nuances of a particular situation
- Makes decisions based on what has occurred in previous situations without assessing significant differences in current circumstances
- Acts in a self-righteous or revengeful way as a personal judging authority
- Defends others inappropriately

∽ 34 ~ Kindness ∾

Kindness is considering the needs or wants of others and acting in a deliberately warm-hearted and empathetic manner to meet them.

Someone practices Kindness effectively when he/she:
- Looks outside of himself/herself and makes efforts to meet the needs of others
- Shows a warm, pleasant, and considerate attitude towards others
- Offers positive, understanding, hopeful, and uplifting words and gestures to calm, comfort, or assist others or himself/herself in difficult circumstances
- Acts or speaks spontaneously with concern and understanding to assist someone and uplift his/her spirits, sometimes privately without the recipient knowing the source of assistance

Someone needs to strengthen Kindness when he/she:
- Insists on or seeks the most severe consequences for other people's mistakes
- Lives a self-centered life, ignoring the needs and wishes of those around him/her
- Behaves in a harsh, mean, cruel, rude, neglectful, or critical way
- Holds a resentful, grudging, or bitter attitude towards others
- Sees the needs of others but ignores them and chooses not to take any action

Someone misuses the strength of Kindness when he/she:
- Lets others take advantage of his/her willingness to help
- Pretends to care, while actually manipulating others
- Acts only when it is to his/her own advantage or benefit
- Spends so much time helping others that his/her own responsibilities are neglected

∽ 35 ~ Love ∾

Love is connecting to others through affection and joining with them to express the powerfully magnetic and caring force that unites the universe.

Someone practices Love effectively when he/she:
- Prays and meditates to maintain a spiritual bond of connection with a loving God
- Uses words, gestures, and actions to communicate warm, affectionate, and appreciative feelings towards others and himself/herself
- Expresses affection consistently to others in ways they prefer
- Maintains a healthy and unified relationship with a partner or spouse, his/her children, parents, and other close relatives
- Bases actions on genuine caring and commitment to the well-being of others
- Recognizes and respects his/her own worthiness and the vital importance of giving and receiving affection as part of living life to its fullest
- Acts with tolerance and respect to create positive change in families, neighborhoods, communities, organizations, companies, countries, and the world

Someone needs to strengthen Love when he/she:
- Acts in a self-centered or careless way, taking for granted the affection of others or ignoring ways of making a difference for others
- Hesitates to take actions that might build a positive connection or bond with others
- Holds a bitter, critical, contemptuous, hateful, or condemning attitude towards others
- Treats other people as if they are opponents or enemies
- Backbites, gossips, or spreads slander about the character of others
- Ignores, refuses, or belittles someone's request for him/her to express affection in a specific and appropriate way
- Ends relationships because he/she feels personally unworthy of others or superior to them
- Spends time with others only if they meet his/her standards or if the relationship seems personally beneficial
- Equates infatuation or the experience of intimate or sexual touch from someone as signs of lasting affection and respect in the absence of other words, actions, or commitments

Someone misuses the strength of Love when he/she:
- Smothers others with so much attention that they have little space or time to be themselves or live their own lives
- Fails to set healthy boundaries
- Allows feelings or excessive concerns about reactions to blind him/her to someone's poor character or unjust actions; hides their flaws or problems from important others
- Manipulates or punishes someone by alternating between giving and withholding affection

∾ 36 ~ Loyalty ∾

Loyalty is honoring, belonging to, supporting, and remaining devoted and faithful to someone or something beyond oneself; such as, a friend, partner, spouse, family, employers, organizations, community, religion, country, or the world.

Someone practices Loyalty effectively when he/she:
- Honors and defends the character and actions of a person who is close to him/her or of an entity he/she respects
- Gives high priority and attention to the people and causes he/she values, even when they disappoint or hurt him/her
- Speaks positively and respectfully about whatever he/she belongs to or gives allegiance to, working to advance its interests and defend it as needed
- Helps the well-being of those he/she cares about
- Guards private information as confidential and chooses carefully who to share information with about others

Someone needs to strengthen Loyalty when he/she:
- Backbites, gossips, or slanders the character of others
- Undermines the legitimate or lawful authority of people or entities
- Uses disrespectful language and actions towards those he/she is affiliated with
- Betrays others or fails to keep his/her promises
- Fails to maintain relationships or lets go of them for petty reasons
- Shows envy of others, abandoning pride in his/her chosen group
- Fails to defend due to fear of consequences or the views of others

Someone misuses the strength of Loyalty when he/she:
- Maintains allegiance to others who are negative or destructive, who habitually treat others poorly, or who participate in negative and harmful activities, such as backbiting or criticism
- Obeys or follows people or groups who are acting unwisely or illegally
- Treats others possessively or jealously, working to prevent them from having other friendships and connections

❦ 37 ~ Mercy ❧

Mercy is treating the mistakes or harmful actions of others in a forbearing and lenient way.

Someone practices Mercy effectively when he/she:
- Gives someone the opportunity to start over by accepting what happened and moving forward
- Accepts apologies and amends that others make kindly and sincerely
- Forgives and detaches from the mistakes of others, letting incidents be in the past
- Allows himself/herself and others to learn from mistakes while moderating the consequences of actions
- Lets someone else have something they seem to need
- Gives others the freedom to live as they choose, without commentary or interference

Someone needs to strengthen Mercy when he/she:
- Finds shortcomings in others routinely and acts or feels irritated by them
- Reminds others of their failures or past mistakes frequently and punishes the offenders
- Focuses rigidly on what is right or just without tolerance for human failings
- Holds grudges and resentments against others
- Annoys others by making repeated comments, complaints, or requests
- Refuses to grant someone a second chance after a problem occurs

Someone misuses the strength of Mercy when he/she:
- Ignores or enables unkind, harmful, or unjust behavior
- Allows others to get away with very harmful actions without experiencing the logical consequences, such as legal action or loss of money or property

∽ 38 ~ Moderation ↝

Moderation is recognizing and avoiding extremes in use of time, words, actions, and other choices, to seek a balance that creates positive outcomes.

Someone practices Moderation effectively when he/she:

- Evaluates his/her schedule and commitments regularly to keep relationships, work, service, spirituality, learning, and leisure in appropriate balance for health and well-being, prioritizing or seeking help as needed
- Balances activity levels to allow time to maintain relationships of all types as a priority, ensuring that this includes opportunities to share his/her thoughts and feelings and listen to those of others
- Takes time and needed actions to rest, relax, and lower stress levels or to raise energy levels and involvement as needed to move with balanced purpose, grace, and ease
- Budgets, saves, and spends financial resources in a responsible and balanced way
- Responds calmly and consistently to situations, avoiding extreme emotional highs and lows
- Uses more than one character strength at a time to guide his/her actions in a balanced way and make appropriate choices

Someone needs to strengthen Moderation when he/she:

- Fluctuates wildly from one extreme to another, creating conflict or causing harm
- Fails to take appropriate actions or make necessary choices to balance words and actions
- Works too hard, becoming so exhausted that he/she is unable to participate in routine activities or spend time and energy with important others
- Gives too much to others, talks too much, participates in many frivolous activities, or indulges compulsions or appetites; such as, over-eating, over-spending, over-exercising...
- Regards appropriate enjoyment of entertainment, food, travel, beautiful objects, or good company as frivolous or improper

Someone misuses the strength of Moderation when he/she:

- Criticizes the habits, actions, and words of others, using statements such as, "You should...", "You should not...", "You cannot..."
- Acts in an overly cautious, timid, or reserved manner with others or when making choices

◌ 39 ~ Patience ◌

Patience is maintaining steady awareness and control of one's thoughts and responses while waiting for or seeking an outcome; controlling one's words and actions while willingly and calmly taking the time to respond to difficult, inconvenient, hurtful, delaying, or troublesome situations.

Someone practices Patience effectively when he/she:

- Listens attentively, stays aware, holds back a hasty or angry reply, thinks before speaking, and responds in a calm and level-headed way
- Works carefully through a task that has many steps, going at an even pace, or waiting for someone else to do the same
- Appreciates and even enjoys the moment without agitating for it to move forward
- Shows acceptance of and tolerance for differences and limitations in others
- Tolerates a delay, waiting alertly and calmly for what is in motion to unfold or for difficulties to be resolved
- Taking calm and appropriate actions as needed to move something forward
- Accepts calmly and with a positive and hopeful attitude what he/she cannot change
- Allows himself/herself and others the time, attention, and practice needed to develop character strengths, learn new skills, accomplish tasks, and give effective service to others
- Maintains quiet, steadfast hope and intention for positive outcomes, trusting that matters will come together in the best way possible

Someone needs to strengthen Patience when he/she:

- Acts in an unreasonable, irrational, or short-tempered way because things do not go the way he/she wants
- Forces someone to rush or pushes for something to happen faster than is wise, denying the reality of circumstances
- Criticizes, agitates, yells, and becomes anxious or angry about the pace of something or the slow actions of others or himself/herself
- Shows signs of irritation or agitation; such as, finger-tapping, a strained facial expression, or wandering eyes
- Speaks impulsively or rushes ahead or into a situation without assessing it or consulting with others, thereby causing harm

Someone misuses the strength of Patience when he/she:

- Causes delays, passively ignores issues, becomes apathetic, or acts too slowly or not at all to address important matters or needs
- Waits an unreasonable amount of time to respond to a problem, trouble, or danger, resulting in the possibility of greater loss, difficulties, harm, or injury
- Withholds attention, affection, or input for extended lengths of time to manipulate the other person and get his/her own way

40 ~ Peacefulness

Peacefulness is being physically, mentally, and emotionally calm and serene and working to reduce conflict and build harmony between people.

Someone practices Peacefulness effectively when he/she:

- Seeks points of agreement and harmony between himself/herself and others, seeing unity as a building block for family, community, and global peace
- Communicates in respectful, truthful, loving, and positive ways, sowing in all interactions the seeds of peace; learns new communication skills to build agreement and reduce conflict
- Handles his/her own responsibilities and responds to whatever issues arise in his/her life without feeling anxiety, anger, or inner agitation about what is not being done
- Maintains an inner sense of calm, tranquility, and happiness
- Utilizes positive or spiritual practices; such as, gratitude, meditation, or prayer
- Focuses on love, appreciation, and reconciliation between people
- Listens to calming or uplifting music, watches upbeat media, or goes to places that increase his/her serenity
- Stops discussions that cause disunity with others, replacing thoughts of conflict with thoughts of harmony and peace

Someone needs to strengthen Peacefulness when he/she:

- Fights, argues, swears, or provokes or participates in disagreements or conflicts with others
- Criticizes, judges, corrects, or attempts to dominate others
- Backbites, gossips, or spreads slander about the character of others
- Refuses to communicate with others or take actions towards reconciliation in a conflict
- Holds a grudge or seeks revenge for the perceived hurtful words and actions of others
- Attempts to manage other people's responsibilities without their agreement
- Worries about potential negative outcomes
- Sees violent, abusive, or forceful action as the only solution to an issue or as a way to dominate others
- Allows others to disrupt his/her sense of inner serenity

Someone misuses the strength of Peacefulness when he/she:

- Suppresses his/her emotions to hide appropriate anger; neglects to take decisive action towards resolution or to call in appropriate authorities
- Allows himself/herself to become so mellow that he/she does not experience even such positive emotions as happiness or excitement
- Fails to act in situations that call for strength and decisiveness

❧ 41 ~ Perseverance ❧

Perseverance is persisting and pressing onward towards worthwhile goals, particularly in the face of challenges or adversity.

Someone practices Perseverance effectively when he/she:

- Stays on task and finishes what he/she starts
- Values his/her goals and focuses on steadfastly achieving them
- Stays in relationships or situations long enough to attempt to work through issues together with others and to determine their probability of a successful outcome
- Commits to and acts according to his/her moral values and beliefs, even when it is difficult
- Continues to develop his/her character and relationship skills over time
- Makes plans to overcome whatever obstacles get in his/her way where possible and appropriate
- Carries on steadfastly even after responding to and grieving from crushing emotional blows or crippling grief

Someone needs to strengthen Perseverance when he/she:

- Stops working on tasks or towards important goals at the first obstacle, sign of trouble, or the loss of support or an ally
- Skips from one activity or task to another without completing most of them
- Allows feelings of being overwhelmed deter him/her from continuing with important tasks
- Abandons his/her values and beliefs when someone challenges them or when it is hard to do what he/she believes is right
- Discounts the importance of finishing what he/she has started, abandoning his/her effort, and rationalizing and justifying his/her failure

Someone misuses the strength of Perseverance when he/she:

- Refuses to assess, reconsider, or adjust a goal; change a direction; or seek advice and assistance when things continue to go poorly
- Persists stubbornly in doing something even when it is clearly unwise or causes significant harm or disunity
- Drops most unrelated activities, friendships, and relationships while pursuing a goal

≪ 42 ~ Purity ≫

Purity is maintaining personal physical cleanliness, a clean and orderly environment, uplifting and chaste thoughts, positive words, honest motivations, a loving heart, and a spiritually focused soul.

Someone practices Purity effectively when he/she:

- Maintains good personal hygiene
- Keeps his/her clothes, vehicles, possessions, property, and home tidy, organized, and clean
- Replaces degrading, destructive, or inappropriate sexual thoughts with those that are uplifting, noble, or spiritual
- Prays and/or meditates regularly
- Acts according to spiritual practices and principles
- Makes wise choices and acts out of honest, kind, and selfless motives
- Resists temptations to participate in harmful activities as soon as he/she recognizes their danger
- Keeps his/her body free of non-medicinal alcohol and harmful drugs
- Eats healthy food and drinks clean and healthy beverages to nourish his/her body and keep it functioning smoothly

Someone needs to strengthen Purity when he/she:

- Clutters up or neglects cleaning his/her environment for extended periods
- Views or reflects on violent or harmful sexual images
- Holds resentment, anger, hate, bitterness, envy, or jealousy in his/her mind and heart
- Speaks or acts with manipulative motives or has an unspoken, personal agenda when interacting with others
- Swears, shouts, or uses words that hurt or degrade others
- Gives into temptations to participate in harmful activities that damage his/her body, mind, heart, or soul

Someone misuses the strength of Purity when he/she:

- Obsesses about cleanliness and neatness so that he/she and others cannot relax and live normally around him/her
- Lectures others about what he/she thinks are their harmful lifestyles, or speaks in a way that implies that his/her standards are the only correct ones
- Acts in a superior and self-righteous way, claiming his/her high standards and actions are better than those of other people

◦§ 43 ~ Purposefulness ৯৹

Purposefulness is pursuing meaningful goals and participating in vital activities with determination.

Someone practices Purposefulness effectively when he/she:

- Defines his/her personal life purposes in harmony with his/her beliefs and sets and pursues goals that fulfill his/her individual or shared aims, taking into careful consideration the purposes and goals of others in his/her life
- Works towards his/her goals and dreams with determination, efficiency, and effectiveness, or works with others towards joint goals
- Focuses on developing all aspects of his/her mind, talents, skills, and character, encouraging others to do the same
- Works persistently to make improvements in his/her life, family, and community
- Adjusts his/her environment to help achieve his/her goals, perhaps by rearranging furniture to reduce distractions or creating a work schedule that maximizes efficiency
- Surrounds himself/herself with positive people who help him/her with completing tasks and achieving his/her goals and assists with the fulfillment of the tasks and goals of others
- Works diligently at both assigned and chosen tasks, gaining knowledge and skills as needed to be of effective service to others
- Uses visualization or concentration to picture successful outcomes for projects and relationships

Someone needs to strengthen Purposefulness when he/she:

- Wanders aimlessly through life without any idea of where he/she is going or what he/she will do
- Spends his/her days lazily doing only what brings him/her short-lived or superficial pleasure or allows him/her to live only in the moment, and involves others in the same choices
- Ignores or delays responding to issues and tasks, failing to act when it is timely and appropriate
- Avoids identifying and discussing his/her expectations and desired outcomes with appropriate others

Someone misuses the strength of Purposefulness when he/she:

- Focuses so much on his/her goals that he/she neglects the needs of others and himself/herself and any concerns that arise
- Ignores other activities or experiences that would create a more balanced life
- Behaves rudely or poorly towards those who stand in his/her way when he/she is trying to accomplish a task or goal or when someone expresses concerns about plans or actions
- Sabotages decisions or the plans of others when he/she perceives they could interfere with his/her plans
- Refuses to flexibly bend or change plans as needed when new information or circumstances arise

෨ 44 ~ Resilience ෨

Resilience is accepting, responding appropriately to, recovering from, and coping with adversity, misfortune, change, or illness, and bouncing back from stressful experiences effectively and in a reasonable amount of time.

Someone practices Resilience effectively when he/she:

- Accepts and adjusts to change rather than resisting it
- Acts calmly during crises and takes positive steps to manage them
- Seeks creative and appropriate solutions to problems
- Looks for what he/she can learn from a current challenge to help him/her to prevent or respond effectively to future ones
- Adapts to changing circumstances, staying detached enough from what is occurring to respond appropriately
- Stays reasonably optimistic when faced with unwanted events or experiences, but does not engage in serious denial or avoid responding to circumstances
- Withstands or quickly recovers from the impact of failures, disruptive events, loss, and disappointments; quickly and confidently re-focuses on goals and resumes action

Someone needs to strengthen Resilience when he/she:

- Grumbles, whines, and complains about unexpected or disruptive events
- Ignores, panics, or responds poorly to problems, often making them worse
- Takes an excessive amount of time to recover from challenges and changes
- Becomes helpless in the face of problems
- Talks pessimistically about all the bad things that are occurring and that might occur in the future

Someone misuses the strength of Resilience when he/she:

- Insists on handling challenges without help from others
- Tries to resume normal activities after an adverse experience without adequate time to heal or grieve; denies the impact of the experience on him/her
- Acts as if no problem is really occurring and that he/she can cope with anything anyway

❧ 45 ~ Respect ❧

Respect is interacting with all people and what they value, as well as animals and the environment, in a manner that demonstrates they are worthy of fair treatment, consideration, and honorable regard.

Someone practices Respect effectively when he/she:

- Speaks, acts, listens, and touches in ways that go past first impressions, prejudices, and biases
- Honors the personal limits, boundaries, wishes, and comfort levels of others, both when they are present and when they are not
- Treats his/her own body, mind, heart, soul, beliefs, belongings, history, experiences, and environment, as well as those of others, with interest, honor, dignity, care, appreciation, and consideration
- Appreciates and honors the talents, abilities, specialties, and strengths of others as well as his/her own
- Practices character qualities with consistency and acknowledges the character strengths of others
- Allows others the right to practice their beliefs and values as they choose without interference, as long as their beliefs and values do not violate laws or the just and legitimate rights of others
- Remembers and acknowledges special dates, anniversaries, and other key events in the lives of others
- Gives consideration to others even when their views, experiences, and perspectives differ from his/her own
- Follows and obeys the rules, guidelines, and laws relevant to a situation

Someone needs to strengthen Respect when he/she:

- Behaves rudely, harshly, or negatively towards others or himself/herself
- Backbites, gossips, or spreads slander about the character of others
- Tramples on the rights, property, possessions, boundaries, or needs of others
- Treats valuable or sacred books and objects carelessly or irreverently
- Borrows from others without returning in an agreed and timely way what he/she took
- Acts immorally, unethically, or illegally
- Intrudes on the privacy of others or breaks confidentiality
- Acts arrogantly, as if superior to others

Someone misuses the strength of Respect when he/she:

- Places such a high value upon others that he/she gives them too much time and attention or defends and enables their unwise, cruel, or unjust behavior
- Violates his/her own standards and values to win or keep someone's approval who he/she holds in high esteem
- Assists someone to feel or act arrogantly self-important
- Acts inferior or subservient to others, as if he/she is worth less than they are

❦ 46 ~ Responsibility ❧

Responsibility is claiming personal accountability for one's own life, choices, happiness, commitments, required activities, and relationships with others, as well as sharing accountability for the quality of life in the communities in which one lives and works and in the global society.

Someone practices Responsibility effectively when he/she:

- Expends the necessary time and effort to build and maintain relationships with others
- Seeks to improve all facets of himself/herself in order to achieve his/her potential, using character strengths effectively to navigate through life
- Shows initiative, empowerment, and leadership in relationships, home, education, work, and community
- Assesses words and actions regularly, listening to feedback from others, accepting credit or blame as appropriate, and acting to change behavior or resolve any problems that he/she partially or fully causes
- Initiates action and keeps and completes all promises, commitments, and assigned tasks, honoring and meeting the reasonable expectations of others
- Shows concern and care for the environment, conserving, reusing, and recycling as appropriate

Someone needs to strengthen Responsibility when he/she:

- Resists or complains about what he/she needs to do or sabotages situations to avoid action or accountability
- Blames others instead of accepting accountability when a problem is a logical consequence of his/her own words or actions
- Defends his/her attitude, words, and actions even when he/she knows they are harmful to others; ignores the hurtful effect of his/her attitudes, words, and actions
- Breaks promises or laws; ignores or changes important rules; fails to inform others of applicable rules or changes in them
- Withholds information vital to a successful outcome
- Neglects home tasks, work, studies, or service assignments and duties
- Refuses to apologize or make amends to others for mistakes

Someone misuses the strength of Responsibility when he/she:

- Gives higher priority to work or interests than to relationships without agreement with important people in his/her life
- Over-works and rarely relaxes, has fun, or laughs
- Enables others to avoid doing things that they can and should do themselves

∽ 47 ~ *Self-Discipline* ∾

Self-Discipline is maintaining the inner control to perform needed and important tasks; fulfill one's commitments, goals, and life purposes; and resist what is harmful to others or oneself.

Someone practices Self-Discipline effectively when he/she:
- Monitors and controls his/her thoughts, emotions, desires, intentions, responses, and actions so that they do not harm others or him/her; expresses them or carries them out when appropriate in constructive ways
- Takes charge of his/her own thoughts, character, and behavior and governs himself/herself to achieve self-improvement goals or to address what requires attention
- Sets goals to benefit others and oneself and establishes structures and guidelines to keep himself/herself focused on achieving them
- Speaks and acts wisely, calmly, and appropriately
- Uses delegated and personal power appropriately
- Makes healthy choices to meet his/her nutrition, exercise, and sleep needs, resisting temptations as appropriate
- Creates routines, orderliness, and harmony in his/her environment
- Budgets, controls, and balances his/her spending of time and money, meeting due dates, being punctual, and avoiding excessive commitments
- Follows civil laws, such as speed limits, or spiritual laws or practices, such as prayer or fasting

Someone needs to strengthen Self-Discipline when he/she:
- Loses control of his/her thoughts, emotions, desires, temper, actions, and reactions or speaks or acts impulsively or dominates conversations
- Acts without regard for principles, rules, laws, commitments, beliefs, and cultural or personal values
- Speaks or acts according to habits, whims, or preferences, without considering the effect on others or himself/herself
- Needs repeated reminders from others
- Is regularly late in paying bills or arriving at work, meetings, or other commitments
- Gives up worthy goals for ones that are less challenging without making efforts to get help or make them more manageable
- Spends his/her time primarily on what brings him/her instant pleasure

Someone misuses the strength of Self-Discipline when he/she:
- Acts or speaks rigidly or in an over-bearing manner
- Places more value on following a set of rules or rigid schedules than on the well-being of others or himself/herself
- Establishes such a set personal schedule that he/she does not leave time for effectively building and maintaining a relationship or marriage

≈ 48 - Service ≈

Service is acting selflessly and often sacrificially, directly or indirectly, to improve or enhance the well-being and quality of life of others and their situations and experiences.

Someone practices Service effectively when he/she:

- Offers his/her time, talents, skills, money, and attention proactively to a partner/spouse, friends, family, religion, employer and customers, and community as needed and appropriate
- Works to complete tasks quietly and humbly
- Puts the needs and comforts of others before his/her own in a joyful and willing way
- Contributes time, resources, and energy to improve the health, happiness, well-being, spiritual connection, and prosperity of others or to enhance or improve the situations of others
- Assists, encourages, or accompanies people to help them participate in activities that benefit others; such as, working together on a task or inviting someone to work on a project team or committee
- Makes choices based on an altruistic commitment to bettering the lives of others
- Follows directions or does what needs to be done, even when it is boring, repetitive, or unpleasant

Someone needs to strengthen Service when he/she:

- Fails to notice, acknowledge, or respond to the requests, needs, and problems of others; thinks the problems of others are too much trouble for him/her to respond to
- Acts but boasts about actions or expects notice, reward, reciprocity, or repeated or constant attention and praise for what he/she does for others
- Expects people to wait on him/her, even when that is not physically necessary or not their responsibility
- Stands by while others do what needs to be done, making no sincere effort to participate or cooperate
- Experiences difficulty in accepting helpful and needed actions from others

Someone misuses the strength of Service when he/she:

- Enables others to act irresponsibly or to become unwisely dependent upon him/her
- Seeks actions to do as a means to draw recognition or praise
- Becomes so involved in serving others that he/she neglects other important relationships, health and well-being, commitments, and responsibilities
- Engages in activities for others as a way to avoid dealing with issues, responsibilities, or relationships

∽ 49 ~ *Sincerity* ∾

Sincerity is being genuine and earnest about one's motives, words, and actions.

Someone practices Sincerity effectively when he/she:
- Maintains harmony between his/her inner thoughts and outer words and actions
- Shares aspects of his/her true self with others
- Acts with integrity, according to his/her beliefs and values
- Shows genuine concern for others through his/her words and actions
- Builds trust between people with honest words and deeds
- Tells others what he/she appreciates about them and celebrates what is special in their lives
- Seeks spiritual guidance and prays with careful thought and genuine feeling

Someone needs to strengthen Sincerity when he/she:
- Expresses appreciation or affection to get something from someone else, instead of as an unconditional and genuine acknowledgement or emotion
- Manipulates someone
- Hides who he/she really is from himself/herself or others
- Fakes his/her responses to others
- Pretends to have virtues, moral or religious beliefs, or principles, that he/she does not actually possess or believe in

Someone misuses the strength of Sincerity when he/she:
- Assumes naively that everyone is honest, letting himself/herself be easily fooled or deceived
- Gives so much serious attention to something that it prevents him/her from enjoying life
- Acts impulsively without assessing whether his/her motives are honest and pure
- Speaks bluntly and hurtfully and justifies it as genuine feedback

⤚ 50 ~ *Spirituality* ⤙

Spirituality is nurturing your heart and soul through maintaining a close, interactive relationship with God, drawing on spiritual sources for divine guidance, dedicated or devoted to the service of God or religion, and acting and speaking in alignment with the teachings in the Word of God.

Someone practices Spirituality effectively when he/she:
- Converses or communes with God or His Messengers in prayer, meditation, or through reading spiritual guidance, being certain of receiving Divine love and assistance
- Learns about spiritual topics through a variety of sources; such as, faith communities, study groups, spiritual gatherings, or books; treats spiritual books and places with reverence and respect
- Meditates, prays, then and reflects to seek inspiration and guidance for wise character and relationship choices, and develops and practices character qualities effectively
- Participates in a spiritual or religious congregation, community, or organization, and/or in interfaith activities; participates in inspiring activities and events
- Bases his/her identity, words, purposes, beliefs, and actions upon spiritual principles and values
- Shares his/her spiritual insights and beliefs authentically with others as requested or as appropriate, while respecting theirs in return
- Grows and develops faith, beliefs, and confidence in the blessings and assistance of God
- Maintains a hopeful and optimistic outlook
- Believes in a life beyond this one where he/she will be accountable for his/her actions and continue to grow and serve others

Someone needs to strengthen Spirituality when he/she:
- Chooses words and actions that reflect his/her lower physical nature rather than his/her higher spiritual nature or that project a negative or hopeless outlook
- Focuses his/her energy primarily on material possessions or physical pleasures
- Lacks confidence that God will provide for his/her needs and guide him/her and attempts to live only on his/her own strength
- Fails to follow through on the guidance received through prayer, meditation, reflection, reading, and consultation and decisions made with others
- Resists character quality development, misuses qualities, or attacks the characters of others
- Acts in ways inconsistent with his/her beliefs or moral standards; fails to raise moral or ethical concerns with those who can address them

Someone misuses the strength of Spirituality when he/she:
- Isolates himself/herself indefinitely to focus on his/her spiritual growth, while neglecting his/her responsibilities, the needs of others, or the opportunity to develop full, loving relationships
- Considers himself/herself too holy, lofty, or spiritual to associate with or work with others
- Tries to force his/her beliefs on others
- Chooses to endlessly sit and be inactive while waiting for Divine aid instead of acting and requesting guidance in the process

❦ 51 ~ Tactfulness ❧

Tactfulness is choosing whether and when to act or speak and, when speaking, using gentle and kind words with the intention of not offending others or hurting their feelings.

Someone practices Tactfulness effectively when he/she:

- Assesses carefully what he/she is about to say to others and communicates with gentleness, courtesy, love, and sensitivity
- Ensures that his/her words, gestures, body language, and tone of voice are positive, truthful, timely, constructive, and wise
- Waits for his/her emotions to calm down before responding respectfully to the thoughts, opinions, or feelings of others
- Makes requests of others rather than demands
- Stays silent, ignores something, or is brief when appropriate to avoid hurting another person's feelings or embarrassing him/her
- Chooses to either stay present or to leave a person or situation so that others are more comfortable

Someone needs to strengthen Tactfulness when he/she:

- Responds hastily, hurting someone's feelings as a result, and ending up regretting his/her words and actions
- Speaks unwisely without pausing to consider the effect on the listener
- Speaks in a rude, insensitive, embarrassing, or inconsiderate way

Someone misuses the strength of Tactfulness when he/she:

- Keeps silent inappropriately or lies because he/she is overly worried about someone's possible reaction
- Becomes so preoccupied with what to say that he/she withdraws and does not speak about an issue at all
- Takes offense easily or overreacts in response to what he/she considers inappropriate words and actions by others

∼ 52 ~ Thankfulness ∼

Thankfulness is expressing warm, genuine feelings of praise, appreciation, and gratitude for such aspects of life as loved ones, blessings, benefits, lessons learned, challenges that prompt growth, and warm gestures.

Someone practices Thankfulness effectively when he/she:
- Appreciates or celebrates what is good or beneficial in his/her life and in himself/herself
- Appreciates all that is good about other people, especially those closest to him/her
- Accepts and learns from the difficulties he/she experiences, appreciating that they help with developing character and strengthening faith
- Focuses on the positive aspects of his/her life and the world around him/her, appreciating the beauty or bounty around him/her; such as, nature, art, music, food, people, money, spirituality…
- Expresses gratitude to God, from the spiritual promptings of a radiant heart and soul, for the grace and blessings in his/her life
- Shares with others how much he/she appreciates who they are and what they do
- Notices and rejoices in the abundance of good in the world

Someone needs to strengthen Thankfulness when he/she:
- Fails or refuses to acknowledge what others do for him/her, taking their assistance for granted and neglecting to say thank you
- Discounts the appreciation that others express to him/her
- Remains stuck in self-pity, ignoring what is good about himself/herself and in his/her life and circumstances
- Acts self-centeredly as if he/she deserves all the good things in his/her life without acknowledging those who provide them or giving forth any personal effort to provide them
- Stops or delays doing important actions because others do not express appreciation

Someone misuses the strength of Thankfulness when he/she:
- Uses excessive or insincere compliments or flattering appreciation to manipulate others
- Does favors for others to make them feel grateful and with the expectation that they will do a favor in return
- Expects gratitude from others in return for actions or service

∾ 53 ~ Thoughtfulness ∾

Thoughtfulness is being concerned in a deliberate and genuine way about the well-being and happiness of others, acting in anticipation of and in loving awareness of their needs.

Someone practices Thoughtfulness effectively when he/she:

- Stays aware to identify and carry out ways to meet the needs of others, often putting others before himself/herself
- Takes actions to make life easier or more pleasant for others
- Plans positive and enjoyable activities for others
- Makes choices based upon love, respect, and consideration for the interests, needs, and wishes of others
- Pays attention to and considers the preferences of others when choosing activities, gifts, expressions of affection, and communication styles
- Discusses options and plans with others before making decisions that involve or affect them; makes decisions together with those involved
- Uses careful, prayerful, and reasoned thinking about the consequences of his/her words, choices, and actions

Someone needs to strengthen Thoughtfulness when he/she:

- Speaks or acts impulsively without giving due consideration to the feelings of others or the consequences
- Ignores or does not notice and respond to the wishes and needs of others
- Focuses selfishly on his/her own needs without considering the effect on others
- Withdraws and neglects to communicate with others
- Creates or participates in conflicts that result in hurt feelings or distance from others

Someone misuses the strength of Thoughtfulness when he/she:

- Tries so hard to assist someone that he/she seems intrusive or smothering
- Analyzes details excessively and tries so hard to take the right approach that he/she becomes fussy and overly absorbed with a project, often resulting in no action or too much action

∽ 54 ~ Thriftiness ∾

Thriftiness is managing ones economic situation and expenditures in a wise and frugal way to meet needs adequately, create prosperity, and successfully plan positive outcomes.

Someone practices Thriftiness effectively when he/she:
- Meets financial needs and obligations
- Keeps careful records, understands and monitors the flow of income and expenses, and sets and follows a budget
- Economizes on purchases, reduces expenses where possible, and carefully manages expenditures
- Chooses a simple lifestyle, eliminating non-essentials
- Saves money for future needs, seeking and following expert advice about investments
- Plans for large needed expenditures
- Negotiates for fair prices
- Stays happy and content with his/her financial situation and focuses on creating a thriving family

Someone needs to strengthen Thriftiness when he/she:
- Spends extravagantly, especially when he/she could save money elsewhere
- Plans poorly and wastes money and time
- Makes choices based on uncontrolled desires to acquire material possessions
- Spends excessively for physical pleasures
- Covets the possessions or lifestyle of others

Someone misuses the strength of Thriftiness when he/she:
- Behaves miserly with resources that he/she has and others need
- Acts stingy with time, energy, and money
- Makes money more important than relationships

◦◦ 55 ~ Trustworthiness ◦◦

Trustworthiness is handling tasks, responsibilities, possessions, money, and information reliably and honestly, thereby earning the confidence of others.

Someone practices Trustworthiness effectively when he/she:
- Fulfills agreements, promises, and commitments consistently, meeting agreed-upon expectations and providing timely and dependable service
- Acts with integrity and honesty when handling money, others' possessions, and responsibilities
- Listens carefully to personal sharing from others and keeps that information confidential
- Uses good judgment to avoid being swayed by inappropriate or harmful influences or acting in ways that damage the confidence of others
- Practices truthfulness, faithfulness, and loyalty with others, thereby gaining their confidence, building credibility, and acquiring a positive reputation
- Returns borrowed possessions without having to be reminded
- Extends confidence to others at an appropriate pace for the relationship and situation

Someone needs to strengthen Trustworthiness when he/she:
- Uses deceit, lies, or dishonesty to get things done or to get out of commitments
- Acts or speaks in ways that are not in alignment with words or beliefs or that prompt the suspicion of others
- Fails to do what he/she promises
- Overestimates his/her ability to earn someone's confidence
- Mishandles responsibilities
- Avoids positions of leadership or service to others that he/she could fulfill because he/she fears or is annoyed by being accountable to others
- Backbites, gossips, or spreads slander about the character of others
- Tells secrets or sensitive matters to others, failing to respect confidentiality or privacy

Someone misuses the strength of Trustworthiness when he/she:
- Values rules, policies, or his/her reputation more than the well-being of others and his/her relationships with them
- Assumes authority and power without considering the needs of others or what is best for the circumstances
- Clings rigidly to a commitment or promise that seems harmful or too difficult, instead of renegotiating it or asking for help

∽ 56 ~ Truthfulness ∾

Truthfulness is communicating accurately to convey one's best understanding of facts and feelings.

Someone practices Truthfulness effectively when he/she:
- Communicates carefully, accurately, and consistently in speech or writing, building trust with others, even when it is difficult
- Recognizes and appreciates the accurate words of others and appropriately challenges exaggerations and lies
- Investigates important matters fully, independently, and objectively before making decisions about what is factual or best for himself/herself or for others
- Speaks of matters accurately and factually, making it clear when he/she is voicing an opinion or personal understanding rather than facts
- Promises others only what he/she can reliably fulfill
- Knows and shares his/her true self accurately and authentically with others
- Admits to appropriate others when he/she makes a mistake, apologizes, and makes amends
- Shares stories and information accurately and without exaggeration or deceit

Someone needs to strengthen Truthfulness when he/she:
- Lies or exaggerates to deceive, manipulate, or impress others with false information; leaves out important details that would reflect poorly on him/her
- Defends or covers up actions with lies or partial truths
- Misuses his/her imagination or creativity to concoct inaccurate, exaggerated, or misleading stories to gain power, sympathy, or attention from others or to get what he/she wants
- Slanders the reputation or defames the character of others through backbiting, gossip, exaggeration, partial truths, or lies
- Accepts information from others or shares information without verifying its accuracy
- Distorts facts or misunderstands information and situations due to hidden motives, biases, or prejudices

Someone misuses the strength of Truthfulness when he/she:
- Speaks accurate words rudely, harshly, or hurtfully
- Backbites or gossips, defending the sharing of harmful information because it is true
- Speaks too much beyond the interest of others, often telling more than what people need or want to hear
- Focuses on the small details of an event or situation beyond necessity

ᴥ 57 ~ Unity ᴥ

Unity is consciously looking for and strengthening points of commonality, harmony, and attraction, as well as working with others to build a strong foundation of oneness, love, commitment, and cooperation.

Someone practices Unity effectively when he/she:

- Draws out the diverse achievements, talents, and abilities of others and guides them to act for the benefit of all
- Builds bonds of friendship with others who are different than him/her and invites them into an ever-widening circle of fellowship and inclusive loyalty
- Emphasizes points of agreement and de-emphasizes points of conflict, reconciling differences with others to bring all together in harmony and love
- Involves as many as possible of those affected by a situation in the problem-solving discussion and decisions, bringing multiple perspectives into concord and agreement
- Encourages full participation of everyone involved in an activity
- Fosters diverse individual initiatives that work together for the benefit of others
- Practices respect, justice, and fairness in his/her relationships, service, and work
- Attempts to solve a problem or conflict that is between two people only with them directly, in order to protect unity and confidentiality within a larger group

Someone needs to strengthen Unity when he/she:

- Fails to help or protect others, especially family and friends, from disruptive attacks, injustices, or neglect
- Acts superior to and separates himself/herself from people who are different from him/her
- Gives orders to friends, family, or coworkers instead of treating them as equal human beings and asking for their participation, input, and help
- Undermines group discussions and decisions
- Acts out of his/her lower nature in ways that are hostile, indifferent, cliquish, prideful, selfish, biased, prejudiced, impatient, contentious, vengeful, jealous, envious, disrespectful, unforgiving, argumentative, hateful, insulting, hypocritical, sabotaging, hasty, ill-tempered, violent, destructive, abusive, or otherwise negative

Someone misuses the strength of Unity when he/she:

- Ignores actual differences, safety issues, and unequal values between people and circumstances and tries to promote unity without responsibility, wisdom, reconciliation, or amends
- Promotes that harmony always requires people to be together physically
- Insists on uniformity, acting the same or doing the same thing in the same way it has been done in the past or by all/most people involved, not allowing room for leadership, creativity, and individual initiative
- Defers to others or avoids giving his/her legitimate or needed thoughts and opinions, thinking that his/her motive is reducing conflict by not participating

❦ 58 ~ Wisdom ❧

Wisdom is making good choices based upon knowledge gained from observation, education, and experiences, and reflecting and determining whether it is best to speak, remain silent, act, or be inactive.

Someone practices Wisdom effectively when he/she:
- Learns from his/her mistakes, experiences, and problems, as well as those of others, gaining knowledge of how to do better in similar situations in the future; does not repeat the same mistakes
- Uses listening, reflection, discernment, good judgment, experience, and common sense to assess whether his/her silence, words, or actions would be timely, helpful, and appropriate and sharing his/her knowledge and understanding in respectful ways
- Gathers factual information and feelings patiently and thoroughly from a variety of people and resources before making a decision or choice
- Acknowledges his/her strengths and limitations, admitting when he/she is overdoing it or does not know something, and demonstrating willingness to learn more about it
- Discerns when to give help and guidance to others and when to request and accept help and guidance from others
  Adjusts to changes calmly, knowing that they are a natural part of life

Someone needs to strengthen Wisdom when he/she:
- Speaks or acts without appropriate reflection and planning or urges others to do the same
- Takes little or no responsibility for directing his/her life and actions or for learning from the logical consequences or difficult outcomes of his/her choices and improving from them
- Ignores prayer and other spiritual resources when seeking knowledge and guidance
- Fails to learn from observation, experiences, and knowledge of others or himself/herself

Someone misuses the strength of Wisdom when he/she:
- Talks to others in arrogant or prideful ways about how much more he/she knows than they do, and critiquing, belittling, or judging them, thereby making them feel stupid or small
- Insists that others listen to his/her knowledge or advice and act on it
- Makes simple things complicated or difficult to understand
- Shares what he/she knows without assessing its timeliness, appropriateness, and consequences

BACKGROUND AND RESEARCH NOTES

There is increasing attention occurring towards character and virtues as people search for meaning in their lives and ways to be happier. Therefore, many people are researching the topic of character, and we wish to acknowledge some of them here.

John Gottman, PhD, emeritus professor of psychology at the University of Washington and executive director of the Relationship Research Institute in Seattle, Washington, determined through studying couples that one of the most destructive interactions they experience is attacking or criticizing the character of each other (The Seven Principles for Making Marriage Work, pp. 27-29, coauthored with Nan Silver). His finding led me to look at how to assist couples to encourage one another's character development instead of engaging in criticism. Character knowledge and encouragement is a positive and nurturing practice that is vital in building strong and lasting marriages.

Bill Gothard and his book *Research in Principles of Life Basic Seminar Textbook*, started my associate John Miller on his quest to understand character and the concept of misusing character qualities. University-based researchers like Christopher Peterson, Professor of Psychology, University of Michigan, and Martin E. P. Seligman, Fox Leadership Professor of Psychology, University of Pennsylvania, are experts in positive psychology and are studying and classifying qualities such as creativity, integrity, and kindness. They are authors of *Character Strengths and Virtues: A Handbook and Classification*. Blaine Fowers at the University of Miami, and author of *Beyond the Myth of Marital Happiness*, focuses his work on the qualities of loyalty, generosity, justice, and courage. A team at Brigham Young University is developing ways to measure character in marriage. Life Innovations includes some aspects of character in its relationship assessment model (www.prepare-enrich.com).

Many other people globally are drawing people's attention to the importance of character. Among these is Linda Kavelin Popov of The Virtues Project™ (www.virtuesproject.com). She and her husband, Dan Popov, PhD, one of the founders of the project, have studied the world's religious scriptures and identified in them over a hundred qualities that guide human attitudes, words, and actions. Linda Kavelin Popov has incorporated the virtues into her books, *The Family Virtues Guide*, *The Virtues Project™ Educator's Guide*, and *A Pace of Grace*. As the Popov's travel internationally, they are finding universal application of these qualities for families, religious organizations, businesses, governments, youth organizations, and more. Some of their research and their encouragement have helped the development of this work.

Character education is also developing and spreading throughout the world's education systems, particularly at the primary school levels. The Dibble Institute (www.dibbleinstitute.org) is including character in its relationship skill building courses with teens. In homes, parents are learning how to help the development of their children's characters. How character applies to relationships and marriage, however, is in the early stages of both university research and incorporation into relationship and marriage education.

ABOUT THE AUTHOR AND PUBLISHER

Susanne M. Alexander is a Relationship and Marriage Coach specializing in character development and certified by PREPARE-ENRICH. She is President of Marriage Transformation LLC, a publishing and coaching company based in Chattanooga, Tennessee, USA, (www.marriagetransformation.com). It has the mission of helping people create happy, lasting, character-based marriages. She is the author or co-author of *All-in-One Marriage Prep: 75 Experts Share Tips and Wisdom to Help You Get Ready Now*; *Can We Dance? Learning the Steps for a Fulfilling Relationship*; *Marriage Can Be Forever—Preparation Counts!*; *Pure Gold: Encouraging Character Qualities in Marriage*; and *A Perfectly Funny Marriage* cartoon book.

Susanne has conducted many workshops for individuals and couples in the United States, Canada, and China. She has been quoted in or written articles published in: *Washington Woman, Marriage Partnership, Inc., Ladies Home Journal, Newsweek, Chicago Sun Times, The Washington Times, NBC Online,* Yahoo.com, Match.com, Hitched.com, ParentsConnect.com, Entrepreneur.com, and more. She is a contributing columnist and eCourse leader with www.simplemarriage.net.

Susanne is a member of the American Society of Journalists and Authors and a Competent Communicator with Toastmasters International. She founded Marriage Transformation with her husband Craig Farnsworth, who passed away from cancer in 2009. She is a member of the Bahá'í Faith (www.bahai.org; www.bahairelationships.com). She has one married daughter, three married stepchildren, and four grandchildren.

ACKNOWLEDGEMENTS

I have been assisted along the journey of more deeply understanding character through my colleague John S. Miller. His insights and edits have enriched all of my work about character. John is a Character Specialist and Founder of Solving Conflicts LLC, which has a system of relationship and character coaching (www.solvingconflicts.com). He is also coauthor of *Pure Gold: Encouraging Character Qualities in Marriage* and *Can We Dance? Learning the Steps for a Fulfilling Relationship* and is producer of the TV show "Eden to Eden".

I also deeply appreciate the editing of Jane Ives and Hannah Yanega, as well as the input of Laurie Cunningham.

CONTACT MARRIAGE TRANSFORMATION

I welcome hearing back from you about your experiences with this book. Please share anything about how it has helped you, as well as any **feedback** that would improve its usefulness in future editions.

Please contact me if I can be of service to you with my coaching or marriage-readiness assessment services, or with any additional information.

CONTACT INFORMATION

Marriage Transformation LLC
Susanne M. Alexander,
President; Relationship & Marriage Coach;
Character Development Specialist
Chattanooga, Tennessee, USA

E-mail:

Susanne@marriagetransformation.com
or staff@marriagetransformation.com
Skype: MarriageTransformation

Websites:

www.marriagetransformation.com
www.bahaimarriage.net; www.bahairelationships.com
www.allinonemarriageprep.com

Social Media:

www.twitter.com/Marriage4ever
www.facebook.com/MarriageTransformation
www.linkedin.com/in/susannemalexander

Please be sure to visit our website **to purchase an ever-growing selection of exciting new books, eBooks, coaching services, workshops, and training materials**. Sets of worksheets from various books are also often available for purchase through: www.marriagetransformation.com/store.htm.

Please **subscribe**, on our websites, to our free e-newsletter, which has great articles and information for you about relationships, marriage, new books, and book sales. Our books are also often available through your favorite distributor or a local or on-line bookseller!

CPSIA information can be obtained at www.ICGtesting.com
Printed in the USA
LVOW051648200113

316455LV00021B/1184/P